The English Judges

Their Role in the Changing Constitution

ROBERT STEVENS

·HART·
PUBLISHING

HART PUBLISHING
OXFORD AND PORTLAND, OREGON
2005

Published in North America (US and Canada) by
Hart Publishing
c/o International Specialized Book Services
5804 NE Hassalo Street
Portland, Oregon
97213–3644
USA

Distributed in Netherlands, Belgium and Luxembourg by
Intersentia, Churchillaan 108
B2900 Schoten
Antwerpen
Belgium

First published 2002, reprinted 2003 (twice)
Published in paperback, with revisions, 2005

Hart Publishing is a specialist legal publisher based in Oxford, England.
To order further copies of this book or to request a list of other publications
please write to:

Hart Publishing,
Salters Boatyard, Folly Bridge, Abingdon Rd,
Oxford, OX1 4LB
Telephone: +44 (0)1865 245533 Fax: +44 (0) 1865 794882
email: mail@hartpub.co.uk
WEBSITE: http//:www.hartpub.co.uk

British Library Cataloguing in Publication Data
Data Available

ISBN 1–84113–226–8 (hardback)
ISBN 1–84113–495–3 (paperback)

Typeset by J&L Composition, Filey, North Yorkshire
Printed and bound in Great Britain by
MPG Books Ltd, Bodmin, Cornwall

To my colleagues at Covington and Burling,
Essex Court Chambers,
Pembroke College, Oxford and
Yale Law School,

for their tolerance, support and insights

Preface to the Revised Edition

There was a time when writing about the English Constitution was a genteel activity. In the 1950s, struggling to survive as a pupil, when the Bar was far less hospitable financially than it is today, I manufactured a slim bar exam crib entitled *Questions and Answers in Constitutional Law*. There were precious few recent cases which might have been described as constitutional. Beyond the outline of *ultra vires* which might curb local authorities, there was almost nothing by way of modern administrative or constitutional law. The study of courts was limited to judicial structures; no one seriously thought that the role of judges was any part of constitutional law. The judges themselves cultivated an image of passivity, based on the objectivity of the common law and the literal meaning of statutes.

How that world changed is described in Chapters 3 and 4. One needs a loose leaf service to keep up with judicial review and the Human Rights Act. Politically New Labour, when it was returned in 1997, promised constitutional reform and joined-up government. It delivered on the first, but coherence is not a word one would associate with its constitutional innovations. The eclectic nature of its constitutional reform was put into the shade by developments roughly a year after this book was first published. In June 2003, as part of a cabinet reshuffle, the Prime Minster—Tony Blair—announced that the Office of Lord Chancellor would be abolished, a Judicial Appointments Commission would be established, and, perhaps most significantly, there would be a Supreme Court, with the law lords no longer being members of the legislature. The changes, while supported by many, were seriously undercut by the inept -and inexcusable – method of their announcement. Consultation had been non-existent. Working out solutions was to take nearly two years. As this revised version of *The English Judges* went to press, the constitutional battle still raged. The exact status of the Lord Chancellor remained to be decided, while the government had been forced to give statutory form to judicial independence and largely to exclude the politicians from any part in the selection of judges.

In a new chapter—chapter 11—I have sought to bring the story up to date at least to the beginning of 2005. In speaking of the political battles surrounding reform of the senior judiciary and the final appeal in the 1870's, several politicians of that time expressed sympathy with later historians who would have to sort out what actually happened. The years 2003 and 2004 surely competes with those years in the difficulty of 'sorting out'.

In adding an additional chapter I have relied on 'Reform in haste and repent at leisure: Iolanthe, the Lord High Executioner and *Brave New World*', (2004) 24 *Legal Studies*, 1. This in turn was developed in a faculty talk I gave when I was at George Washington University in the Fall of 2003 and a public lecture when I was Cardozo Law School in the Winter of 2004. At both institutions I received valuable feedback and thank the faculties of those two institutions. I have also benefited from the review of the first edition of the book by Lord Goodhart in the *Law Quarterly Review*[1] and the review article by Diana Woodhouse in the *Modern Law Review*[2]. Developing a program about the constitutional changes for BBC Radio Four was also instructive, as I was in a position to interview many of those most closely concerned with the legislation. I also benefited from the insights of my producer, Brian King, and Executive Producer, Bruce Hyman.

Needless to say, I am also grateful to many more who have helped shape my thoughts and helped me avoid errors. I thanked most of those in the Preface to the First Edition, for their support over a ten year period. To these names I should now like to add Derek Morgan, who edited the *Legal Studies* article. I must also thank those who read the penultimate draft and saved me from various errors—Sir Thomas Legg, Kate Malleson and William Twining. Once again Lord Smith of Clifton offered help of a political science and research nature. Remaining faults are obviously my own.

I should also like to thank my secretary at Covington & Burling, Manuela Henrique, who has organised my life so that I have had time to undertake this modest revision. Finally, I should also thank her for her willingness to compensate for my technological backwardness, as well as her willingness to help with research demands. I should also like to thank Jennifer Green, Information Officer at Covington & Burling, and her staff for their support. As usual, Richard Hart's team have been eminently civilised and helpful.

Robert Stevens
Constitution Unit, UCL
February 1, 2004

---

[1]   (2004) 120, *LQR*, 174.
[2]   (2003) 66, *MLR*, 920.

Preface

Since the 1950s, I have been trying both to understand and record what has been happening to the English judiciary. The scene has changed dramatically since my first article forty-five years ago. Frustratingly, the change has been at its most dramatic in the last ten years, with a serious possibility of a further restructuring of the Constitution in the next ten. Richard Hart—that most civilised of publishers—has now encouraged me to bring together in this book the themes of various lectures and articles over the last decade. I am especially grateful for this encouragement since this is a period when most of my energy has gone into attempting either academic administration or the practice of law.

Chapter one reaches back into the seventeenth and eighteenth centuries to look at the English Civil War and the slow emergence of responsible government and judicial tenure. It is, of course, hazardous to tread where Maitland and Macaulay have trod; but I have attempted, in a telegraphic way, to set the stage for later developments. At a time when, both in England and America, there is no longer a shared knowledge of English constitutional history, I hope I shall be forgiven for this excursion.

While chapter two dwells on the first sixty years of the twentieth century, the remainder of the book is primarily concerned with the politics of the judiciary in the second half of the century; a story continued in chapter three. Chapter four outlines the Thatcher and Major years. Chapters five, six and seven tread water historically in order to review the English approach to law and to deal with the independence of judges individually and collectively during the twentieth century. Chapters eight and nine deal with the Blair years and chapter ten looks to the future.

The book is the product of a series of seminars, papers and public lectures. Chapter one relies heavily on a lecture given at the Chief Justices' Conference on the Act of Settlement at Vancouver in May 2001, now published in the *Oxford University Commonwealth Law Journal* (2001). Chapters two and three rely on 'Government and Judiciary' in Vernon Bogdanor's *The British Constitution in the Twentieth Century* (OUP/British Academy, 2002). Those chapters have also benefited greatly from a British Academy seminar in the winter of 2001, led by Vernon Bogdanor and David Butler.

Chapters four to seven have a more complex genesis. Seminars on the role of the judiciary, held at the University of Bristol (1994), the University of Hong Kong (1995), the University of Ulster (1996), Pembroke College,

Oxford (1996) as well as the Harcourt Chambers' lecture (1997), ultimately led to 'Judges, Politics, Politicians and the Confusing Role of the Judiciary', published in *The Human Face of Law: Essays in Honour of Donald Harris* (OUP, 1997). A second source was a series of meetings on the meaning of judicial independence. Meetings of the Comparative Political Science Association in Boston in 1998 led to a chapter in *Judicial Independence: A Comparative Study*, edited by Peter Russell and David O'Brien, (University of Virginia Press, 2001). Some of that research had, as the result of a conference on Judicial Independence and Accountability at the University of Southern California in 1998 appeared as 'Judicial Independence: The Case of England' in (1999) 72 *University of Southern California Law Review* 101. Finally, to prove the basic principle of academic freedom, namely the right to publish the same article under various titles, an extended version of the piece appeared as 'Loss of Innocence: The Separation of Powers and Judicial Independence', in (1999) 19 *Oxford Journal of Legal Studies* 365. The final shape of these three chapters, however, owes much to a faculty seminar at the Yale Law School, when I was Georges Lurcy Visiting Professor of Law in 1999.

Chapters eight, nine and ten are basically new, although no doubt containing material from various lectures and Yale faculty seminars. I am, moreover, conscious that chapters nine and ten have benefited from the Constitution Unit's seminar on the Future of the United Kingdom's Highest Court, held at the British Academy in July 2001, based on the ESRC's project directed by Andrew Le Sueur and Richard Cornes.[1]

This litany cannot, nor should not, disguise the fact that this book is primarily the result of a series of public lectures. While I have sought to avoid repetition and have endeavoured to bring the discussion up to the early spring of 2002, I have consciously retained the less formal style of the speech and the lecture. I do this in part in the hope that this book will be read by laymen as well as lawyers. If I have failed to avoid all repetition, I shall claim the book to be a legal version of the *Alexandria Quartet*.

As always, I have benefited enormously from the insight of those who read or in other ways contributed to the various lectures. In this connection, I should like to thank Bruce Ackerman, Jack Balkin, J Barton Beebe, Michael Beloff, Boris Bittker, Vernon Bogdanor, Joe Chubb, Jill Cottrell, Ruth Deech, John Eekelaar, Robert Elickson, Peter Farthing, William Felstiner, Yash Ghai, William Goodhart, Robert Gordon, Adrian Gregory, John Griffith, Keith Hawkins, Robert Hazell, Anthony Holland, Geoffrey Howe, Christopher Kingsland, Anthony Kronman, John Langbien, Paul

---

[1] I also benefited greatly from the book and papers on which that seminar was based. See *The Future of the United Kingdom's Highest Courts* (Constitutional Unit, UCL, 2001).

Langford, Martin Lee, Thomas Legg, Anthony Lester, Charles Lister, Kate Malleson, Geoffrey Marshall, Christopher McCrudden, Michael Mustill, Philip Otton, Dan Prentice, Judith Resnik, David Robertson, Peter Russell, Andrew Sanders, Stephen Sedley, Colin Sheppard, Katherine Booth Stevens, Johan Steyn, William Twining, Paul Verkuil, Michael Wheeler-Booth, Stephen Whitefield and David Williams. I should also like to thank especially those who undertook the painful task of reading the whole manuscript in draft: John Bell, John Eekelaar, Richard Hart, Thomas Legg, Kate Malleson and Katherine Booth Stevens. Their contributions were particularly important in ensuring closure. Of course none of these persons should be held responsible for my views or the errors in this volume. Indeed, all would disagree with some of my views; some with most. Yet all have had an impact on my thinking.

The preparation of the book, including editing and typing, fell to Sue Embley, my assistant at Pembroke for four years and even now virtually the only person who can read my writing—for my typing skills, while improving, are scarcely professional. To Sue I am immensely grateful; as I am to Tracey Roberts, my secretary at Covington and Burling. I should also like to thank Jenny Green and Gay Jenkins, the Library/Information Group at Covington and Burling, who have tirelessly helped me with books and references. I must also thank Ellena Pike, the Librarian at Pembroke; Bonnie Collier, the Deputy Librarian at the Yale Law School and Gene Coakley of Reader Services there, who claims (I hope wrongly) that I have exploited him for forty years; I should also like to thank the librarians at Gray's Inn and the Reform Club. I must also thank David Grief of Essex Court who, in addition to running the world, has found time to help me in various ways in connection with this book. Finally, I should like to thank Alison Morley and Hannah Young for bringing the book to publication. All have been incredibly supportive.

Robert Stevens
Constitution Unit, University College, London.

Easter Day, 2002

Contents

Prologue

Traditionally, the growth of the English Constitution has been organic; the rate of change glacial. Until recent times, there has perhaps been only one exception to this—the period from 1640, the end of Charles I's Eleven Years Personal Rule, to the arrival of Robert Walpole as Prime Minister around 1720. This period represented the transformation of the Constitution from the admittedly weak English version of the Divine Right of Kings to a dimly perceived form of constitutional monarchy and responsible government. The intervening eighty years saw the Civil War, the execution of Charles I, the Protectorate, the Restoration, the Glorious Revolution of 1688, the Bill of Rights in 1689, the Act of Settlement of 1701 and the arrival of the Hanoverians in 1714. Jacobites might occasionally rise and George III might forget the rules of the new game, but the Constitution had been revolutionised.

There were, of course, important constitutional developments over the following centuries. The reform of the suffrage in the Great Reform Act of 1832, followed by the extensions of the franchise in 1867, 1884, 1919 and 1928 were vital, as was the reform of local government in 1835 and 1888. Much of the machinery of government—the Civil Service, substantive law and the courts—was reformed between 1832 and 1875. The early part of the twentieth century was marked by the curbing of the House of Lords by the Parliament Act of 1911 and the establishment of the Irish Free State, finally achieved in 1922. Yet vital as these Acts were in moving England—and Britain—towards a modern democracy, they were essentially independent acts rather than part of a dramatic period of constitutional restructuring.

For lawyers and the courts, however, the period from 1970 to 2000 provided a practical and psychological transformation comparable with the earlier constitutional revolution. In 1960, it had seemed that judges, barristers and solicitors were becoming marginal to society, whether in terms of the economy or the Constitution. As the result of a series of events, some not easily explained, the courts in the later 1960s took on a new lease of life. Litigation revived; legal aid expanded and by the early 1970s the courts were regaining their importance. Restrictive practices, whether in management or unions, became once more the responsibility of the courts. The judiciary rediscovered the English version of judicial review to exert pressure on the executive. Most important of all, with Britain's accession to the Common Market (European Union), perhaps without most people appreciating what was happening, the basis of parliamentary sovereignty—the cardinal principle of the English Constitution sanctified by Dicey—began to erode. In England, Parliamentary supremacy had already given way to Executive supremacy; in the EU the European Court had become the primary agent of change. Both psychologically and practically, again without full realisation, the judges were in a position to adopt a far more proactive view of their role.

By the 1980s, a new influence was at work. As the administration of Margaret Thatcher established its ascendancy, it began to undo the basic social assumptions of post–1945 Britain. No longer would Britain be a dirigiste, consensus society. It was to be a society driven—at least in some respects—by a market economy and individual enterprise. The judges, already in the 1960s and 1970s becoming more activist and outspoken, slowly found themselves transformed from establishment figures into survivors of the consensus society. From being seen by the public as sometimes rather ludicrous guardians of the status quo, they were increasingly seen as enemies of the enterprise society.

The situation was further transformed in May 1997 with the return of Tony Blair and New Labour. Despite misgivings, the enterprise atmosphere was continued, and the judges increasingly adapted to that. What was most significant, however, was that Tony Blair inherited from the previous Labour leader, John Smith, a series of constitutional commitments which, while they lacked coherence, were to have a profound impact on the future role of the judiciary. British entry into union with Europe had transformed parliamentary sovereignty and given the judges their own British version of American judicial review, allowing British judges to invalidate British legislation in the light of EU legislation. The incorporation into English law of the European Convention on Human Rights and devolution in Scotland and Wales more clearly than ever weakened parliamentary sovereignty and left the judges with immense—if thus far not fully used—powers.

The effect of two landslide elections in favour of New Labour and the apparent collapse of the old Conservative party meant that the role of the House of Commons as a brake on government was decaying. Once again the courts were needed. While some control over constitutional niceties was provided by a partially reformed House of Lords, a fully reformed upper house might well have the effect of transfering more power to the judges. As it was, the absence of coherent constitutional reform meant that the judges were in an increasingly powerful position. England—and Britain—was moving from a classical version of parliamentary supremacy towards a constitutional democracy. The reign of Dicey was coming, relatively peacefully, to a close.

1

Setting the Tone: the Act of Settlement and the Emergence of the Balance of Powers

THE ROLE OF judges as an independent force within the British Constitution dates, from an historian's point of view, only from the Stuarts. The Act of Settlement is seen by most as the basis of judicial independence in the common law world. To understand the Act of Settlement 1701, however, one must realise what an incredible century had preceded it. Christendom itself seemed to be threatened. The forces of the Ottoman Empire were once again at the gates of Vienna in 1683. Within Christendom, meanwhile, Reformation and Counter-Reformation (or Catholic Reformation as fashionable historians now call it) ensured strife and instability. Central Europe had been torn apart by the Thirty Years War. By the time that that war ended with the Treaty of Westphalia in 1648, the action had moved further west to France, where Louis XIV, not only the 'Sun King' of Versailles, but also 'the most Catholic King', took away the rights of French Protestants by revoking the Edict of Nantes in 1685, and engaged in almost perpetual wars with the Protestant Netherlands and, perhaps more for economic than religious reasons, England. Some understanding of the militant role of religion during the period is, however, essential for understanding the background to the Act of Settlement.

England in the sixteenth century had been trying, theologically, to steer between religious extremes while, in the seventeenth century, it was attempting to find a suitable royal family for a country beginning to be touched by the Enlightenment. The problem in the late sixteenth century was what to do when it became clear that Elizabeth, the last of the Tudors, would die childless. There was really no alternative to James VI of Scotland (to be James I of England), descended from a daughter of Henry VII. Scotland was a backward country, split between Catholics and Presbyterians, with a tendency to alliances with France. Indeed that tendency had led Elizabeth to execute Mary Queen of Scots, James I's mother. While James was happy to take over an Anglican country, he was not equipped with the Tudors' political wisdom, which had enabled Elizabeth to survive as an autocrat while working with her Parliaments. James' lack of skills in this area led to increasing clashes with his Parliaments and the Parliamentarians. This resulted, in the law, in driving his Chief Justice, Sir Edward Coke, into the arms of the Parliamentarians, for whom he 'discovered' or 'invented' (depending on your political persuasion) Magna Carta.

James I at least survived, but the fragments of a religious radicalism grew stronger. While James I's successor, Charles I, originally tried to work with Parliament, by 1629 he had begun a period of personal rule, embodied in Strafford and the policy of 'thorough', while the Anglican hegemony and the tradition of Armenianism were protected by Archbishop Laud and the Court of High Commission. When the scheme eventually collapsed in 1640 and Parliament reconvened, the King's powers were threatened by Parliaments in which dissenters were increasingly represented. Civil War, the execution of the King in 1649 and ultimately a Protectorate under Oliver Cromwell brought the chill wind of a Republic to the Anglican settlement.

Cromwell was a Congregationalist, although he did not hesitate to persecute those more Protestant or more politically radical—Levellers, Baptists and proto-Quakers. He ultimately wearied of dealing with Parliaments and declared himself Protector. When Cromwell died in 1658, however, the country was tired of war and religious strife. Economically the century had been one of decline. While it was by no means clear that the Stuarts would be restored, General Monck's march on London was rapidly followed by the Declaration of Breda and the reappearance of Charles II in 1660. The Restoration was on. Parliament, no doubt in a mood of guilt, made appropriate financial provision for a monarch for the first time and Charles, while by no means abandoning Divine Right, at least went to Parliament for war supplies and, as to the evolution of the judiciary, respected the concept that judges held office 'during good behaviour', at least until the fall of Clarendon in 1667.

At this point Charles began a campaign of attempting to control the senior judges, and by 1680 Parliament was holding hearings on why various judges had been fired while the House of Commons actually passed a Bill (not taken up by the Lords) to protect judicial tenure 'during good behaviour'. As early as 1668, Charles was appointing judges during his pleasure and, to fill such posts, he began appointing King's Counsel (KCs) from among the younger (and loyal) members of the Bar. (The distinction between barrister and solicitor was already some two hundred years old.) Whereas only three barristers were made KCs during the first seven years of the reign, eighteen patents were issued in the 1670s. In 1671, KCs were granted precedence over the Serjeants whose loyalty was suspect, while royal influence ensured the KCs automatically became Benchers of their

Inns. The new royal men received preference. After only seven years at the Bar, Francis North became a KC in 1668, Solicitor-General in 1671, Attorney-General in 1673, Chief Justice of Common Pleas in 1675 and Lord Keeper in 1682.

The office of KC, together with minor local judgeships, was given to royal supporters in the House of Commons. This was part of a wider pattern of placemen and pensioners whom Charles and his ministers appointed. As the King went to Parliament for support for his Dutch wars, such placemen, and the gradual emergence of Cabinet committees, caused increasing frustration to the emerging Whig class in the Commons. Together with banning placemen went ensuring tenure for the judges and an effort to prevent the emergence of cabals advising the King. The emergence of a Whig oligarchy, coinciding with the beginning of what we now call the Enlightenment, meant that God and King seemed less important.

Charles II, however, had a good deal going for him. He was governing a country which was tired of tumult; he was generally popular and he maintained the Anglican settlement, only converting secretly to Roman Catholicism on his death bed; and he took money only covertly from France. James II, when he came to the throne in 1685 had none of these advantages. While not unpopular at the beginning of his reign, his open Roman Catholicism and his policy of toleration was alarming both to the Anglican establishment and to a squirearchy and aristocracy which, in a significant number of cases, occupied land which had formerly been the property of monasteries. The distaste of the Whig oligarchy was matched by the fears of the dissenters who threw their support behind the unsuccessful rising led by Charles II's illegitimate son, the Duke of Monmouth.

When Parliament expressed concern about repeal of the Test Acts, which supported the Anglican settlement, it was dissolved. Catholics were slipped into many of the most important positions and a new Model Army created. James II began using his dispensing power to avoid parliamentary rules. Attacks on the universities and the Inns of Court went hand in hand. James's plans to re-Catholicise the country were anathema even to his hand-picked judges. Thus even Chief Justice Jones of Common Pleas, who had accompanied Judge Jeffreys in hanging Monmouth's troops at the Bloody Assizes, had doubts about the dispensing power. 'A man', as Macaulay said, 'who had never before shrunk from any drudgery, however cruel and servile, now held in the royal closet language which might have become the lips of the purest magistrates in our history'. When told by King James that he must allow the dispensing power in favour of Catholics, according to Macaulay the Chief Justice said: 'For my place I care little. I am old and worn out in the service of the Crown: but I am mortified to find your Majesty thinks me capable of giving a judgment which none but an ignorant or a dishonest man could give'. The King replied: 'I am determined to have twelve judges who will be all of my mind as to this matter'. Jones replied: 'Your Majesty may find twelve judges of your mind, but hardly twelve lawyers'.

Jones, together with the Chief Baron of the Exchequer, was dismissed, along with two other puisne judges. The Solicitor-General, Finch, was dismissed for refusing to argue for the dispensing power; the Attorney-General for refusing to allow Roman Catholics to hold benefices belonging to the Church of England. With a packed bench, in *Hales* case, eleven of the twelve judges held that the King did have the right to dispense with the Test Acts in favour of a Catholic. (Only Baron Street dissented, a man, so Macaulay reports, 'of morals so bad that his own relatives shrank from him'.) The King then sought to ally himself with the dissenters by a Declaration of Indulgence which he ordered to be read in all churches. Seven Anglican Bishops refused the order, petitioned the King, and were imprisoned in the Tower. Prosecuted for publishing a criminal libel against the King, they were eventually cleared by a jury, to the delight of the mob of London, not normally admirers of the Anglican Bishops.

Even then the situation did not seem impossible. By his first wife, James had two daughters, Anne and Mary, both Protestants and Anglicans. Then in June 1688, James's second wife, Mary of Modena, gave birth to a son. The succession would now be a Roman Catholic one. The situation began to deteriorate. William of Orange, Stadtholder of the Netherlands and husband of Mary, James II's younger daughter, had extensive contacts in England and had been testing the mood of English politics, since he was constantly engaged in wars with France and James II was close to Louis XIV. By July 1688 William was being sounded out about, in some way, preserving the Protestant tradition in England. He refused to appear in England unless formally invited; that written invitation was forthcoming after the trial of the Bishops.

By November, William had landed in the West Country, avoiding the English navy. Within days local magnates joined the force of professional soldiers, even though it was not yet fully clear what William's ultimate goal was. James marched with his troops to Salisbury. John Churchill, (later Duke of Marlborough), commander of the King's forces, recommended an advance and when that advice was not accepted, he deserted to William and shortly thereafter, with the Bishop of London, went James' elder daughter, Anne. The situation was confused. William claimed he wanted not the throne but 'to right wrongs'. He agreed to stay forty miles from London but, in December, James fled in disguise. The army was disbanded unpaid. Twenty-one peers met at the Guildhall and invited William to London to keep order. James, brought back from his disguised flight, was later allowed to leave openly for France. By Christmas Day 1688, England was kingless, although the Dutch leader was sitting in Whitehall.

Modern historians reject the idea that Locke was influential in the political settlement of the 1690s. Yet a contractual approach to the State was in the air. More than that was going on. The beginning of the era of the Enlightenment was allowing in England, if not in Scotland and Ireland, a spirit of tolerance. While the prosperity of Elizabethan England had been damaged by a century of social and religious conflict, there was a yearning for peace and reasonableness—a settled order and prosperity. The Crown was increasingly a commodity. To dispose of it satisfactorily was a precondition to the return of prosperity.

As soon as James had gone, an election was held, not legally for a Parliament, but for a Convention. Meeting in February 1689, the Convention, with the Commons controlled by the Whigs and the Lords of a more Divine Right bent, agreed that James had, 'with the assistance of evil counsellors and judges', subverted the Protestant succession, and had abdicated the throne by his desertion. The Convention then had no choice but to invite William to succeed, but before doing so, it passed the Bill of Rights, which dealt with the dispensing and suspending powers, standing armies, the right to bear arms and frequent Parliaments. The early draft of the Declaration of Rights, dated second of February, provided that judges' commissions were to be made *quamdiu se bene gesserint*, salaries were to be ascertained and established, to be paid out of the public revenue only, 'and judges were not to be removed nor suspended from the execution of their office, but by due course of law'. As part of the reform, judges were to lose their lucrative right to fees. Later that same month, however, the Convention decided that the Declaration of Rights should contain only a restatement of ancient rights and that the heads requiring changes in the law—including the provisions for the judges—were dropped. In that form, the Convention Parliament passed what had by then become the Bill of Rights, although it did find time to dismiss all twelve of James II's judges.

With the Bill of Rights out of the way, the throne was offered to William and Mary. William rejected any compromise that did not give him an equal right to the throne with his wife and threatened to return to the Netherlands if he were thwarted. At the same time he was prepared to have Anne succeed if he and Mary did not have children. William thus took the throne in his own right, to share it with James's second daughter during her lifetime, then to hold it in his own right and then to be succeeded by James's first daughter. A century of civil strife had made a severe dent in the Divine Right of Kings, but it had also made possible the beginning of judicial independence and a Cabinet system. The compromise of 1689 also meant the monarch had to work through Parliament.

That co-operation William managed, frequently with feelings of frustration. Parliament, with William unenthusiastic, passed the Triennial Act in 1694 to provide for regular elections. He continued to clash with Parliament for, basically, he had taken the Crown of England in part to continue his continental wars against France and wars were expensive. Annual Parliaments became the norm; statute law proliferated. The Toleration Act 1689 allowed considerable latitude to non-conformists and indirectly to Catholics. William spent much of his reign overseas, he relied heavily on foreign advisors, and while he did not pack the bench, placemen in Parliament became ever more important.

William's reign had seen a great improvement, over those of Charles II and James II, in the matter of judicial tenure. Yet, while judges' patents by then guaranteed tenure during good behaviour, in 1692 William vetoed a Bill to establish a Commission to set judicial salaries for fear that it would make the judges 'stiff'. Burnett in his *History* says that the judges urged the veto but he was unable to remember why. It is unlikely that the judges would have opposed the mandating of judicial tenure during good behaviour, although the King may have feared having to pay the judges out of his hereditary or traditional revenues. Perhaps the thing which swayed the judges most was the proposal to take away their right to fees, an increasingly lucrative form of income and something not fully addressed until after the legislation of 1825 and 1832 which finally established modern judicial salaries.

Be that as it may, the idea that there was no modern notion of separation—or even balance—of powers was underlined later in 1692, when the royal placemen were able to defeat a Bill in the Commons which would have set judicial salaries, on the ground that 'it did entrench upon the King's prerogative and would render judges independent of the Crown'. Nor was Parliament fastidious about judicial independence. In the 1690s, the Commons took Chief Justice Holt to task for his decisions in *Ashby v White* and *Paty's Case*, while the Lords summoned him to explain *Ashby v White*. In fairness, however, when he was summoned by the Lords in 1698 to explain his decision in *R v Knollys*, Chief Justice Holt refused to appear.

Meanwhile politics was made more complex by the fact that William and Mary had no children. Indeed Mary died in 1694 and the Stadtholder of the Netherlands remained King of England in his own right. The succession therefore passed to her elder sister Anne, married to Prince George of Denmark, with one sickly child, although she also had sixteen miscarriages. In 1700 the son, the Duke of Gloucester, died. Since William showed no interest in remarrying, the future of the succession to the English throne was once more open. Some secretly hoped that James's son would become King, if it could be guaranteed he would be a Protestant. In fact James II died in 1700 and Louis XIV immediately recognised James's son, a Catholic, as James III of England and VIII of Scotland. Something had to be done to ensure the Protestant succession. The most obvious choice was the most legitimate Protestant, the Electress Sophia of Hanover, granddaughter of James I. William had unsuccessfully urged that her succession be included in the Bill of Rights. Fearing that war with France, interrupted by the Treaty of Ryswick in 1697, was about to restart, Parliament passed the Act of Settlement in the summer of 1701. It received the Royal Assent in June.

The Act of Settlement

The Act of Settlement was passed with precious little opposition. In the House of Commons only one MP spoke against it and there was no division in either Commons or Lords. The Protestant succession had been secured. Part of the concern had of course been religious. After all, much of the previous hundred years had seen a series of religious fights, interspersed with periods of almost theocratic control, whether it was Charles' eleven years personal rule in favour of the Church of England or the Puritan control of England by the Dissenters during the Interregnum. There were, however, other factors. Much as the country may have resented William's continental wars, it feared France and especially Louis XIV—the most Catholic King—even more. Charles II surreptitiously and James II openly were dependent on Louis' money, while the Parliamentarians' theory was that they should have sought supply from Parliament. Finally there was an economic base encouraging the Protestant succession. If the seizing of the lands of the monasteries was beginning to fade into the background, government was by then funded through loans and, especially after the founding of the Bank of England in 1694, fiscal stability had become linked with the Protestant succession. It was little wonder that the Act of Settlement sailed through.

The Act itself seemed primarily designed to remedy the many perceived defects of the reign of William. Already the English were establishing a reputation for chauvinism. After ensuring that, in default of Anne's offspring, the succession would pass to the Electress Sophia and her heirs providing they were communicating members of the Church of England, Parliament turned its attention to William's defects. The first provision was a response to the more or less constant wars fought by William, often perceived as being of more value to the Netherlands than to England: 'That in case the crown and imperial dignity of this realm shall hereafter come in any person, not being a native of this Kingdom of England, this nation be not obliged to engage in any war for the defence of any dominions or territories which do not belong to the crown of England, without the consent of Parliament'. The next provision was even more insulting: 'No person who shall hereafter come to the possession of this crown shall go out of the dominions of England, Scotland or Ireland, without the consent of Parliament'. That, of course, had to be repealed in the first year of the reign of George I the son of the Electress Sophia—only thirteen years later. George, was, after all, Elector of Hanover, as well as King of England but, by then, Whig politicians had decided that having a King spending much of his time abroad had its advantages.

The next section of the Act of Settlement reflected the frustrations at the slow and often painful evolution of Cabinet government. There was a hankering for the golden days of the King's Council:

> all matters and things relating to the well governing of this Kingdom, which are properly cognizable in the Privy Council by the laws and customs of this realm, shall be transacted there and all resolutions taken thereupon shall be signed by such of the Privy Council as shall advise and consent to the same.

This artificial restriction on the growth of the Cabinet was repealed by statutes in 1707 and 1714 as the Whigs became convinced of the value of a Cabinet, especially when controlled by them. Next, the Act of Settlement purported to make it illegal for foreigners to be members of the Privy Council, the Houses of Parliament, or to enjoy any office or place of trust, either civil or military, or to have any grants of lands, tenements or hereditaments from the crown. It was scarcely a vote of thanks to William.

Again, in an effort, Canute-like, to turn back the growth of parties, the Act of Settlement once more addressed the issue of placemen, declaring that 'no person who has an office or place of profit under the King, or receives a pension from the Crown, shall be capable of serving as a member of the House of Commons. Placemen had first attracted hostility during the reign of Charles II. During William's reign roughly a third of MPs (between 120 and 160) held such offices of profit. Without them, however, government was not possible and the system of government we know as responsible government would not have developed without them. Within five years after 1701, the Act of Regency provided partial relief and the Offices of Profit Act completed the work. By the beginning of the Hanoverian reign, the requirement that any MP, who was the recipient of a place, resubmit himself to the voters in his constituency, had replaced the ban on placemen in the Commons. The stage was set for Sir Robert Walpole, the first modern Prime Minister, and for Cabinet or responsible government. That also meant that England chose the balance of powers rather than the separation of powers, with the judiciary ranking after both legislature and executive.

The next provision was the one that had made its appearance in an early draft of the Bill of Rights. It was in response to the interference with the judges by Charles II and James II, for, in this matter, William III had a reasonably clean record. The Act of Settlement provided that: 'judges commissions (shall) be made *quamdiu se bene gesserint* and their salaries ascertained and established; but upon the address of both houses of Parliament it may be lawful to remove them'. Since the provisions have never been directly tested in the case of an English judge, it is difficult fully to understand their implications. Is the arrangement like impeachment? If the judges have committed a crime can they still avoid addresses? If they have not committed a crime can they still be dismissed? Is the procedure an entirely political one? Inevitably today, one must also ask how the procedure is affected by the Human Rights Act.

Historically the Act of Settlement marks the crossroads of the English Constitution. The provisions of the Act, both with respect to placemen and judges, represented an inarticulate effort to have the kind of separation of powers which was to be spelled out with much greater clarity at the Constitutional Convention in Philadelphia eighty-five years later. The effort to keep the executive out of the legislature and to offer a measure of protection to the judiciary could have led to a concept of the separation of powers along what became the American model. Almost at once, however, the English decided that they preferred a balance of powers rather than the separation of powers. Yet both Blackstone in his *Commentaries* and Montesquieu in his *Esprit des Lois,* for different reasons, talked as if the British had opted for the separation rather than the balance of powers. It had confused the patriots in Massachusetts, particularly in their 1780 constitution. It seems to have confused at least some of the delegates at Philadelphia in 1787. Yet balance of powers rather than separation of powers was the British choice. This was an understandable choice, but it makes more difficult a rationale for the independence of the judiciary.

There was another constitutional wrinkle. The Act of Settlement was, of course, an English Act. While Scotland had gone along with William and Mary and then with Anne as sovereigns, they were, after all, members of that Scottish House—the Stuarts. When the Act of Settlement was passed in London, the Scottish Parliament was outraged. They thought it a typical case of English arrogance and imperialism. There were calls for a formal severing of the links with England. The English saw the solution as quite simple: merge the two Parliaments. Scotland, or at least the Presbyterian majority, had benefited from William. Charles II's solution of imposing the Episcopal church in Scotland had been abandoned in favour of the

Presbyterian establishment. Whatever the Catholic Highlanders might feel, the Presbyterians had no interest in seeing the return of a Catholic King, still recognised by Louis XIV as King of Great Britain.

London put great pressure on Edinburgh to merge the legislatures. In 1702 London appointed Commissioners and, in a dubious constitutional move, Edinburgh did the same. Scotland did not help agreement by passing legislation to say that the Scottish Parliament had to be consulted before a war involving Scotland was declared (Act Anent Peace and War). While an Act said that on Anne's death there should be a Protestant succession, Edinburgh declined to follow the English choice unless Scotland were guaranteed freedom of government, of religion and of trade (Act of Security). Meanwhile in 1705, the English Parliament passed the Alien Act saying that unless Scotland accepted the Hanoverian Succession by Christmas Day 1705, the Scots would be treated as aliens in England. The threat of being deprived of what Samuel Johnson was to describe later in the century as 'the finest sight a Scotsman ever sees, . . . the high road to England' was sufficient to encourage the Commissioners to thrash out an agreement in 1706 in London. Despite much opposition, the Treaty was accepted by the Scottish Parliament in 1707, probably with the assistance of bribes, a not uncommon form of political discourse in that period.

Quamdiu se bene gesserint

It will come as no surprise that, despite the newly drafted patents, many in the eighteenth century feared that the English judges were not free of political influence. Much influence is, of course, indirect. In the twentieth century, Harold Laski observed that 'the English judges cannot be bribed—with money' and there is little doubt that in earlier centuries flattery, honours and royal or ministerial favours were even more relevant. Moreover there were powerful legal levers which might be used on the judges.

Lemmings' studies show that between 1689 and 1714, 85 per cent of the senior judges had been MPs and 92 per cent had 'crown service'. Of the puisne judges, 41 per cent had been MPs and 52 per cent had 'crown service'. While the Act of Settlement may have been intended to prevent royal interference with the judges, Parliament showed no interest in curbing its tradition of interfering with the judges. The Tories during their period of control (1702–04) had inserted their man, Sir Thomas Trevor, as Chief Justice of Common Pleas. During their period in power between 1705–10, the Whigs inserted as Chief Justice of the Court of Queen's

Bench, Sir Thomas Parker, and he helped protect Whig supporters from Tory prosecution.

Moreover, the Act of Settlement did not abolish the right of the Crown not to reappoint judges on the change of a monarch. In 1702, on the accession of Anne, the opportunity was used to fire Mr Justice Turton of the Court of Queen's Bench, a Whig, and Baron Hatsell of the Court of Exchequer. In 1714 the Whigs convinced the new King, George I, to fire Tory judges including Trevor, by then Chief Justice of the Court of Queen's Bench and two other judges. They were rapidly replaced by Whig judges. This was, of course, the moment when the Hanoverian succession laid down in the Act of Settlement came to fruition. There were fears of Tory loyalty to the Pretender, James III; partially borne out by Jacobite risings of 1715 and 1719. The right not to reappoint judges on the change of sovereign nevertheless continued. When George II succeeded in 1727 one judge was not renewed; and the right not to renew judges was not abolished until 1761, one year after George III came to the throne.

Getting rid of existing judges was not the main way of ensuring a pliant bench. As the system of responsible government took off—and by the early 1720s Sir Robert Walpole was unquestionably Prime Minister—more barristers than ever served in the House of Commons. As the Bar itself was contracting, barrister MPs could be rewarded not only with the patent of King's Counsel and Serjeant-at-Law, but with local judgeships and, increasingly, counsel to various government departments. Between 1714 and 1760, two-thirds of all judges had served in the House of Commons and nearly 90 per cent had accepted crown patronage. Moreover, Chief Justices and Chief Barons were increasingly given peerages and expected to vote with the government in the Lords. Even if they were not given peerages, political work was expected. Sir Peter King, Walpole's Chief Justice of Common Pleas in the 1720s, was responsible for distributing rotten boroughs in the West Country. He was ultimately rewarded with the Lord Chancellorship.

The head of the judiciary, the Lord Chancellor, continued to be a politician and to rise and fall with Ministries and it was he and the Prime Minister who appointed the judges. The rise of responsible government, with Ministers being dependent on the House of Commons, meant that judges were increasingly seen as inferior to Parliament even if there was a glowing reluctance on the part of Parliament to interfere with them. Yet judges continued to fall out of favour with Parliament. Page, a Whig MP, who had argued as counsel in *Ashby v White*, was promoted to be a Baron of the Exchequer in 1718. By 1722 he came within four votes of censure by the House of Commons for allegedly attempting to corrupt the Corporation of Banbury. Walpole appointed his friends and political cronies to the bench. While Lord Hardwicke was Chief Justice between 1733 and 1737, he continued to advise the Walpole administration and eventually became Lord Chancellor.

This merging of judiciary and crown servant continued throughout the century. Lord Mansfield was a product of the Whig machine and was made Chief Justice of the Court of King's Bench in 1756. That did not discourage him from serving as a member of the Newcastle and Pitt governments from 1757 to 1760, despite Blackstone, one of his puisne judges, warning about the dangers of merging the power of Minister and judge. The only consolation one might offer is to say that Mansfield's Whigism led him to give libertarian decisions in the early years of George III's reign. Certainly George III and his Ministers did not hesitate to write to judges to express their views on cases and in one famous case in 1767 a judge received lottery tickets from Ministers. Expectations about judicial independence in the eighteenth century reflected the mores of the times.

The absence of separation of powers was mirrored in the country at large. Towns and counties were run by Justices of the Peace. While their primary responsibility was to hear misdemeanours and to prosecute more serious cases before the King's judges, their ambit went far further than that. They were responsible for maintaining the highways and the prisons, for policing and the militia, for licensing and the price of bread. It was only after 1835 in the towns and 1888 in the counties that their responsibilities became largely judicial.

There as a similar, albeit slow, transformation in the senior judiciary. As the nineteenth century dawned, Lord Ellenborough, as Chief Justice, was serving in the Cabinet during the Napoleonic Wars, and the interaction between law and politics, with its inevitable impact on judicial independence, continued. In 1832 Lord Denman, in a political deal, accepted the job of Chief Justice of the Court of King's Bench at a lower salary (£8,000) than the £10,000 laid down by statute. In 1850, when Lord John Russell appointed Lord Campbell as Chief Justice, he agreed to do the job at the same discount. Such deals were scarcely what we now think of as classic cases of judicial independence.

By the time the great era of liberal reform of the courts had begun in the 1860s both Conservative Lord Chancellors (Cairns) and Liberals (Hatherley and Selborne) sought to professionalise the judiciary and to make merit the primary consideration for appointment to the bench. With respect to the final court of appeal, the House of Lords, these purposes suffered a setback as the result of the Appellate Jurisdiction Act 1876, by which a group of backbench Tories reinserted the final court of appeal into the upper house of the legislature. For a while it had looked as if the bench would follow the professionalised civil service by drawing a clear line between law and politics. That was not to be. Utilitarian solutions suffused most aspects of the State, but not the political settlement underlying the Whig ascendancy.[1]

[1] Lord Campbell, *Lives of the Lord Chancellors* (London, 1869); G Clark, *The Later Stuarts, 1660–1714* (Oxford, 1955); JCD Clark, *English Society 1660–1832* (Cambridge, 2000); G Davies, *The Early Stuarts, 1603–1660* (Oxford, 1937); J Goldsworthy, *The Sovereignty of Parliament: History and Philosophy* (Oxford, 1999); A Havighurst, 'The Judiciary and Politics in the reign of Charles II' (1950) 66 *Law Quarterly Review* 62, 229; A Havighurst, 'James II and the Twelve Men in Scarlet' (1957) 69 *Law Quarterly Review* 522; C Hill, *The Century of Revolution* (London, 1981); J Hoppit, *A Land of Liberty? England 1689–1727* (Oxford, 2000); H Horwitz, *Public Policy and Politics in the Reign of William III* (Manchester, 1977); P Langford, *A Polite and Commercial People: England 1727–1783* (Oxford, 1989); D Lemmings, 'The Independence of the Judiciary in Eighteenth Century England' in P Birks (ed), *The Life of the Law* (London, 1993) 125; D Lemmings, *Gentlemen and Barristers: The Inns of Court and the English Bar 1680–1730* (Oxford, 1990); Lord Macaulay, *History of England* (London, 1877); F O'Gorman, *The Long Eighteenth Century: British Political and Social History 1688–1832* (London, 1997); LG Schwoerer, *The Declaration of Rights* (Baltimore, 1981); B Williams, *The Whig Supremacy, 1714–1760*, 2nd edn (Oxford, 1962).

2

1900–1960 The Declining Role of the English Judiciary

The Edwardian Era

IF ONE WERE to have stopped the clock in 1900, it would not have been obvious that the transformation to a depoliticised judiciary had occurred in England. The second Home Rule Bill and the 'strange death of liberal England' in the 1890s left the Lord Chancellorship in the hands of Lord Halsbury who, in many ways, was a type of Tory who had thrived a hundred years earlier. Both in terms of appointments and decisions, Halsbury saw the senior judiciary as part of a system of spoils that Prime Minister Walpole or President Andrew Jackson would have understood. The partial depoliticisation of judicial appointments under Hatherley, Cairns, Selborne and Herschell in the 1860s, 1870s and 1880s had been quietly abandoned.

To Halsbury it seemed entirely normal that undistinguished Conservative backbenchers with indifferent practices at the Bar should be appointed to the High Court bench. It was a view that was supported by Halsbury's Prime Minister, Lord Salisbury:

> It is . . . the unwritten law of our party system; and there is no clearer statute in that unwritten law than the rule that party claims should always weigh very heavily in the disposal of the highest legal appointments. In dealing with them you cannot ignore the party system as you do in the choice of a general or an archbishop. It would be a breach of the tacit convention on which politicians and lawyers have worked the British Constitution together for the last two hundred years. Perhaps it is not an ideal system—some day no doubt the Master of the Rolls will be appointed by a competitive examination in the Law Reports, but it is our system for the present: and we should give our party arrangements a wrench if we threw it aside.

Assuming that Salisbury's view of the Constitution was the correct one, Halsbury fulfilled the expectation. He took particularly to heart Salisbury's view that 'within certain limits of intelligence, honesty and knowledge of the law, one man would make as good a judge as another, and a Tory mentality was *ipso facto* more trustworthy than a Liberal one.'[1]

Typical of the appointments Lord Halsbury made was Mr Justice Ridley. A former undistinguished Tory MP, the brother of the Home Secretary, he had been made an Official Referee. His appointment as a High Court judge was greeted with horror. The *Law Journal* announced that 'The appointment can be defended on no ground whatsoever. It would be easy to name fifty members of the bar with a better claim.' The *Law Times* said bluntly: 'no-one will believe that he would have been appointed to the High Court Bench but for his connections. . . . This is Ridleyism.' The appointment of John Lawrence, another Tory MP, was greeted with hoots of derision. The *Law Times* reported the 'bad appointment' with the observation that 'Mr Lawrence has no reputation as a lawyer, and has been rarely seen of recent years in the Royal Courts of Justice.'[2] The warning was fair. Lawrence was such an incompetent judge that it is said his decisions led to the creation of the Commercial Court.[3] Yet these two appointments were not alone. The Granthams and the Darlings were to bedevil the courts for years into the future.

From the point of view of the Conservative party there was logic to the Salisbury-Halsbury position. Conservatives were not committed to the separation of powers; they were ambivalent about the balance of powers. That wing of the party had, in the 1870s, re-established the House of Lords as the final appeal court, with the Law Lords sitting in the legislature. In Salisbury's words, since 'practically they have often to make law as judges, they will do it all the better from having also to make it as legislators.'[4] Political peers—although no longer those without legal training—still made up the quorum in panels in the Privy Council. The Attorney-General was still thought to have the right of reverter to the Chief Justiceship. The mystique of the King's Council was not dead.

Halsbury was not, however, totally unaffected by the political philosophy of the times. Albert Venn Dicey's spirit was increasingly dominating legal thought. At least as expounded in his *Introduction to the Study of the Law of the Constitution* (1885), Dicey praised the absence of a distinctive constitutional and administrative law in England, arguing that the common

---

[1] RFV Heuston, *Lives of the Lord Chancellors 1885–1940*, (Oxford, 1964) 52; A Roberts, *Salisbury: Victorian Titan* (London, 1999) 684.
[2] Heuston, (n 1 above) at 36–37.
[3] Heuston, (n 1 above) at 45.
[4] R Stevens, *Law and Politics: The House of Lords as a Judicial Body 1800–1976* (N Carolina, 1978) 55. For the debate about the revival of the House of Lords as the final court of appeal, see R Stevens, 'The Final Appeal: Reform of the House of Lords and Privy Council, 1867–1876', (1964) 80 *Law Quarterly Review*, 343.

law was sufficiently strong to protect citizens' rights and to hold individuals personally liable for administrative acts. Moreover, in propounding his concept of the Rule of Law, Dicey demanded pre-existing principles, and left virtually no room for judicial discretion or creativity. This position was, in so many ways, the flowering of Utilitarian thought, far closer to Austin than to Maine, superficially at variance with the Halsbury style. A utilitarian state of mind which had led to reform of the franchise, the court structure and the civil service, left an intellectual tradition of mechanical formalism in substantive law. Democracy was to be protected by Acts of Parliament, but not by the judges.[5] Parliamentary supremacy— or sovereignty—finally drove out any sense of Blackstone's balanced Constitution.[6] Dicey's concept of the Rule of Law was to dominate legal thinking until the 1960s and to be important throughout the twentieth century.[7] A Harold Laski or Ivor Jennings might rail against the canon; but Dicey ruled.[8]

Salisbury and Dicey were, however, right that the judges could be relied on for a Conservative spirit. Halsbury had ensured that the High Court was overstocked with Conservative MPs *manqués*, but he also appointed Conservative Lords of Appeal. While Loreburn, when he became Lord Chancellor with the great Liberal landslide in 1906, sought to lessen the importance of politics in appointments to the High Court bench, politics remained significant in appointing Lords of Appeal. Under the Liberals, Lord Shaw, the Lord Advocate, and Lord Robson, the English Attorney-General, were both appointed Lords of Appeal for, as Robson put it, the Lords were handling 'disputes that are legal in form but political in fact.'

---

[5] AV Dicey, *Introduction to the Study of Law of the Constitution* (London 1885) (1991) XII.
[6] On this see P Craig, 'Sovereignty of the United Kingdom Parliament after *Factortame*' (1991) 11 *Yearbook of European Law* 221, 234–38.
[7] R Cosgrove, *The Rule of Law: Albert Venn Dicey, Victorian Jurist* (N Carolina, 1980); see especially chs 4 and 5; Sir T Bingham, 'Dicey Revisited', (2002) *Public Law* 39.
[8] The irony was that by the end of his life Dicey had resiled from his earlier position. In 1898, in lectures delivered at Harvard (published in 1905 as *Lectures on the Relation between Law and Public Opinion in England during the Nineteenth Century*), Dicey expressed some alarm about the 'growth in collectivism'; and whereas in 1885 he had talked of judge-made law in the past tense, by 1905 he assumed it was very much alive. By then, jurisprudentially, he accepted that 'the best part of the law of England is judge-made law . . . Nor let anyone imagine that judicial legislation is a kind of law-making which belongs wholly to the past, and which has been put an end to by the annual meetings and the legislative activity of modern Parliaments'. In fact by this time Dicey had given up his unqualified enthusiasm for parliamentary Sovereignty, the Rule of Law and democracy. He by then welcomed the fact that judges are 'for the most part persons of a conservative disposition'. He admired the *Taff Vale* decision and was shocked by the legislative politics of Home Rule for Ireland. Yet, it was his earlier position on parliamentary Sovereignty, based on a democratic franchise and the Rule of Law, defining a formalistic role for the judges, which dominated the twentieth century. Stevens, *Law and Politics* (n 4 above) at 104.

He added: 'it would be idle to deny the resolute bias of many of the judges—there and elsewhere.'[9] It all sounded a little like de Tocqueville writing of the new United States seventy-five years earlier.

The interaction of Utilitarianism, High Toryism, and the collectivism of a Lib-Lab administration produced fascinating juxtapositions in decisions in the final court of appeal. Lord Halsbury had developed in *London Street Tramways v London County Council* (1898) what appeared to be a formalistic view of stare decisis: 'a decision of the House once given upon a point of law is conclusive upon this House afterwards, and [that] it is impossible to raise that question again.'[10] Or as Halsbury announced in the *Earldom of Norfolk Peerage Case* (1907): 'to alter it [the law] or even modify it is the function of the Legislature and not of your Lordships' House.'[11] Yet while Halsbury seemed anxious to endorse a declaratory formalistic theory of law, that claim may have been more a political statement than at first sight appears. He did not hesitate to manipulate the composition of panels in the House of Lords, whether the matter was Scottish ecclesiastical history or charities.[12]

Halsbury had, however, more important matters to address. *Allen v Flood*[13] was the first in a series of cases whereby he sought to weaken the unions. The Court of Appeal held there was a tort of conspiracy where the unions pressed for the sacking of a worker even where no breach of contract was involved. In the Lords, Halsbury found that only two persons in the panel of seven Law Lords were willing to support him and uphold the decision of the Court of Appeal. Without consultation, he then called up the High Court judges to appear before the Law Lords and offer their advice—a constitutional device not used since the reform of the courts in the 1870s. Because many of the judges had been appointed for their Tory views, it is scarcely surprising that six of the eight sided with Halsbury. The Law Lords, however, were not impressed. Of the nine Law Lords sitting, six voted to overrule the Court of Appeal.[14]

The point of law was, however, rapidly resurrected. Three years later, *Quinn v Leatham*[15] raised the issue of whether *Allen v Flood* had made all boycotting illegal. This time Halsbury chose the hearing panel more carefully—excluding the Liberals and including the Conservatives.

---

[9] Heuston (n 1 above) at 151.
[10] [1898] AC 375, 379.
[11] [1907] AC 10, 12.
[12] *General Assembly of Free Church of Scotland v Lord Overtoun* [1904] AC, 515; *I RC v Pemsel* [1891] AC 531. See also, Stevens, *Law and Politics* (n 4 above) at 87–88.
[13] [1898] AC 1.
[14] Stevens, *Law and Politics* (n 4 above) at 92–94.
[15] [1901] AC 495.

Moreover Halsbury appeared to go back on the jurisprudential implications of *London Street Tramways*, announcing: 'A case is only authority for what it actually decides. I entirely deny it can be quoted for a proposition which may appear to flow logically from it'.[16] Halsbury won this time, admitting it was a policy decision; but he had more in store for the unions. In 1901 in *Taff Vale Railway v Amalgamated Society of Railway Servants*,[17] the Court of Appeal had held that an injunction was not available against the threat of a strike nor could the officers of the union be personally responsible for damages flowing from such a strike. Halsbury once again chose the House of Lords panel carefully and, to the horror of the unions, the Court of Appeal was overruled. The Lords' decision in *Taff Vale* drove the unions into a formal alliance with the Labour Party and was a significant element in the Liberal landslide of 1906.[18]

It was this election which helped change the form and substance of the English judiciary. From 1905 to 1915 the Lord Chancellorship was in the hands of Loreburn and Haldane. They were very much politicians, but politicians who saw that the Halsbury system could not survive in a democratic society, particularly one in which political power—at least a meaningful part of it—had passed to the working classes. It was necessary to remove the judges from trade union law and to keep them out of the proposed welfare state. As a way of protecting the judiciary, the more formalistic view of the common law, which could be traced back to the reform of law, procedure and the courts between the 1850s and the 1870s, was re-emphasised. The more judges could appear to have no control over the outcome of decisions, the less the newly empowered left could complain. Initially, however, it was the new legislation that attracted attention.

The Trade Disputes Act of 1906, putting the unions to a very large extent outside the law, horrified Halsbury who, in the legislative debates, announced that: 'the Bill is most unjust . . . it is contrary to the spirit of English liberty . . . [it was a] Bill for the purpose of legalising tyranny.'[19] The new Liberal Lord Chancellor, Loreburn, however, was determined to see that the new legislation was interpreted neutrally and this was significantly achieved in 1909 in *Conway v Wade*.[20] While the more conservative Law Lords hit back by striking down the mandatory political levy that same year in *Amalgamated Society of Railway Servants v Osborne*,[21] the

---

[16] At 506.
[17] *Taff Vale Rly Co v Amalgamated Society of Railway Servants* [1901] AC 426.
[18] Stevens, *Law and Politics* (n 4 above) at 92–94.
[19] Parl. Debs (series 4) vol 166, col 704 (4 December 1906). While Halsbury's response was an overreaction, the unhappy history of union disruption of the British economy during the twentieth century was not unrelated to the 1906 Act.
[20] [1909] AC 506.
[21] [1910] AC 87 (1909).

government took legislative action to negate the decision in the Trade
Union Act 1913. Halsbury's legacy—and the reaction to it—was not a
happy one as the country began to build a welfare state. Lloyd George, as
the responsible Minister, carefully excluded the judges from the National
Insurance Bill and related legislation, while the Home Secretary, Winston
Churchill, told the House of Commons in 1911 that 'where class issues are
involved . . . a very large number of our population have been led to the
opinion that they (the judges) are, unconsciously no doubt, biased'.[22] A
combination of legislation, self-protection and a change in legal style was
removing courts and judges from the political arena.

Dicey had seen the absence of a separate system of administrative law
as one of the great advantages of the English legal system; Loreburn and
Haldane worked to ensure that the elements of administrative law which
did exist would be excised. Lord Loreburn, who had a practical sense of
politics denied to Haldane, set a balanced tone in *Board of Education v
Rice in* 1911[23] where he drew a distinction between procedural due process
('natural justice'), where the courts had a vital role, and substantive due
process where the courts had none. Haldane, who became Lord Chancellor
in 1912, with a reputation of being more intellectual and, in theory at least,
more of a radical than Loreburn, nevertheless destroyed the rational
distinction in *Rice* in the case of *Arlidge v Local Government Board*.[24]
Haldane put together a panel of Law Lords, all of whom had been active
Liberal politicians. As Lord Shaw put it, to require even procedural due
process:

> would be inconsistent, as I say, with efficiency, with practice, and with the true
> theory of complete parliamentary responsibility for departmental action . . . that
> the judiciary should presume to impose its own methods on administrative or
> executive officers is a usurpation.[25]

By denying the courts even a limited role in protecting procedural due
process, British administrative law was to sleep for the next fifty years.

The idea of a written Constitution, or even fundamental laws, by which
executive or legislative decisions might be judged, was traditionally alien
both to the royal prerogative and to parliamentary sovereignty. It is an

---

[22] Stevens, *Law and Politics* (n 4 above) at 94–96. Parl. Debs (series 5) vol 26, col 1022 (30 May 1914). In that same year, Churchill was reported in a TUC document to have said: 'statements have been made from the bench reflecting on the trade unions in language which is extremely ignorant and wholly out of touch with the general development of modern thought, and which has greatly complicated the administration of justice and created a sense of distrust in the ordinary administration of the law'. Stevens, *Law and Politics* (n 4 above) at 97; D Pannick, *Judges* (Oxford, 1988) ch 2.

[23] [1911] AC 179.

[24] [1915] AC 120.

[25] [1915] AC at 137–38.

absence which confuses—or mystifies—North American and continental lawyers, as well as being frustrating to some British reformers. The closest the English legal system came to a flirtation with such ideas was the Judicial Committee of the Privy Council which had taken on a new lease of life with the expansion of the British Empire in the nineteenth century. It was given even greater prominence as the Dominions came into being, with British statutes serving as written Constitutions in Canada in 1867, Australia in 1900, New Zealand in 1907 and South Africa in 1909. The sad thing was that the British judges showed little flair for constitutional matters, and from 1900 onwards, each successive Imperial Conference complained about the casual staffing of the Judicial Committee and the failure of the Law Lords to comprehend the nature of constitutional decisions.[26]

It is perhaps not surprising that while the British North America Act (the Canadian Constitution) allowed appeals in all matters, the Commonwealth of Australia Act restricted constitutional appeals and the South Africa Act virtually excluded them. The royal prerogative and parliamentary sovereignty had so permeated thinking that the idea that a parliamentary statute might be unconstitutional—the basis of the new Dominions' Constitutions—eluded some of the British judges. In *Webb v Outrim*, an Australian appeal in 1906, Halsbury, faced with judicial review, in the American sense—that is the ability to strike down statutes—recoiled in horror: 'That is a novelty to me. I thought an Act of Parliament was an Act of Parliament and you cannot go beyond it . . . I do not know what an unconstitutional Act means.'[27] Halsbury therefore refused to listen to arguments based on American precedents going back to *Marbury v Madison*.[28] Even those Law Lords who were more conscious of the realities had little sense of the organic nature of constitutions.

The War to End All Wars, Economic Strife and the Long Weekend

Under Loreburn and Haldane then, Liberal Party policy came to be that High Court and Court of Appeal judges were appointed on the basis of success at the Bar to the general exclusion of party affiliation, a remarkable switch in which success in a private profession (albeit determined by a politician) was substituted for political claims. This policy was in general pursued by their Conservative successors, although political experience was still thought appropriate for Law Lords in the final court of appeal—

[26] R Stevens, *The Independence of the Judiciary: The view from the Lord Chancellor's Office* (Oxford, 1993) 30–39.
[27] [1907] AC 81. On the quote see Stevens, *Law and Politics* (n 4 above) at 137–38, 178–79.
[28] 5 US (1 Cranch) 137 (1803).

witness the appointment of the Irish Protestant politician, Carson, by Lloyd George. Lord Chancellors, however, remained very much politicians, presiding in the Lords as a legislative body, sitting in the Cabinet, running the Lord Chancellor's Office and still sitting frequently—some of them— as judges in both Lords and Privy Council. With the exception of the few politically weak Lord Chancellors, it was they who set the judicial tone.

The Lord Chief Justiceship was also a highly political office. It was still regarded as belonging by right of reverter to the Attorney-General and the post of Chief Justice was still thought of as a political office. In this tradition Richard Webster, Salisbury's Attorney-General, succeeded to the Chief Justiceship as Lord Alvestone in 1900. Alvestone was not intellectually distinguished, but perhaps one did not need to be to run the King's Bench Division. His lack of judgment came to the fore, however, when he sat as one of the six arbitrators in the Alaska boundary dispute. Against much of the evidence, he sided with the US arbitrators, an act still regarded as treacherous, especially in British Columbia.

In 1913, Alvestone was replaced by Rufus Isaacs, a man with virtually no formal education, great ability and, at least in the eyes of his political enemies, dubious ethics. The world was of course about to be plunged into the First World War, but even taking account of that, Isaacs' (by now Lord Reading) time as Lord Chief Justice was remarkable. With the outbreak of war, he was called to the Treasury to run the legislative and economic side of the war. In 1915 he led the Anglo-French mission to Washington, achieving a badly needed war loan. He returned to judicial work for a while—presiding over the conviction of Sir Roger Casement for treason in 1916—but by 1917 he was back in Washington as High Commissioner to the US and Canada. By January 1918 he was Ambassador to the US as well, returning to the UK in the summer of 1919, when Lloyd George claimed that he had been the catalyst in persuading the US to commit troops to Europe. In 1920 Lloyd George made it clear that he needed him as Viceroy to India. Thither Reading went in 1921, this time resigning as Chief Justice.[29]

Even then, as was so often the case during the Prime Ministership of David Lloyd George, things were not simple. His Attorney-General, Gordon Hewart, wanted to exercise his right of reverter to the Chief Justiceship, but Lloyd George felt he could not be spared. One of Halsbury's better appointments, AT Lawrence, was appointed Lord Chief Justice with the title of Lord Trevethin. The quid pro quo was that he gave an undated letter of resignation, a letter of resignation which Trevethin then read in *The Times* when, in 1922, the administration broke up. Hewart, who turned out to be a poor judge—as well as a difficult man—became Chief Justice.

[29] J Simon, 'Rufus Isaacs', *DNB 1931–1940* (Oxford, 1949) 467.

Much water was to flow under the bridge, but symmetry was achieved in 1940, when Downing Street asked for Hewart's resignation in order that Churchill might insert Lord Caldecote into the Chief Justiceship. Caldecote had been removed as Dominions Secretary on the outbreak of war in 1939. He was compensated by being made Lord Chancellor. Eight months later when that post was needed for Sir John Simon, Caldecote found himself Lord Chief Justice. The post was little more than a commodity.

Meanwhile, in the courts, with the exception of the Judicial Committee of the Privy Council, the public law element was growing irrelevant. *Arlidge* and *Rice* had left very little of English administrative law. In 1931, *Minister of Health v R, ex p Yaffé* [30] confirmed that this was the situation. Increasingly, delegated legislation operated under 'Henry VIII' clauses, providing that even subsidiary legislation should have effect 'as if enacted in this Act'. Coupled with statutory clauses preventing challenges in the courts, such developments meant that delegated legislation could not be challenged at all. Defects in an order, once confirmed by a Minister, were automatically cured. [31] There was also a wide range of discretionary acts based on the exercise of the royal prerogative, which the courts were reluctant to question, as they were those of most administrative tribunals. Dicey's vision of a legal system devoid of administrative law was close to being accepted, but in the English context it meant that control of the administration was left to the vagaries of the parliamentary question rather than systematic control by the courts.

While the judges had been primarily responsible for the tepid state of UK administrative law, this did not prevent the Chief Justice, Lord Hewart, the former Liberal Attorney-General, from complaining bitterly about the state of affairs. Hewart in 1928 discovered 'that there (was) a long-standing plot (hatched among part of the civil service and fostered by Royal Commissions) to alter the position of the judiciary'. [32] The Civil Service felt the pressure. Sir Claud Schuster, the powerful Permanent Secretary of the Lord Chancellor's Office complained:

> In recent years . . . it has been difficult for the State to obtain justice from the judges of the High Court. It is not too much to say that in recent years, the weight of prejudice against the State in the minds of many members of the Court of Appeal and judges of the High Court has been such as seriously to affect the administration of justice. [33]

---

[30] [1931] AC 494.
[31] For this Dicey must take a significant share of the blame: Cosgrove, (n 7 above) at ch 5. Parliamentary sovereignty, said Dicey, was 'the dominant characteristic of our political institutions': *Law of the Constitution* (n 5 above) at 71.
[32] Stevens, *Law and Politics* (n 4 above) at 193.
[33] Stevens (n 26 above) at 27.

The conflict ultimately led to the establishment of the Committee on Ministers' Powers in 1928.

The Committee not surprisingly found that since 1905 an increasing amount of social legislation excluded the jurisdiction of the courts entirely, while disputes under such legislation were handled by tribunals outside the scope of the regular courts. Rather than urge reconciliation, however, the Committee blessed the dichotomy between legal decisions (the rightful province of the regular courts) and policy decisions (the domain of the executive and tribunals). It was Dicey's original concept of the Rule of Law carried to the outer limit.[34] The Committee apparently had no doubt that a line could be drawn between a judicial decision 'which disposes of the whole matter by a finding upon the facts in dispute and an application of the law of the land to the facts so found' and a quasi-judicial situation (not appropriate for the judges) where such process was replaced by 'administrative action' that might involve 'consideration of public policy' or 'discretion'. The report assumed the objectivity of legal rules and the feasibility of interpreting statutes 'impartially'. Formalism (and in particular the declaratory theory of law) had achieved public and political respectability.

It was in short a sad period in British history and a petulant period for the judiciary. While deferring to the legislature—as Dicey had decreed—the judges seethed. One of the few powers they did retain was the right to declare delegated legislation ultra vires. With the bloody memory of the First World War fading, in *Roberts v Hopwood*[35] the Law Lords struck down, in speeches loaded with class assumptions, Poplar Council's minimum wage of £4 per week. As Harold Laski observed, the decision might be 'fatal to the esteem in which judges should be held. . . . It is an easy step from the *Poplar* judgment to the conclusion that the House of Lords is, in entire good faith, the unconscious servant of a single class in the community.'[36] The judiciary appeared increasingly out of touch with an England which was rent by class divides and economically in decline. The situation was not helped when Mr Justice Astbury decided that the General Strike

---

[34] 'Not only the ideas but the language of Dicey spiced the report, *Law of the Constitution* permeated every page. The Donoughmore Committee, as it was known, cited Dicey so often and so favourably that Sir Cecil Carr remarked that the Committee investigated whether Britain had gone off the Dicey standard in regard to administrative law and, if so, what was the quickest way to return. The Committee accepted Dicey as gospel, inquiring whether his constitutional teachings were being betrayed by delegated legislation heretics. In particular, the Committee embraced Dicey's antithesis between *droit administratif* and English law. "In our opinion Professor Dicey's conclusion is no less true than it was in 1915." Recommendation XI of the Report exhorted that no system of administrative law in any guise should be established in England.': Cosgrove (n 7 above) at 95–96.
[35] [1925] AC 578.
[36] Stevens, *Law and Politics* (n 4 above) at 193.

was illegal.[37] As if to confirm the class basis of the appeal judges, the House of Lords, which under Loreburn had sought to take a balanced approach to tax statutes, became caught up with the idea that tax statutes must be construed narrowly to protect civil liberties. The high point of this was *IRC v Duke of Westminster*[38] where the House of Lords, over the objections of Lord Atkin who wished to look to the substance of the transaction, held that by a series of formal arrangements, the Duke might pay his servants out of untaxed income. For the next forty years, Britain, even in the period of 'socialistic' taxation, was able to provide a way for the wealthy, with good tax advisers, to avoid much of their tax burden.

In that tawdry atmosphere, it was perhaps not surprising that the judges were not minded to join in the general sacrifice expected of all Civil Servants during the Depression. When the National Economy Acts axe was wielded in 1931, judicial salaries were cut. Stanley Baldwin, the Chancellor of the Exchequer, unwisely wrote to the judges that he had not consulted them because 'it seemed to me best . . . to rely on the patriotism of the eminent and patriotic body to which you belong and to assume their acquiescence'. The judges had a legitimate concern; as Mr Justice Maugham put it, perhaps unfortunately, they had been treated 'as if they were policemen or postmen'. The judges published a memorandum and threatened a Petition of Right to challenge the cuts. The government understandably worried about who would hear the Petition. In the end the government had a defensive Bill drawn up. Schuster wrote to the parliamentary draftsman:

> Begin with a recital, which should be as long and pompous as possible, asserting the independence and all the rest of it and negating any idea that the Economy Act or the Order in Council affected that in any way . . . Then declare that notwithstanding all this, they are affected by the cut.[39]

The interaction between the judiciary, the legislature and the executive in the 1920s and 1930s left much to be desired. The increasing judicial obsession with deference and status seemed to be in inverse proportion to the declining importance of the judiciary in constitutional and other disputes. The courts were increasingly limited to crime, property, tort and contract. While property matters still heavily involved the profession, much of social, commercial and industrial life was passing the courts—and the profession—by. Increasingly the centre of judicial life was the criminal cases of the judges on circuit. The majesty of the law, embodied in the circuit system, moving from assize town to assize town, accompanied by

---

[37] *National Sailors and Firemen's Union of Great Britain v Reed* [1926] Ch 536. JAG Griffith, *Judicial Politics since 1920* (London, 1993) 11–15.
[38] [1936] AC 1.
[39] Stevens (n 26 above) at 98.

Lords-Lieutenant, trumpeters, pikemen, marshals and the butler, became a symbol for the irrelevance of the judiciary's role in modern England. For judges like Lord Goddard, who became Chief Justice in 1946, the right to order hanging and the wearing of the black cap created a false impression of the importance of the senior judiciary.[40] In truth the legal system was increasingly irrelevant to the functioning of modern England.

It would be wrong, however, to think that the judges had been completely excluded from the Constitution. As judges became less important in hearing public law cases and in dealing with new areas in the courts, they were used more frequently to chair commissions and committees. Judges were increasingly seen as 'impartial' and capable of 'objective' solutions. For most of the nineteenth century committees of one or other House of Parliament had investigated both narrow factual issues and general policy areas—hence the ubiquitous Blue Books. The Pigott forgeries in the 1880s, however, had led to a judicial inquiry, although one conducted by good Unionist judges. The norm, nevertheless, remained for Parliament to police itself; as for instance the investigation of the Marconi scandal involving Rufus Isaacs and other of Lloyd George's Ministers (1913). By the end of the First World War, however, the tide turned and the Tribunals of Inquiry Act 1921 gave status and certain privileges to judicial enquiries. Already Shaw, a Law Lord, had been used in 1919 to handle the dock strike; Sankey, a High Court judge, was used to project the future of the coal industry (recommending a form of nationalisation); Scott completed the Committee on Ministers' Powers. A regular new role for the judges had emerged.

Moreover the judges still had important constitutional roles in the Commonwealth, sitting as judges of the Judicial Committee of the Privy Council. It was probably with respect to Canada that the British judicial influence in constitutional interpretation was most obvious. Earlier in the century the formalistic pro-provincial views of Watson, Davey and Haldane contrasted with the more instrumental and balanced views of Loreburn. Sankey (Lord Chancellor 1929–35) returned to the broad approach:

> the British North America Act planted in Canada a living tree capable of growth and expansion within its natural limits . . . their Lordships do not conceive it to be the duty of this Board—it is certainly not their desire—to cut down the

---

[40] Goddard was the object of sycophantic praise during his lifetime, and for sometime afterwards: see F Bresler, *Lord Goddard: A Biography* (London, 1977). The first serious criticism came at the time of his death in 1971, when Bernard Levin in *The Times* opined that 'Goddard, as Lord Chief Justice, was a calamity'. This led to a shouting match between the legal establishment and the critics who had emerged during the 1960s. S Shetreet, *Judges on Trial* (Amsterdam, 1976) 184–85.

provisions of the Act by a narrow and technical construction, but rather to give it a large and liberal interpretation.[41]

Sankey was dismissed as Chancellor in 1935 to be replaced by Hailsham. In 1936 Hailsham was faced with a series of appeals testing the constitutionality of Ottawa's 'New Deal'. He tried to persuade Sankey to preside, but Sankey was still sulking as a result of his dismissal. Lord Atkin, a distinguished commercial lawyer, presided instead and disassociated the Judicial Committee from the Sankey view:

> while the ship of state now sails on larger ventures and into foreign waters she still retains the watertight compartments which are an essential part of her original structure'.[42]

(It is believed that this was a 3–2 decision, the swing vote being Mr Justice Rowlatt, a difficult tax judge who had been persuaded to resign from the High Court with the inducement of a Privy Councillorship.[43]) The Canadian New Deal was struck down; responsible opinion in Ottawa was outraged; the Canadian Senate's O'Connor Report of 1939 recommended abolition of appeals, something which, with the intervention of the Second World War, was ultimately achieved in 1949.[44]

High Formalism, World War and Increasing Irrelevance

The period from 1939 to the early 1960s marked the depths of the irrelevance of the courts in the development of the Constitution. During the Second World War, Lord Greene, at that time Master of the Rolls (Head of the Court of Appeal), announced:

> The function of the legislature is to make the law, the function of the administration is to administer the law and the function of the judiciary is to interpret and enforce the law. The judiciary is not concerned with policy. It is not for the judiciary to decide what is in the public interest. These are the tasks of the legislature, which is put there for the purpose, and it is not right it should shirk its responsibility.[45]

---

[41] *Edwards v A-G for Canada* [1930] AC 124, 136.
[42] [1937] AC 326, 354.
[43] After the case was heard, but before the decision came down, Hailsham, the Lord Chancellor, who had not sat, wrote to Lord Atkin who had presided: 'I think that you and I are both agreed as to the paramount importance of retaining the Appeal to the Privy Council from the Dominions of the Crown ... I expect the decisions, when given, will carry conviction, which after all is the best test of the strength of the tribunal.': Heuston, (n 1 above) at 487.
[44] CG Pierson, *Canada and the Privy Council* (London, 1960) 69 *et seq.*
[45] W Greene, 'Law and Progress', (1944) 94 *Law Journal* 349.

The workload of the House of Lords as a judicial body, declined steadily. In 1953 only nineteen cases were heard—half as many as in 1939. They took, however, twice as long to hear; some four days rather than two; and almost half of them concerned tax.[46] Far from being a Supreme Court for the United Kingdom, the House had lost its way as a final court of appeal. With legal aid not at that point extended to the House of Lords, it was scarcely surprising that Gerald Gardiner, writing in 1963, the year before he became Harold Wilson's Lord Chancellor, recommended the abolition of the second appeal.[47]

Tax law itself had become an elaborate form of chess or crossword puzzle with the courts giving an appearance of joining in the game. Even the Lord Chancellors of the period—Lord Simon (1940–45), Lord Jowitt (1945–51) and Lord Simonds (1951–54)—took pleasure in emasculating anti-avoidance devices. In purely public law cases only the 18B case—allowing detention without trial—*Liversidge v Anderson*[48]—became well known and that chiefly for the vigorous dissent of Lord Atkin. Elsewhere public law was a wasteland. *Duncan v Cammell Laird*[49] gave carte blanche to crown privilege. In *Franklin v Minister of Town and Country Planning*[50] the House of Lords denied that the law had any responsibility for procedural due process under the New Towns Act, while the same response was given with respect to the Central Land Board—the epitome of central planning—in 1951 in *Earl Fitzwilliam's Wentworth Estates Co v Minister of Housing and Local Government*.[51] It could be argued that the massive majority of the Labour government in 1945 justified judicial caution. The depths of judicial abdication, however, were reached in *Smith v East Elloe RDC*,[52] at a time when the Conservative Party was back in power. There the House held there was no way the courts could entertain a case even if fraud had been alleged in making or confirming a compulsory purchase order.

The flight of the courts from public law was, in some ways, understandable. In one famous interchange, James Reid, who later became a Law Lord, but at that time was a Conservative MP, moved an amendment to the National Health Bill concerning the Standing Committee of the National

---

[46] L Blom-Cooper and G Drewry, *Final Appeal: A Study of the House of Lords in its Judicial Capacity* (Oxford, 1972). For a study of the actual operation of the Law Lords, see A Paterson, *The Law Lords* (London, 1982).
[47] Stevens, *Law and Politics* (n 4 above) at 415.
[48] [1942] AC 206. See AWB Simpson, *In the Highest Degree Odious: Detention Without Trial in Wartime Britain* (Oxford, 1992).
[49] [1942] AC 624.
[50] [1948] AC 87.
[51] [1952] AC 362.
[52] [1955] AC 736.

Health Service, which had the right to fire physicians or other employees of the Service. The Bill provided a final right of appeal to the Minister. The Reid amendment suggested the appeal should go to a High Court judge. Aneurin Bevan, the Health Minister, opposed the change:

> we cannot admit that the courts should interpret whether the doctor has, in fact, been a good servant of the people . . . (this) would be real judicial sabotage of socialised services in which the functions of industrial dispute are entrusted to the judiciary.

Reid saw this as a charge that 'His Majesty's judges . . . desire to commit judicial sabotage on the introduction of Socialism'. While Bevan claimed he had been 'monstrously misconstrued', the exchange was scarcely an invitation to judicial activism; and, at the same time, it made it even odder that the Labour government should be willing to use judges so freely outside the courts to settle wage disputes and other industrial issues.[53]

The charade of independence and irrelevance was taken to a remarkable degree. The Lord Chancellor, Lord Jowitt, was proud of the fact that he had never appointed a Labour man to the bench (he did eventually appoint Donovan) and he was clearly anxious to retain his Diceyan credentials, telling the American Bar Association:

> Never has there been a time when the rule of law has been more firmly entrenched in my country. Never has there been a time when the acts of the executive are more completely subject to the opinions of an entirely independent judiciary.[54]

Jowitt's powers of self-delusion were considerable.

The Labour government (1945–51) was, in this sense, a study in contrasts. The judges did, however, continue to influence politics in other ways. It had always been a murky constitutional convention about which subjects it was appropriate for Law Lords to speak on in the legislative debates in the House of Lords. In the 1950s and 1960s Lord Goddard, the Chief Justice, defended capital punishment and supported flogging, two causes initially taken up by his successor, Lord Parker. Goddard, a Conservative, although appointed by a Labour government, saw no reason to extend legal aid to criminal cases. While the government was anxious to reform divorce law, such reform was vigorously (and largely successfully) opposed by Lord Merriman (and later Lord Hodson) in the legislative sessions of the Lords.[55]

---

[53] Griffith (n 37 above) at 80.
[54] Stevens, *Law and Politics* (n 4 above) at 337.
[55] Stevens (n 26 above) at 114–15.

Even more powerful was the role of the judges as Chairs of Royal Commissions and Departmental Committees. Between 1945 and 1969, judges—mainly Law Lords—chaired seven of the 24 Royal Commissions and 118 of the 358 Departmental Committees. The Law Lords might increasingly be seen as eunuchs in legal appeals, but they were virile in investigating, advising and prescribing. Lord du Parcq, for instance, chaired the Royal Commission on JPs, Lords Cohen and Radcliffe shared the Royal Commission on the Taxation of Profits and Income, Lord Morton chaired the Royal Commission on Marriage and Divorce, while Lord Uthwatt chaired the Committee on Leaseholds and Lord Donovan chaired the Royal Commission on Industrial Relations. Lord Asquith chaired the Royal Commission on Equal Pay, Lord Cohen chaired the Committee on Company Law, both Lord Evershed and Lord Devlin chaired committees on the Port Transport Industry and Lord Jenkins chaired a Committee on Intermediaries. On a more controversial level, Lord Denning reported on the Profumo Affair, Lord Devlin on the Riots in Nyasaland; and Lord Radcliffe on the Vassell affair and 'D' Notices. Pay disputes were increasingly referred to judicially chaired bodies. Lord Wilberforce dealt with electricity supply and the mines; Mr Justice Lloyd Jacob with the pay of doctors. In a brief space of time, as the decline in the importance of the courts in public policy became obvious, the judges' time was increasingly spent in activities which many societies would define as political.[56]

---

[56] C Guarnieri and P Pederzoli, *The Power of Judges: A Comparative Study of Courts and Democracy* (Oxford, 2002), *passim*.

3

The Gradual U-Turn

The Old Order Regroups

WITH THE END of the Second World War in 1945 and the
arrival of the first Labour government with a majority in the
House of Commons, there were pressures in the Cabinet for a
radical restructuring of the court system and hence of the judiciary. Would
the legal system survive the arrival of a socialist majority? In Cabinet ideas
advanced included the abolition of the adversary system and the substitu-
tion of a civil law approach to litigation. Fortunately from the point of
view of the judiciary and the divided profession, the Lord Chancellor was
the conservatively minded William Jowitt. To thwart serious reform, and
especially to maintain judicial prestige and a separate Bar, Jowitt was only
prepared to tinker with the status quo. He wanted the Bar preserved in its
traditional form. He was opposed to any Continental influences. To protect
the High Court bench and the barristers' traditional role, he persuaded the
Cabinet Committee that what was needed was two committees—one on
the High Court and one on the county court—thereby ensuring that the
existing structure and monopolies would not be threatened.[1] Indeed, Lord
Chief Justice Goddard and the Master of the Rolls, Lord Greene, saw little
point in having a committee on the High Court at all; and certainly did not
want any non-lawyers on it. Jowitt put his conscience at rest by appointing
a committee including non-lawyers, but making Raymond Evershed chair,
since 'I know from previous correspondence that he does not want to do
anything so drastic as to substitute for our procedure something analogous
to French procedure'.

The 'previous correspondence' was important. In the waning days of the
Churchill administration, in 1945, Evershed had written to Viscount
Simon, the outgoing Chancellor, arguing that the supremacy of the Rule of
Law in England 'is largely bound up with the immense prestige and
personal position accorded to the judges.' There were at least four reasons
for this. First, the judges were chosen from a 'cloistered' and 'aristocratic'

---

[1] LCO 2/4012 (Lord Chancellor's Office papers, Public Record Office).

profession. Secondly, the judge was 'the complete master of the trial.' Thirdly, the strict rules of procedure 'make the proceedings not only solemn (if not Olympian) but secure a real impartiality.' Fourthly, 'the rules as to dress (wigs and gowns) plus the rules of common law and precedent have made the law something of a mystery'.

From all this, Evershed drew certain conclusions. First:

> if very far reaching reforms were made so as to make our procedures more like the Continental, the result might well be to impair the position of the judges. *Per contra* if it is desired to maintain the personal position of the judges, certain limitations to the scope of the reforms which are possible have got to be realised.

First there could be no fusion of the professions: the distinction between barristers and solicitors was sacrosanct. Secondly, Evershed was:

> inclined to think that a complete codification of our law plus the abolition of our rules of precedent would tend to make our law simpler and therefore cheaper. On the other hand, it would tend to make it less certain and authoritative and it would tend to derogate seriously from the supremacy of our Courts.

Finally, Evershed thought:

> that a complete and radical change of our whole system so as to make it conform more to the 'centralised' system would or could greatly cheapen our law . . . But in considering such a change, the main thing to bear in mind is, I believe, the effect such a change might have on the position of Judges.

Such was the provenance of the Evershed Committee.[2] Its conservative assumptions were to shape English legal culture for the remainder of the century.

By this time in the civil courts the work was inevitably primarily of a private nature, and it was approached in the most formalistic manner. While, in succeeding decades, there were more imaginative judges—Reid, Denning, Radcliffe and Devlin—theirs was a voice little heard in the 1940s and 1950s. The tone was set by the Lord Chancellors—Simon, Jowitt and Simonds—who at that time still sat regularly in the judicial committees of both Lords and Privy Council and their view allowed little by way of judicial creativity in the common law or statutory interpretation. Jowitt was obsessed with the idea of certainty, which may have insured technical competence in private law decisions at first instance; it was the antithesis of what was needed in public law cases in the final court of appeal. Jowitt, however, believed the establishment of fixed rules to be 'an inevitable tendency in civilized society.' In talking of one possible appeal he emphasised that:

---

[2] Evershed Memorandum, dated 27 July 1945, LCO 2/3827.

we should loyally follow the (earlier) decision of the House of Lords . . . it is not really a question of being a bold or timorous soul . . . we are really no longer in the position of considering what the law ought to be . . . the problem is not to consider what social and political considerations do today require, that is to confuse the role of the lawyer with the task of the legislator. It is quite possible that the law has produced a result which does not accord with the requirements of today. If so put it right by legislation, but do not expect every lawyer . . . to decide what the law ought to be . . . do not get yourself into a frame of mind of entrusting to the judges the working out of a whole new set of principles which does accord with the requirements of modern conditions. Leave that to the legislature, and leave us to confine ourselves to trying to find out what the law is.[3]

In short, judges should apply objective rules (to be determined by strict principles of stare decisis and ratio decidendi) and interpret statutes according to their 'plain meaning'. How could a socialist government object to such a policy-neutral bench even if its members were public school and Oxbridge educated with an alleged Conservative bias? Moreover, Lord Simonds, who became Lord Chancellor when Churchill returned to power in 1951, continued the Jowitt approach. Even the mischief rule of statutory interpretation was offensive to Simonds:

it is sufficient to say that the general proposition that it is the duty of the court to find out the intention of Parliament—and not only of Parliament but of Ministers also—cannot by any means be supported. The duty of the courts is to interpret the words that the legislature has used; these words may be ambiguous, but, even if they are, the power and duty of the court to travel outside them on a voyage of discovery are strictly limited.

To modern eyes the style was not helpful.[4]

Simonds' approach to developing the common law was similarly negative:

I will not be led by an undiscerning zeal for some abstract kind of justice to ignore our first duty, which is to administer justice according to law, the law which is established for us by Acts of Parliament or the binding authority of precedent.[5]

---

[3]   R Stevens, *Law and Politics: The House of Lords as a Judicial Body 1800–1976* (N Carolina, 1978) 338–39.
[4]   *Magor and St Mellons RDC v Newport Corporation* [1952] AC 189, 191. In *IRC v Ayrshire Employees Mutual Insurance Association* [1946] 1 All ER 637 Simonds opined: 'It is at least clear what is the gap that is intended to be filled and hardly less clear how it is intended to fill that gap. Yet I can come to no other conclusion than that the language of the section fails to achieve its apparent purpose and I must decline to insert words and phrases which might succeed where the draughtsman failed' (at 641).
[5]   *Midland Silicones v Scruttons* [1962] AC 446, 467–69.

He was, moreover, firm about binding authority. In *Jacobs v LCC* the law of invitees and licensees was pushed back some fifty years by his insistence on treating both reasons for an earlier decision as binding:

> There is in my opinion no justification for regarding as obiter dictum a reason given by a judge for his decision, because he has given another reason also . . . it would, I think, be to deny the importance, I would say the paramount importance, of certainty in the law to give less than coercive effect to the unequivocal statement of the law made after argument by members of this House . . . nor . . . are your Lordships entitled to disregard such a statement because you would have the law otherwise. To determine what the law is, not what it ought to be, is our present task.'[6]

It was Simonds who presided in *Smith v East Elloe RDC*.[7] To administrative law he applied the same brand of formalistic deference as he did to stare decisis. It was scarcely surprising that public law was moribund in the 1940s and 1950s, with private law approaching judicial catatonia.

The Changing Political Environment

There was, however, a slow and gradual change of style. While a detailed analysis of the jurisprudential aspects of this falls outside the scope of this book, one can see obvious pointers by the late 1960s. Lord Radcliffe, who had gone straight from the Bar to be a Law Lord in 1949, offered one:

> [t]here was never a more sterile controversy than that upon the question whether a judge makes laws. Of course he does. How can he help it? . . . Judicial law is always a reinterpretation of principles in the light of new combinations of facts.

He also added the political justification—singularly appropriate for one so involved in 'political' work off the bench—for the then current situation:

---

[6] [1950] AC 361, 368–69.

[7] [1956] AC 736, see especially at 750–51. 'I think anyone bred in the tradition of the law is likely to regard with little sympathy legislative provisions for ousting the jurisdiction of the Court, whether in order that the subject may be deprived altogether of remedy or in order that his grievance may be remitted to some other tribunal. But it is our plain duty to give the words of the Act their proper meaning and, for my part, I find it quite impossible to qualify the words of the paragraph in the manner suggested. It may be that the legislature had not in mind the possibility of an order being made by a local authority in bad faith or even the possibility of an order made in good faith being mistakenly, capriciously or wantonly challenged. This is a matter of speculation.' Reid and Somervell, the two Law Lords with political experience, dissented. In *Earl Fitzwilliam's Wentworth Estates Co v Minister of Housing and Local Government* [1952] AC 367, the House of Lords held that the Central Land Board might use its powers to force owners to sell underdeveloped land, although the Board's powers had previously been thought to be limited to the collection of development charges.

> Personally, I think that judges will serve the public interest better if they keep quiet about their legislative function . . . The judge who shows his hand, who advertises what he is about, may indeed show that his is a strong spirit, unfettered by the past; but I doubt very much whether he is not doing some harm to general confidence in the law as a constant, safe in the hands of the judges, than he is doing good to the law's credit as a set of rules nicely attuned as the sentiment of the day.[8]

The next alighting point might well be Lord Reid, a Scottish law officer who was made a Law Lord in 1948. He felt the time had come to end 'fairy tales'. He pushed the English judicial style back from that which Karl Llewellyn had described as being 'like a Victorian virgin tubbing in her nightgown'. Reid raised the constitutional issue: 'In so far as we can get the thing back on the rails let us do so.'[9] Reid's position was the antithesis of Simonds. What had happened?

While political wisdom may have guided Lord Chancellors Jowitt and Simonds in their efforts to protect the judiciary from anything that might be thought to be political—or even involve a policy choice—a reaction to what was, after all, an intellectually indefensible position, had been inevitable. One can begin to detect a change during the Chancellorship of Lord Kilmuir. In 1954, in his first year of office, he announced that 'the law should be brought in to help in the solution of the great problems of a modern state.' Early in the Churchill administration, when Kilmuir was President of the Board of Trade, he had wanted to appoint a judge as Chair of the Monopolies Commission, but he was thwarted by Sir George Coldstream, the Permanent Secretary to the Lord Chancellor, who did not want 'to ask the judiciary to descend into the arena of public affairs.' By the time the matter was raised again in 1955, Kilmuir had become Lord Chancellor. The permanent officials took the Diceyan position: 'public interest questions are not justiciable issues such as are appropriate for determination by a truly judicial body: the function is more nearly executive or administrative.' When later in the year a Cabinet Committee opted for registering restrictive agreements and having them investigated by High Court judges, the civil servants were shocked.

The Deputy Permanent Secretary minuted the Permanent Secretary that 'the whole nonsense had been caused by the agitation about tribunals . . . a High Court Judge . . . is ill suited to decide the sort of cases that will be at issue here.' That same day, the Permanent Secretary presented a paper to the Lord Chancellor, pointing out that the Permanent Secretaries of all the relevant departments were agreed that the proposals were 'thoroughly unsound' and should be 'remitted to officials.' He was eventually convinced

---

[8]   Lord Radcliffe, *Not in Feather Beds* (London, 1968) 271.
[9]   Lord Reid, 'The Law and the Reasonable Man' (1968) *Proceedings of the British Academy* 193.

that the only justification for using the judges was 'the wretched state of business in the Chancery Division.' (The truth was that the Chancery judges were such a disagreeable group that litigation in that Division had virtually dried up.) In the event, however, the Chancery judges had 'grave objections' because of the 'political element' which 'must play a part in the deliberation of the court as proposed.' All the Queen's Bench judges except Mr Justice Devlin opposed the new court. Perhaps unsurprisingly, Devlin was selected as President of the new court.[10]

The Labour Party opposed the Restrictive Trade Practices Bill because the 'Bill hands over to this court governmental and parliamentary power. All judgments are founded on law or upon facts, but in this case the decision which really matters will be a decision founded neither upon law nor upon fact. It will be a political and economic decision.'[11] *The Economist* warned that the 'idea that a decision should change if the climate of opinion changes, even though other things remain the same, is not an idea that will be easily digestible by trained legal minds.' *The Times* thundered: '[c]lose thought must be given to the probable effect on the judiciary itself. Will judges . . . weighing these highly controversial questions of expediency . . . carry back to the Queen's Bench and Chancery quite the same unassailable reputation for detachment from political considerations that they have hitherto enjoyed?'[12]

Within a decade one could see a slowly changing attitude to judicial decision-making. Lord Denning, who had become Master of the Rolls in 1962, became a publicist for the creative role of the judges. *Hedley Byrne v Heller*[13] had, in the early 1960s, suggested that the judges—even in the House of Lords—were waking up from several decades of a formalistic approach to the common law. Ironically, and probably unintentionally, the return of Labour in 1964 actually accelerated this trend toward the instrumental. Lord Gardiner, while intellectually belonging to the narrow formalistic tradition of the liberal left, by allowing dissents in the Privy Council and, more importantly, allowing the House of Lords to overrule its

---

[10] R Stevens, *The Independence of the Judiciary: The View from the Lord Chancellor's Office* (Oxford, 1993) 101–8.

[11] 'This is not really a matter suitable for judicial decisions according to the rules and the ordinary way in which we conduct matters in the courts of law in this country. It is a matter of a decision to be made from the greatest accumulation of knowledge and experience which is available, and the greatest knowledge and experience available in this country is only available, in the last resort, to the Minister. It is essentially a government decision.': Sir Lynn Ungoed-Thomas, *Hansard* HC Deb (5th Ser), vol 549, col 2033 (6 March 1956). On this, see RB Stevens and BS Yamey, *The Restrictive Practices' Court: A Study of the Judicial Process and Economic Policy* (London, 1965).

[12] Stevens, (n 9 above) at 101–2.

[13] [1964] AC 465. R Stevens, '*Hedley Byrne v Heller*: Judicial Creativity and Doctrinal Possibility' *Modern Law Review* 14 (1964) 27.

own earlier decisions, which he thought would be used to remedy primarily legal and logical inconsistencies, changed the psychology and perhaps the very nature of the appeal process in England.[14] It was not to be long before the judiciary was taking power from both executive and legislature.

The next convenient milestone on the road to the politicisation of the judiciary was the Industrial Relations Court, created by Edward Heath in 1971, before he made the U-turn from dry to wet or, if one prefers, from ideologue to consensus politician. Before the court was dismantled by the returning Labour administration in 1974, its President, Sir John Donaldson, later to be Master of the Rolls, joined the Roll of Honour with Page, Barrington and Grantham, of having had a brush with impeachment— when 187 Labour MPs moved an address to remove him from the Presidency for 'political prejudice and partiality.'[15] That move was to persuade Lord Diplock, in discussing the 1974 Trade Disputes and Labour Relations Act that:

> at a time when many more cases involve the application of legislation which gives effect to policies that are the subject of bitter public and parliamentary controversy, it cannot be too strongly emphasised that the British Constitution, though largely unwritten, is firmly based upon the separation of powers: Parliament makes the laws, the judiciary interprets them.[16]

It is in this rather narrow context that one must look at the evolution of administrative law, especially the growth of judicial review. *Anisminic*, thwarting parliamentary efforts to exclude review by the courts, had been decided in 1968. The evolution of administrative law over the next thirty years cannot but have been heavily influenced by the political tone of the years that followed. Heath's undistinguished administration from 1970 to 1974 was marked chiefly by Britain's acceptance into the EEC. Whatever was appreciated at the time, it came to mean continental influences and, in particular, a Treaty of Rome whose federalist thrust was hidden primarily amid the powers and potential powers of the European Court of Justice. It is only in recent years that the implications for English law have finally become clear.

It was with the unwinding of the Wilson-Callaghan administration between 1974 and 1979 that the judges felt pushed to strike out on their own. With the appearance of Mrs Thatcher in 1979, the game changed still further. It gradually became clear that Britain now had a radical Government of the right, with a Labour Party, soon to be led by Michael Foot, appearing to lurch to the left. There was a vacuum of power in the centre

[14] Stevens (n 3 above) at 417–20; 472–73; 543–44; 551–52; 572–75; 617–20.
[15] Stevens (n 10 above) at 172.
[16] *Duport Steels v Sirs* [1980] 1 All ER 529, 541 (HL).

and, consciously or not, the judiciary began to move into it or, if one prefers, was forced into it. If this was not clear at once, it may be attributed to the fact that, until 1987, there was a Lord Chancellor, Lord Hailsham, protective of the traditional roles of judges and the profession, insisting on the continuation of the Kilmuir Rules on judicial silence out of court.

And Who Were these Judges?

One could wish there were a more sophisticated literature in the socio-legal field relating to the judiciary. We know so little about who the judges were and who the judges are. What quantifiable information we have is basically so unrevealing, although we do know that judges today are from a slightly more diverse background than their predecessors and are much more likely to have read law at university. In general, however, one is driven to 'bar-room sociology', or perhaps, in deference to our distinguished and sophisticated profession, one should say 'wine bar sociology'.

Inevitably one has to begin with ambience. In the 1950s, the profession was indeed dramatically different. Court of Appeal and High Court judges were barely one-third their current number (in 1948 there were twenty Queen's Bench Division judges); the county court bench was one-fifth the size of the current Circuit Court bench; solicitors about one-quarter of their present numbers; barristers less than one-fifth their present strength. The bench, however, could not have been held in greater awe.[17] As Churchill put it in Cabinet, the judges were 'a national asset the Conservative Party should feel honoured to uphold.'[18] Yet for all this deference, in the words of Anthony Sampson who was beginning his *Anatomy of Britain* industry, the judges were 'increasingly out of touch with the movements of contemporary Britain.'[19]

The bench surely contained its share of scholarly, fair, and decent men. It also had more than its share of cantankerous, prejudiced, intimidating, and boorish judges, constrained by no retirement age. In an age when the

[17] The Lord Mayor's Banquet set the tone. During the 1950s the judges were told 'if British judges were ever biased at all, it was always in favour of the accused'; 'our judiciary today stood unchallenged by friend and foe and remained the bulwark of our nation and a guarantee of peace'; the judges 'maintained, with glorious continuity, the high standards which they, and they alone in the world, had created'; and by 1956 'her Majesty's judges had a greater understanding of human nature than any other body of men in the world': B Abel-Smith and R Stevens, *Lawyers and the Courts: A Sociological Study of the English Legal System* (London, 1967) 290; see also Abel-Smith and Stevens, *In Search of Justice: Society and the Legal System* (London, 1968) 181–85.

[18] Stevens (n 10 above) at 128.

[19] Abel-Smith and Stevens, *Lawyers and the Courts* (n 17 above) at 290.

courts were under-utilised, the bar was financially impoverished, and what we would now call High Street practice was the norm for solicitors, judges were, with rare exceptions, accustomed to deference and sycophancy. Conservatism, both political and personal, with both a capital and a small 'c', was the order of the day among the judges. Henry Fairlie, in *The Establishment* (1963), claimed, with justification, that the intellectual revolution sparked by Freud had had no impact on the England of that day or the thinking of persons such as the judges. It was a period when, as we have seen, the socialist Lord Chancellor Jowitt could boast to the slightly bemused Canadian audience that all the High Court judges he had appointed had been members of the Conservative Party,[20] just as he had equally mystified an Australian audience by stating that the judges should take pride in not considering the needs of society. A bench composed almost exclusively of those educated at public schools and either Oxford or Cambridge would not have dissented.

England today has a remarkably competent judiciary, marked by a bench the overwhelming majority of whose members are gracious, scholarly, imaginative, and fair compared with the 1950s. They are even 'in touch'. The days of 'Who is this Mr Gordon Richards?' (then the leading jockey) and 'What are The Beatles?' have passed.[21] So too have days when High Court judges took pleasure in looking at widows to assess damages by attempting to judge their chance of remarriage from their appearance, or when Divorce Commissioners filled the *Evening Standard*, *Evening Star*, and the *Evening News* with inappropriate comments on the morality of divorce and the behaviour of petitioners, respondents and co-respondents.

What changed the judges? Partly it was a societal change in the approach to authority, partly it was due to what might be called the Joan Littlewood factor. The Second World War had an infinitely better general staff than the First, largely, so historians now accept, because the young subalterns in Flanders were so appalled by the awfulness of Haig's and Kitchener's operations they vowed never to repeat them. In the spirit of *Oh What a Lovely War*, it may be that the leaders of the current judiciary made a similar pledge when they saw the worse side of the judges in the 1950s and 1960s.

---

[20] Elsewhere he claimed he 'would far rather have a true blue Tory of the extreme Right who was an honest and respectable man than somebody of his own line of thought who was not.' *Ibid*.

[21] If one needs an exception to prove a rule, there is always Mr Justice Harman of the Chancery Division. During the 1990s he affected to be ignorant of Oasis. He had earlier, when leaving his home to hear an emergency petition for equitable relief, aimed a kick at journalists and their photographers. Unfortunately, he connected with his own taxi driver, earning the profound caption from *The Sun*; 'It's me nuts, m'Lord': *Independent on Sunday*, 31 March 1996. He was voted the worst judge on the bench by solicitors in 1993: *Legal Business*, *passim*; and again in 1996. 'Gentlemen of the Jury find Harman 'the Terrible' Guilty': *Sunday Times*, 12 May 1996.

Of course there were other influences. Across society the aura of deference began to decline in the 1960s. The sudden prosperity of the Bar, beginning in the late 1960s and never fully explained,[22] undoubtedly changed attitudes. The massive financial success of the whole legal profession in the 1980s and 1990s, coupled with the knowledge that London was by then a largely unchallenged international legal centre, was important. No longer was the Bar dominated by the rather childish high jinks of circuit life. The legal profession was once more attracting more than its fair share of academic talent. Women entered the profession in significant numbers. Discrimination against Jews, which had driven the likes of Herbert Hart away from the Chancery Bar and caused even Lord Goddard to rail, largely disappeared after Lord Schuster—of Jewish origins but vigorously anti-Semitic—ceased to be Permanent Secretary to the Lord Chancellor.

The change opened the bench to an important intellectual tradition that did not shy from the theoretical, and even thought it might be possible to learn from the United States and continental Europe. With the demise of Lord Jowitt, there was no longer prejudice against Catholics on the bench. After Lord Simonds there was less prejudice against divorcees on the bench. Within the narrow parameters of the Bar, the bench was increasingly open to talent and, as specialities in commercial and corporate law took off, the availability of talented barristers who also knew about business and commerce, in addition to more general common lawyers, once again changed the style. Today, commercial lawyers, with their more learned approach, dominate the English law lords. In particular at the appellate level, where England had rarely distinguished itself, by the 1970s a new style was afoot. It only required the advent of the first Scottish Lord Chancellor, Lord Mackay, willing to appoint to both the Court of Appeal and the House of Lords not merely those who had reached a certain point on the *cursus honorum*, but those who might have real talent as appeal judges, to allow this broader style to reach fruition.

The 1960s and 1970s: Confusion and Renewal

Periods in history are inevitably fuzzy.[23] The period of high formalism had been consistently in the ascendant during the 1940s and 1950s its demise was erratic. As we have seen, some effort to make the courts more relevant

---

[22] The advent of well-remunerated criminal legal aid in the 1960s and the expansion of the judiciary following the Courts Act 1971 undoubtedly helped.

[23] Perhaps the last gasp of the old order came with the 1988 appeal in 'the Birmingham Six' case, where the 'heavies' of the West Midlands Constabulary had 'encouraged' six Irishmen to admit to being IRA terrorists. While all the evidence in the Court of Appeal pointed to police

and less formalistic can be traced back to Lord Kilmuir (Sir David Maxwell-Fyfe). He was a law reformer. He changed the rules for occupiers' liability, put in a retirement age for judges, began devolution of the courts, and even suggested that political service ought to be taken into account for appointments to the bench so that the judges had the experience to enable them to handle public law cases. (In this last endeavour he found he was far too late to turn back the tradition of choosing High Court judges on the basis of success in advocacy.) Yet he may have been the last Lord Chancellor to take Dicey at face value—establishing the Franks Committee on Administrative Tribunals. He also restated the rather platitudinous position on judicial objectivity and denied the need for rights to be entrenched, insisting that the common law and the judges were an adequate protection of civil liberties.[24]

The 1960s saw more obvious changes. In 1962, Lord Reid, the former Scottish Conservative politician, became the senior law lord. His broad Scottish approach, coupled with his earlier political experience, made him eschew the formalism of the earlier period. In 1972 he wrote:

> There was a time when it was thought almost indecent to suggest that judges make law—they only declare it. Those with a taste for fairy tales seem to have thought that in some Aladdin's cave, there is hidden the Common Law in all its splendour and that on a judge's appointment there descends on him knowledge of the magic words Open Sesame. Bad decisions are given when a judge muddles the pass word and the wrong door opens. But we do not believe in fairy tales anymore.

Reid's was an approach which enabled the judges to regain the initiative in public law.[25] In 1964 in *Ridge v Baldwin*[26] the House of Lords began the process of restoring procedural due process; in *Conway v Rimmer* (1968)[27] they began taking back the initiative in Crown privilege; *Padfield v Minister of Agriculture* (1968)[28] and *Anisminic v Foreign Compensation Commission* (1969)[29] pointed towards re-establishing judicial review of administrative actions. Life was once again poured into the old prerogative writs. The courts not only restored procedural due process but, with the restatement

---

brutality and unreliable forensic evidence, Lord Lane, the ailing Chief Justice, insisted that the police could not have lied and the forensic expert must have been mistaken. The miscarriage of justice was eventually remedied in 1991. Obituary: 'Sir Patrick O'Connor', *Daily Telegraph*, 5 May 2001.

[24] See generally, Stevens (n 3 above) at 420–25.
[25] *Ibid*, at 466–88.
[26] [1964] AC 40 (1963).
[27] [1968] AC 910.
[28] [1968] AC 997.
[29] [1969] 2 AC 147.

of the so-called *Wednesbury* doctrine, added, in the view of some, a hint of substantive due process.[30] While the House of Lords crafted a new role for the judges in public law, Lord Denning, by then installed as Master of the Rolls was, more flamboyantly, advertising the potential and real power of judges.[31]

In the 1960s, too, there was a fillip from an unexpected source. In 1964 Harold Wilson was returned as Prime Minister and the new Labour Lord Chancellor was Gerald Gardiner. As we saw earlier, Gardiner was professionally conservative, and his Law Commission was designed to reform and restate black letter rules. Another reform, as we have seen, originally made with the internal logic of the law in mind, was to allow the House of Lords to overrule its own earlier decisions. A third of Gardiner's attempted reforms had a similar unintended impact. He picked up the Kilmuir suggestion that the Privy Council should become a peripatetic court. The cruel rejection of the idea brought home the fact that English judges were not necessarily held in the Commonwealth in quite the high regard they had always assumed. More importantly, the Commonwealth countries reminded Britain in different—sometimes inadequate ways—that a legal system needed to take into account the economic and social conditions within which it operated and towards which the judges needed to develop doctrine.[32] At the same time, Gardiner's allowing of dissenting opinions in the Privy Council helped open up further opportunities for judicial creativity.

In the late 1960s, the political environment—and especially the unsatisfactory state of labour relations in the UK—had once more attracted the attention of the courts. In 1964, in *Rookes v Barnard*,[33] the House of Lords held that a person dismissed by his employer after a strike threat by a trade union, might sue the union officials for conspiracy and, in the same year, in *Stratford v Lindlay*[34] the House of Lords extended this principle to boycotts. This apparent expansion of the law caused the appointment of the Donovan Commission, which led to the Labour government issuing *In Place of Strife*, which suggested the establishment of an Industrial Board to police labour relations with a limited power to impose sanctions.[35] The strikes continued and in 1970 the Conservatives, by then led by Edward Heath, were returned to power. Their solution to industrial unrest was the National Industrial Relations Court (NIRC) loosely based on the Restrictive

---

[30] D Robertson, *Judicial Discretion in the House of Lords* (Oxford, 1998), ch 7.
[31] Stevens (n 3 above) at 488–505.
[32] Stevens (n 10 above) at 160–61; Stevens (n 3 above) at 418–19.
[33] [1964] AC, 1129.
[34] [1965] AC, 269.
[35] Ben Pimlott, *Harold Wilson* (London, 1992) 528–35.

Practices Court, with a requirement of registration of unions and openness about their rules for strikes as the basis for staying within the 1906 Act. Sir John Donaldson, a High Court judge, and former Conservative candidate, was appointed President of the NIRC. He soon found his decisions apparently inconsistent with those of Lord Denning, presiding in parallel cases in the Court of Appeal. Heath's Lord Chancellor, Lord Hailsham of St Marylebone, in a remarkable act, appeared to attempt to pressure Denning to change his views, but it was to no avail. By this time the Heath government was caught up in the miners' strike and the two elections of 1974 returned Labour with a small majority and the following year the new government abolished the NIRC and later refused to appoint Donaldson as Master of the Rolls. Labour relations continued to deteriorate. Inflation was rampant; the IMF was brought in; and after the 'Winter of Discontent', the Conservatives, by then led by Margaret Thatcher, were returned in 1979.[36]

While in the 1970s and early 1980s there were Law Lords—particularly Lord Diplock (appointed a Lord of Appeal in 1968) and Wilberforce (appointed in 1964)—who accepted a positive role for the judiciary, they lacked the political acuity of Reid or the flamboyance of Denning.[37] The majority of judges in the Court of Appeal and House of Lords, however, still laboured under the weight of a strongly formalist tradition. Only in legislative debates in the Lords,[38] and, more noticeably as Chairs of Commissions and Committees, were judges heavily involved in public affairs.[39] Such activities inevitably, on occasion, led the judges into trouble.

---

[36] JAG Griffith, *The Politics of the Judiciary* (London, 1997) 63–102.

[37] JAG Griffith, *Judicial Politics since 1920: A Chronicle* (Oxford, 1993) ch 5.

[38] Between 1956 and 1967 in legislative debates, the Law Lords took different sides on capital punishment, artificial insemination, adultery, majority verdicts, corporal punishment and damages for widows. During the period, Lord Hodson attacked the merits of a private members' Bill to reform (and make more liberal) divorce law, intervening no fewer than sixteen times. On the Labour Relations (Amendment) Bill, Lord Salmon made a somewhat emotional speech on communist influence in the unions.

[39] They were used in the 1960s and 1970s for the following Committees: Security in the Public Service (Radcliffe 1961), The Security Service and Mr Profumo (Denning 1963), The Port Transport Industry (Devlin 1964), The Age of Majority (Latey 1965), Legal Education (Ormrod 1967), One Parent Families (Finer 1969), Abuse of Social Security (Fisher 1971), Ministerial Memoirs (Radcliffe 1975), Recruitment of Mercenaries (Diplock 1976), Police Pay (Edmund-Davies 1977), Brixton Disorders (Scarman 1981), Civil Service Pay (Megaw 1981). At the same time in these two decades, there were Royal Commissions on Trade Unions (Donovan 1965), Tribunals of Inquiry (Salmon 1966), The Constitution (Kilbrandon—a Scottish judge—co-chair 1968), Civil Liability (Pearson 1973), The Press (Finer—co-chair 1974), Standards of Conduct in Government (Salmon 1974). In addition, under the Tribunals of Inquiry Act 1921, there was an inquiry into the Official Secrets Act and Vassall (Radcliffe 1962), the Disaster at Aberfan (Davies—co-chair 1967) and the Vehicle and General Insurance Co (James—co-chair 1972). In addition to this, Lord Pearce was, in 1972, made Chair of a Commission on Rhodesian Opinion, to help settle the future of what became Zimbabwe.

Wilberforce's 1972 foray into miners' wages was described by *The Economist* as 'incredible economic nonsense', while others thought the Heath government 'had set up this inquiry to produce a report which would enable them to yield to the miners' claim without total loss of face.'[40] It was, however, also during these years (and early in the 1980s) that Lord Scarman, in a series of inquiries into the disturbances in Red Lion Square, the Grunwick labour dispute and most important of all the Brixton riots of 1981, reaffirmed the significance of the judicial inquiry. The *Brixton Disorders* Report[41] both led to significant legislation and convinced the British public that there were liberal and sensitive Law Lords. Indeed, for the first time in recent decades a Law Lord became a public figure and his prominence may have encouraged other judges to be even more outspoken.

It was, however, in Northern Ireland that the judges were most obviously used—and potentially put in an increasingly impossible position politically. The first appointment was that of Lord Scarman whose report, *Violence and Civil Disturbances in Northern Ireland 1969*, was much criticised partly because it was not published until 1972, by which time the Cameron Report had been published (Cameron was a Scottish judge). Then followed the Widgery Report on Bloody Sunday, where the Lord Chief Justice, while labouring under great difficulties, failed to produce a report that satisfied most sections of the community. *The Independent* later commented that the enquiry was 'so blatantly biased in its findings that it brought British justice into contempt in many parts of the world.' Lord Parker, the next Lord Chief Justice, chaired a Committee of Privy Councillors to look at *Interrogation Methods*. Then followed Lord Diplock's *Legal Procedures for Dealing with Terrorists* (1972), recommending curbing the traditional common law protection to prevent the intimidation of witnesses, which led to the so-called Diplock courts, sitting without a jury. Harold Wilson sent his former Lord Chancellor, Lord Gardiner to look at *Civil and Human Rights in the Province* (1975) and Judge Bennett took a further look at *Police Interrogation Procedures* (1979). To different segments in Ulster all the reports were unacceptable and there is little doubt that they threw doubt on the impartiality and independence of the British judiciary.[42]

Since the English judges were also accustomed to being consulted by departments on Bills and specific problems[43] and in turn to giving advice on the principles of damages and sentencing to lower courts, it is possible to

---

[40] Griffith (n 36 above) at 132–33.
[41] Cmnd 8427, 1981.
[42] Stevens (n 10 above) at 170–71.
[43] For recent examples see Griffith (n 36 above) at 45–46. For the work of the DAC, a private group chaired by Lord Saville, in drafting the Arbitration Act 1996, see A Hughes and B Pilling, 'The Arbitration Act Five Years On' (2001) *New Law Journal* 5 October.

see a surprising internal conflict in the way the English judges and courts saw their roles. It is true that, in the 1960s and 1970s the judges both continued the process of pushing the courts slowly back into public law, as well as reclaiming some responsibility for keeping the common law in line with the needs of society, yet the tone of the approach was tentative. The courts in this sense remained, as a political force, relatively unimportant in the Constitution; and their constitutional contribution was continued significantly outside the courts.

4

The Years of Conservative Government 1979–1997

IN 1979, AS the new leader of the Conservative Party, Mrs Thatcher came to power without the clear political policies that were later attributed to her.[1] As she moved to a more market-orientated approach than Britain had seen since the turn of the century, or perhaps even the mid nineteenth century, she was also accused, with some justification, of moving to a more presidential style of government. Even on Europe, in the early years, Margaret Thatcher's later reputation was not entirely justified. Parliamentary sovereignty may already have been undermined, as Labour had argued at the time when Mr Heath finally took Britain into the Common Market, but Mrs Thatcher's acceptance of the Single European Act confirmed that trend. With a more presidential system of government, coupled with the declining importance of Parliament (Mrs Thatcher's Lord Chancellor until 1987—Lord Hailsham of St Marylebone—described the parliamentary system as 'elected dictatorship'),[2] such developments occurred at the very moment when there appeared to be something of a vacancy by way of opposition. The Labour Party, after the economic disasters of the 1970s and the electoral defeat of 1979, chose to lurch to the left under Michael Foot rather than to seek a political formula likely to appeal to a majority of the electorate. It heralded some eighteen years in the wilderness for them. These developments provided the background for a potentially dramatic change in the role of the judges.

---

[1] On the period generally see H Young, *One of Us: a Biography of Margaret Thatcher* (London, 1989); P Jenkins, *Mrs Thatcher's Revolution: The Ending of the Socialist Era* (Cambridge, Mass, 1987); N Wyn Ellis, *John Major* (London, 1991); A Seldon, *Major: A Political Life* (London, 1997); J Major, *The Autobiography* (London, 1999). And see also J Rozenberg, *Trial of Strength: The Battle between Ministers and Judges over Who Makes the Law* (London, 1997).
[2] The title of his Dimbleby Lecture in 1976: G Lewis, *Lord Hailsham: A Life* (London, 1997), 136.

Europe and Its Influence[3]

The atmosphere had also been changed by the European Communities Act of 1972, drafted under the guidance of the then Solicitor-General, Sir Geoffrey Howe, which provided for a broad reception for European Community law; an invitation which the judges, with Lord Denning in the van, accepted. Judicial activism in this area accelerated in the 1980s and 1990s, and the power of the UK courts in enforcing European Directives was underlined with the *Factortame Case*[4] in 1991, when a British statute was suspended while its constitutionality was tested before the European Court of Justice. The *Daily Mail* reported this decision under the headline 'Brussels rules the waves'. The final logical step was taken in 1995, when in *R v Secretary of State for Employment, ex p Equal Opportunities Commission*,[5] the House of Lords held that British legislation relating to part-time employees violated European Directives and was therefore unenforceable. Lord Mackay—Mrs Thatcher's Lord Chancellor after 1987—explained the decision in conventional terms, namely that one British statute had been interpreted in the light of another (the 1972 Act). The press, however, was not convinced. *The Times* concluded that 'Britain may now have, for the first time in its history, a constitutional court' and, together with the other Murdoch-owned newspaper, *the Sun*, there were increasingly virulent attacks on 'elitist', 'liberal', 'unelected' and 'power hungry' judges.

In a paper to Cabinet, Michael Howard, the Home Secretary, and a euro-sceptic, argued that British courts should be forbidden from enforcing European Community law. The paper marked an important step in the ongoing fracturing of the Conservative Party over the issue of Europe.[6] Howard also argued that the European Court of Justice had been 'increasing its competence and adopting its own political agenda.' Relying on a paper by Sir Patrick Neill QC, he adopted the words that 'a court with a mission is a menace. A supreme court with a mission is a disaster.'[7] While both of Mrs Thatcher's Lord Chancellors, Lords Hailsham and Mackay,[8] insisted that parliamentary sovereignty was sacrosanct and continued to

---

[3]   See now D Nicol, *EC Membership and the Judicialization of British Politics* (Oxford, 2001).
[4]   *R v Transport Secretary, ex p Factortame (No 2)* [1990] 1 AC 603.
[5]   [1995] 1 AC 1. Patricia Maxwell, 'The House of Lords as a Constitutional Court—The Implications of *ex parte EOC*,' in B Dickson and P Carmichael (eds), *The House of Lords: its Parliamentary and Judicial Roles*, (Oxford, 1999), 197.
[6]   'Britain Urges Cut in Power of Euro Court', *The Times*, 13 March 1996. The object of hostility at this point was the White Paper before the Inter-Governmental Conference in Turin.
[7]   'Howard Splits Cabinet on Europe' *The Independent*, 18 May 1996.
[8]   Lord Havers was also, for a few brief months, one of Mrs Thatcher's Lord Chancellors.

reside in Westminster and not Brussels—and certainly not in the judges, the mantra was increasingly less convincing.

It is arguable, however, that the English courts themselves have been more enthusiastic Europeans than the courts in other countries. Lord Denning set the tone when he allowed individual parties to sue in English courts for violation of EU competition law as embodied in what were then Articles 85 and 86 of the Treaty of Rome.[9] By the early 1990s, however, the House of Lords was willing to go much further. In *M v Home Office*[10] and *Woolwich v IRC*[11] it rejected the option of two standards of justice—European and national—and reformed national law, in such matters as injunctions against the Crown, in order to homogenise the two systems.[12] This suspicion of europhilia on the part of English judges was further fuelled by the changing attitude to the European Convention on Human Rights. The Convention was developed mainly by the civil law countries of Western Europe, which had suffered at the hands of Hitler, in the years after the Second World War. The reaction of Attlee's Labour administration was fascinating. Lord Goddard and the other judges were satisfied that the common law was the perfect protector of civil rights. Certainly the Labour Cabinet in the 1940s was appalled by the European notion that there should be a Convention on Human Rights. Sir Stafford Cripps, Chancellor of the Exchequer, opposed it because it would provide protection inconsistent with 'powers of economic control which are essential for the operation of a planned economy.' Lord Jowitt showed his general distrust of foreigners:

> We are not prepared to encourage our European friends to jeopardise our whole system of law, which we have laboriously built up over the centuries, in favour of some half-baked scheme to be administered by some unknown court . . . It completely passes the wit of man to guess what results would be arrived at by a tribunal . . . drawn from various European States possessing completely different systems of law. . . Any student of our legal institutions . . . must recoil from this document with a feeling of horror.

Publicly, however, Jowitt opposed the Convention on the ground that it would 'obviously compromise the sovereignty of Parliament.'[13]

---

[9] *Garden Cottage Foods v Milk Marketing Board* [1984] AC 130. Denning later became far less enthusiastic about the influence of EU law.
[10] [1994] 1 AC 377.
[11] [1993] AC 70.
[12] W Van Gerren, 'Bridging the Gap Between Community and National Laws: Towards a principle of homogeneity in the field of legal remedies' (1995) 32 *Common Market Law Review* 579.
[13] E Wicks, 'The United Kingdom Government's Perception of the European Convention on Human Rights at the time of Entry [2000] *Public Law* 438. See now AWB Simpson, *Human Rights and the End of Empire: Britain and the Genesis of the European Convention* (Oxford, 2001) ch 14.

Yet the United Kingdom did adhere to the Convention in 1951 and the Commission and Court began work in 1952. Britain, after the Wilson administration in the 1960s—pressed externally by Terry Higgins MP and behind the scenes by the International Court judge, Lord McNair—allowed individuals to appeal, soon became its second best customer. While Lord Denning had claimed of civil liberties in England, '[w]e have not needed them to be written down in this country. The judges have been able to protect them by their decisions,'[14] such enthusiasm was not shared by the new court. From birching and IRA detainees to freedom of the press and the right of journalists to protect their sources, Britain lost most of the cases that were taken to the Court. It was with this background that the new leader of the Labour Party after 1992, John Smith, agreed to the incorporation of the Convention into English law.

While indirectly the Convention influenced English law, each appeal had to go to Strasbourg. It was not an ideal system, and leading judges, led by two Chief Justices, Lords Taylor and Bingham, lobbied for its incorporation into English law. Finally, in 1995, Lord Lester, a frequent advocate before the Court,[15] introduced the Human Rights Bill to effect that very change. It was supported in the legislative debates by no fewer than eight judicial peers.[16] While, in a watered-down form, the Bill passed the Lords, it was not taken further.[17] The Conservative government continued to fear a weakening of parliamentary supremacy by giving such direct control over civil rights to the judges, since, in effect, their decision might well involve holding UK legislation unconstitutional. Ironically, Sir Ti-liang Yang, the last Chief Justice of Hong Kong under British rule, unwisely and confidentially made an identical argument to the Beijing government, in suggesting that China should eviscerate Hong Kong's British-imposed Bill of Rights because Bills of Rights allowed courts to strike down legislation and that such conflicts led to 'chaos'.[18] In the United Kingdom, meanwhile, the government continued to fear Commission and Court in Strasbourg and in the Spring of 1996 it was reported that Lord Mackay had flown to Strasbourg to remonstrate with the Human Rights Court judges about their expansive tendencies.[19]

---

[14] *Hansard* HL Deb, vol 224, col 1195 (6 July 1960). When Attorney-General, Lord Simon of Glaisdale justified higher judicial pensions because 'the people owe . . . to the judiciary something they value more highly than their material property, and that is their civil liberties.' *Hansard* HC Deb, vol 525, col 1061 (23 March 1954).

[15] A Lester, 'Fundamental Rights: the United Kingdom Isolated?' [1986] *Public Law*, 46.

[16] Not all judges thought the European Convention should be the basis of an English Bill of Rights, eg Stephen Sedley, 'Charter 88: Wrongs and Rights' in (1991) *Citizenship*.

[17] A Lester, 'The Mouse That Roared: The Human Rights Bill, 1995 [1995] *Public Law* 198.

[18] 'Chief's warning over HK Bill', *Financial Times*, 19 November, 1995.

[19] 'Mackay Seeks Curb on European Court' *The Times*, 9 April 1996.

Government and Judiciary

It was these cases that led the press in the mid 1990s to take delight in both highlighting—and, one suspects, fuelling—the split between judiciary and government. The Beaverbrook press claimed there was a 'sickness sweeping through the senior judiciary—galloping arrogance'[20] and, singling out Mr Justice Dyson, noting that '[w]hile European Human Rights Judges, some from countries which once sent political prisoners to Siberia, are venting their spleen on Britain, legal weevils here at home are practising their own brand of mischief.'[21] The Rothermere press joined in: '[n]ow it seems that any judge can take it on himself to overrule a minister, even though Parliament might approve the minister's action. This is to arrogate power to themselves in a manner that makes a mockery of Parliament.' The paper went on to accuse the judges of giving the impression that they were 'acting on a political agenda of their own.'[22] *The Independent* ensured balance: '[t]he Long Arm of the Law: government clashes with the judiciary are mounting—and they won't stop under Labour.'[23] Such a belief made it possible for *The Times*, when Lord Taylor was forced to resign through ill-health in 1996, to demand a Lord Chief Justice who could 'steer his profession away from the sound of gunfire.'[24]

As in olden times, it sounded as if the Lord Chancellor and 10 Downing Street (the appointment of a Lord Chief Justice is by the Queen on the recommendation of the Prime Minister, which normally means the Lord Chancellor) were listening to *The Times*. When the senior judges in the Court of Appeal took soundings, it is reported that fourteen judges wanted Lord Justice Rose and three Lord Justice Woolf. When this information was brought to Lord Mackay, he agreed to pass it on to the Prime Minister. The problem was that Rose had been a strong supporter of Lord Taylor's attack on the Conservatives' criminal law changes. On the other hand, Lord Bingham, the Master of the Rolls had been sympathetic to the Lord Chancellor's plans to curb restrictive practices in the profession and supported Lord Mackay's efforts to keep down the cost of legal aid. He had in addition supported the government's view of public interest immunity certificates, rather than that espoused by Lord Justice Scott in the Arms to Iraq inquiry. When this rumoured appointment of Lord Bingham surfaced, the ailing Lord Taylor called on the Prime Minister to reaffirm the strong preference of the judges for Rose, only to be told the job had already been

---

[20] *The Daily Express*, 4 November 1995.
[21] *The Sunday Express*, 1 October 1995.
[22] *The Daily Mail*, 2 November 1995.
[23] *The Independent on Sunday*, 5 November 1995.
[24] 'Balance in Justice' (leader) *The Times*, 4 May 1996.

offered to Sir Thomas Bingham. In the meantime Bingham announced he would be hearing judicial review cases in addition to criminal ones.[25]

In terms of judicial expansion, the most obvious and public change concerned the expansion of judicial review to provide an extensive power for the courts to intervene in procedural due process over a wide range of public and quasi-public matters. In a subtle use of the so-called *Wednesbury* doctrine, it also provided a hint of substantive due process.[26] There is little doubt that, from the public's point of view, judicial review helped remedy a wide range of injustices. Despite press comment, however, Victorian judges actively used judicial review, although for much of the twentieth century it was quiescent. Again, despite press comment, decisions under it by no means always went against the Crown. The sudden exponential growth, however, had profound political implications.

Later decades expanded on the developments of the 1960s. In a way unthinkable thirty years earlier, ministers and civil servants found a new partner in the public decision-making process: the judges. In 1987 the Treasury Solicitor's Department issued *The Judge Over Your Shoulder*, a guide for civil servants about this new presence. Moreover the presence was felt not only by the civil servants but by their political masters. Michael Howard, the Home Secretary under John Major (who replaced Mrs Thatcher as Prime Minister in 1990), found his efforts to reform sentencing and the Criminal Compensation Programme, as well as immigration and deportation decisions (and sometimes policies) increasingly circumscribed by the judiciary. John Major had a speech to Scotland banned from television by Lord Abernethy, a Scottish judge. The Foreign Secretary was forced to restructure the foreign aid programme after the judges found he had taken into account inappropriate criteria with respect to the Pergau Dam[27] and Douglas Hurd also complained that the judges had usurped the role of Government with respect to immigration.[28] Moreover, even where they were not willing to strike down governmental actions, judges did not hesitate to rattle sabres, in matters ranging from gays in the armed forces to the privatisation of the

---

[25] Rozenberg (n 1 above) 13–16; 'Senior Judges round on the Tories', *The Independent*, 9 October 1996.

[26] The state of the law was most elegantly described in H Woolf and J Jowell (eds), *De Smith's Judicial Review of Administrative Action* (London, 1995) *passim*.

[27] John Griffith has argued that the effect of the Pergau Dam case was to transfer discretionary powers from the Foreign Office to the judges: JAG Griffith, 'The Common Law and the Political Constitution' (2001) 117 *Law Quarterly Review*, 42, 58. It is worth noting that the World Development Movement was able to bring this action only because two House of Commons Committees had done the investigatory work. R Rawlings, 'Courts and Interests' in I Loveland (ed), *A Special Relationship*, (Oxford, 1995) 99, 104–5.

[28] S Curtis (ed), *The Journals of Woodrow Wyatt* (London, 1998) vol 1 at 307.

railways[29] and housing for asylum-seekers.[30] Michael Howard, as Home Secretary, bore the brunt of these later assaults, finding his efforts to reform sentencing, to restructure the criminal compensation programme,[31] to prevent the Moonie leader entering the country[32] and to deport a Saudi dissident, thwarted by judges.[33] Judges, whose music hall reputation was that of out-of-touch conservatives, were now reviled in the press as interfering woolly liberals out of touch with democracy and laissez-faire solutions.[34]

The situation was aggravated because, with the arrival of Lord Mackay as Lord Chancellor in 1987, the Kilmuir Rules, which made it difficult for judges to speak out, had been lifted. There was therefore a much greater willingness for judges to comment on all manner of issues. Psychologically, however, the new regime seemed to give those judges with a seat in the legislative House of Lords a licence to oppose Government policy. Certainly, in penal matters, the judges found the policies of Michael Howard, Major's last Home Secretary, distasteful. Lord Taylor, the Chief Justice, did not hesitate to issue a statement disagreeing with speeches made at the Conservative Party Conference.[35] It was a very different world.

The public came to hear about judicial conflicts with Government mainly over penal policy. In particular, the judges were unhappy about the constant changes of direction reflected in the numerous Criminal Justice

[29] 'Judge "Reluctantly" Denies Housing for Asylum Seekers' *The Times*, 19 April 1996; 'Judge Voices Concern at Asylum Benefits Cost' *The Guardian*, 27 March 1996.
[30] See also the excitement when the appeal courts refused to allow him to extend the sentence of the child murderers of James Bulger. 'Howard Acted Unlawfully over Bulger Sentences' and 'Ruling Further Weakens Minister's Powers over Judiciary' *The Times*, 3 May 1996; 'Howard Furious at Bulger Ruling' *The Independent*, 3 May 1996; 'Mr Howard is Playing with Fire' (editorial), *ibid*.
[31] *R v Secretary of State for the Home Department, ex p Fire Brigades Union* [1995] 2 AC 513. See also E Barendt, 'Constitutional Law and the Criminal Injuries Compensation Scheme', [1995] *Public Law*, 357.
[32] 'Judicial Moonshine: Howard was right to refuse Moon entry to Britain' *The Times*, 3 November 1995.
[33] 'Judge tells Howard to Reconsider Masari Case' *The Independent*, 6 March 1994.
[34] R Stevens, *Independence of the Judiciary: The View from the Lord Chancellor's Office* (Oxford 1993) 261–62. In the last year of the Major government, some of the disputes with Michael Howard were continued by the new Chief Justice (Lord Bingham) and the new Master of the Rolls (Lord Woolf). The *Daily Telegraph* editorialised about the debates on mandatory sentences: 'Yesterday's debates in the House of Lords revealed the growing unwillingness of our judges to confine themselves to an interpretive role. In the United States and most of Europe, judges are overtly political figures whose views are a matter of great public interest. In Italy, they see themselves as champions of the people against political corruption. British judges are moving in the same direction, appearing frequently in the media and speaking on subjects that often have little to do with the law.' 28 January 1997.
[35] A Selden, *Major: A Political Life* (London, 1997) 605. Within two hours of Michael Howard announcing tougher sentences for criminals, Lord Taylor said: 'What deters (criminals) is the likelihood of being caught, which at the moment is small.' John Major said he expected the attack and had answers ready.

Acts after 1979.[36] These changes effectively allowed the Home Secretary to extend the terms of imprisonment imposed by judges by deciding when prisoners should be released, then to have a fixed tariff for certain crimes (mandatory sentences), thus taking away judicial discretion which allowed judges to make the sentence fit the crime. (Ultimately the Strasbourg court was to frown on much of the Howard philosophy.) Finally, in the April 1996 White Paper, the Home Secretary appeared to have endorsed a 'two strikes and you're out' principle, described by Lord Taylor as a 'bonanza for prison architects'.[37] (This was an adaptation of the Californian system of 'three strikes and you're out' which had led to life imprisonment for the theft of a piece of pizza from someone eating it, being the third crime of violence).[38]

The judicial establishment, led by the Lord Chief Justice, felt irritated by policies which not merely took away the traditional powers of the judiciary, but endorsed the naïve belief that punishment rather than detection was the solution to the crime problem.[39] In May 1996, Lord Taylor resigned through ill-health, but as he did, he initiated a debate in the House of Lords where support for his view was overwhelming and that for Mr Howard sparse.[40] Even Ferdinand Mount, head of Mrs Thatcher's think tank from 1982 to 1984 conceded that the Tory Right was motivated by an overenthusiasm for Gingrich's *Contract with America*[41] rather than developing independent policies. The fact that 'three strikes and you're out' appeared to have led to injustice rather than a decline in crime in California was of little interest to the Conservative Right or to Brian Mawhinney, the then Chairman of the Conservative Party, in the lead-up to the 1997 election. (They should have borne in mind Woody Allen's observation that 'the only contribution California has made to civilisation is right turn on red.')

The cry also lapped over into prison policy, where spartan conditions for the IRA and long-term prisoners were matched by demand for boot camps for the young. The North American appeal of such measures was evidenced by the Dole-Clinton Presidential Campaign in 1996, particularly the No-Frills in Prison Act 1996, passed by the US House and Senate, section 2 of which demanded 'the elimination of luxurious prison conditions'. Under it,

---

[36] *The Economist*, 11 November 1995 at 29.

[37] *The Times*, 26 March 1996.

[38] 'Judges claim Howard is on the Wrong Side of the Law' *The Times*, 4 April 1996; 'Repeat of serious crime will carry automatic life sentence': *ibid*.

[39] [1995] *New Law Journal* 1529.

[40] *Hansard* HL Deb, vol 572, cols 1025–76 (23 May 1996). See also P Taylor, 'Howard's Production Line Justice' *The Times*, 23 May 1996. On the debate, see PW Davies, 'Howard Punished in each Sentence' *The Independent*, 24 May 1996; and 'Lord Taylor denounces Howard Reforms', *ibid*.

[41] F Mount, 'From Major to Maurras' *Prospect* , March (1996).

in-cell coffee pots and televisions were to go, as well as prison weight-rooms, computers and 'earned good-time credit'.[42] It came as no surprise that Mr Howard echoed American policy in this and in his demands for curfews for youths,[43] as Britain prepared for the 1997 Election.

The Judges' Work

In this assertive atmosphere it was not surprising to discover that some judges were continuing the more vigorous development of the common law which had, by then, become the norm. Nothing better illustrated its vigour than two public lectures, delivered by Lord Bingham and Lord Hoffmann in the Spring of 1996, calling on the courts to develop a right of privacy if Parliament did not do so.[44] Viscount Jowitt must have been sleeping uneasily and such discomfort was partially shared by Lord Irvine, the then Lord Chancellor in waiting.[45] Within the traditional areas of the common law, the appeal courts had come to accept a clear responsibility to develop the law. Equally dramatic was the change in statutory interpretation. The major innovation was *Pepper v Hart*[46] in which the House of Lords joined the US Supreme Court in turning to legislative debates to determine the 'true meaning' of statutory interpretation. (Only Lord Mackay dissented; some felt he should not have sat.) Like it or not, judicial power was dramatically extended.[47] While the Law Lords attempted to put some limits on the new system, in practice those limits have proved nugatory. The judges had been given a powerful new weapon in instrumental interpretation. From then on, the limited flexibility that had been theirs in interpreting statutes by using the literal, mischief or golden rules had been

---

[42] 'Jail's No Frills Reality Enlightens a Judge' *International Herald Tribune*, 3 April 1996.
[43] *The Economist*, 8 June 1996.
[44] The press was also agitated when Lord Chancellor Irvine suggested that it was up to the judges, not Parliament, to develop a right to privacy. 'The real question is whether the judges should be left to make their own law . . . . It should be a matter for Parliament, in part because the judges Lord Irvine favours are almost all Conservatives.' (Apparently a reference to the promotion of Lords Hobhouse and Millett.) Editorial, *The Observer*, 27 July 1997. See also 'Unchecked judges, arrogant politicians, and those who would prevent you from knowing the truth about Britain's ruling classes': *Daily Mail*, 4 November 1997. For a questioning of the constitutional appropriateness of this, see 'Sitting in Judgment' (editorial), *Financial Times*, 24 May 1996.
[45] 'The Judiciary: Public Controversy', *Hansard* HL Deb, vol 572, col 1257 (5 June 1996).
[46] [1993] AC 593.
[47] K Mullan, 'The Impact of *Pepper v Hart*' in B Dickson and P Carmichael (eds), *The House of Lords* (Oxford, Hart Publishing, 1998) 213.

dramatically enhanced.[48] The powers of judicial creativity seemed to know no bounds.[49]

By the 1970s, with the exception of New Zealand, the old Commonwealth had abolished appeals to the Judicial Committee of the Privy Council, but appeals by no means disappeared. While some newly independent Commonwealth countries, particularly in Africa, rapidly abandoned appeals, Sri Lanka and Malaysia kept that court busy for far longer than had been predicted. By the 1990s, however, most of the appeals were from New Zealand, Hong Kong (until the handover in 1997) and the West Indies. Appeals from the latter included a series of decisions in the mid 1990s, the most famous of which was *Pratt v Attorney-General for Jamaica* striking down, in that case under the human rights provisions of the Constitution of Jamaica, sentences of death where there had been inexcusable delay in carrying out the sentence.[50] While the decision and a number of related ones questioning the death penalty came close to ending appeals from the West Indies,[51] the cases reflected a much more assertive view of the Judicial Committee's role compared with earlier decades. In the Spring of 2002, for instance, in *Reyes v R*, Lord Bingham, for a unanimous Judicial Committee, held that the mandatory death penalty for murder violated the provision of the Belize Constitution protecting against 'inhuman or degrading punishment.'[52] It was in this spirit that Lords Hoffmann and

---

[48] For the argument that *Pepper v Hart* was wrongly decided because insufficient attention was paid to the constitutional implications, particularly the hazardous nature of statements by Ministers as compared with the words of statutes, see Steyn, '*Pepper v Hart*: A Re-examination', (2001) 21 *Oxford Journal of Legal Studies* 59. The author also argued that insufficient attention had been paid to the increased costs of litigation.

[49] D Robertson, *Judicial Discretion in the House of Lords* (Oxford, 1998) ch 5.

[50] [1994] 2 AC 1. The decision effectively followed the European Court of Human Rights in *Soering v UK* (1989) 11 EHRR 439. With respect to the Bahamas, see *Henfield v A-G of Bahamas* [1997] AC 413 and *Fisher (No 2) v Minister of Public Safety and Immigration* [1999] 2 WLR 349. While the Privy Council came to live uneasily with capital punishment in the Caribbean—eg *Reckley v Minister of Public Safety and Immigration (No 2)* [1996] AC 527, individual Law Lords continued to register their discomfort. Eg dissent of Lord Nicholls, *Briggs v Baptiste* [2000] 2 AC 1; and Lords Steyn and Cooke in *Higgs v Minister of National Security* [2000] 2 AC 228. See especially Lord Steyn at *ibid* 258: 'The Commonwealth of the Bahamas have over a prolonged period treated the appellants as sub-human' and Lord Cooke, at *ibid* 263 noted that a 'spirit' informs those who oppose the death penalty and that the spirit informs 'no small number of members of the Privy Council' and the spirit 'ultimately . . . will prevail.' See also D O'Brien and V Carter, 'Constitutional rights, legitimate expectations and the death penalty' [2000] *Public Law* 573.

[51] This has not deterred the Privy Council from strong decisions with respect to the death penalty: *Lewis v Attorney-General of Jamaica* [2000] 3 WLR 1785, questioning the behaviour of the Jamaican Privy Council, with Lord Hoffmann dissenting in favour of the death penalty. See on this, I Hare, 'Prerogative and Precedent: The Privy Council on Death Row', (2000) 60 *Cambridge Law Journal* 1; *Flowers v R*, [2000] 1 WLR 2396.

[52] [2002] UKPC 12. The judgment is also important for Bingham's thoughts on constitutional interpretation. See at 7: 'A generous and purposive interpretation is to be given to constitutional

Nichols were seconded as members of the Hong Kong Court of Final Appeal after the 1997 handover.

The Thatcher Effect

Mrs Thatcher believed in governments taking decisions and she abhorred delegating decisions. There was, therefore, no use of Royal Commissions during her eleven years as Prime Minister. With the arrival of John Major in 1990, there was once again some limited use of them. Lord Nolan, a Law Lord, was brought in to chair a Committee on Standards in Public Life after a series of particularly unfortunate incidents of sleaze among Conservative MPs. While there was some harassment of Lord Nolan by individual Tory MPs, and it is arguable that Lord Nolan failed to get the full support of the Government to implement his recommendations, his treatment was generous when contrasted with that of Vice-Chancellor Sir Richard Scott, brought in to report on the 'Arms to Iraq' affair. The procedure he adopted may have left something to be desired,[53] and Scott was indeed rather naïve about the nature of Government, with an underdeveloped sense of public relations.[54] The opposition, however, had no doubt, in the words of Lord Williams of Mostyn, that 'there was an officially orchestrated, mischievous, wilful campaign to undermine the judge who had done no more than his public duty.' Overall, as judges had taken on a more central role in political decision-making in court, their utility as chairs of inquiries, blessed with the cloak of independence and impartiality, was increasingly questioned.

provisions protecting human rights. The court has no licence to read its own predilections and moral values into the Constitution, but it is required to consider the substance of the fundamental right at issue and ensure contemporary protection of that right in the light of evolving standards of decency that mark the progress of a maturing society. In carrying out its task of constitutional interpretation the court is not concerned to evaluate and give effect to public opinion . . . it is no substitute for the duty vested in the courts to interpret the Constitution and to uphold its provisions without fear or favour. If public opinion were to be decisive there would be no need for constitutional adjudication. The protection of rights could then be left to Parliament, which has a mandate from the public, and is answerable to the public for the way its mandate is exercised, but this would be a return to parliamentary sovereignty, and a retreat from the new legal order established by the 1993 Constitution . . . the very reason for establishing the new legal order, and for vesting the power of judicial review of all legislation in the courts, was to protect the rights of minorities and others who cannot protect their rights adequately through the democratic process.' See also *R v Hughes* [2002] W L 237099.

[53] G Howe, 'Procedure at the Scott Inquiry' [1996] *Public Law*, 445. For support for the Howe view, see H Grant, 'Commissions of Inquiry—Is there a right to be legally represented?' [2000] *Public Law* 377.

[54] Rozenberg (n 1 above) at 203 ('How not to publish a report'). Roy Hattersley remarked that Scott 'did for judicial inquiries what the Boston strangler did for doorstep selling'.

More questions were also being asked about the 1876 compromise whereby the House of Lords remained as the final appeal court, with the Law Lords, while professional judges, also remaining as legislators. The most dramatic of these occurred when Lord Mackay introduced the Green Papers designed to weaken restrictive practices in the legal profession. Led by the Lord Chief Justice, Lord Lane, the Lord Chancellor was accused in legislative debates of authoritarian attitudes. While some claimed that former Law Lords were entitled to make 'political' speeches, the whole episode was a reminder of the murkiness of the separation of—or even balance of—powers, as well as constitutional conventions in Britain. Conventions were indeed vague. Lord Chief Justice Taylor supported the Government Bill to weaken an accused person's right to remain silent; Lord Browne-Wilkinson opposed the Government on electronic surveillance; Lord Woolf opposed mandatory sentencing, while many of the Law Lords supported Lord Lester's Bill to incorporate the European Convention on Human Rights, although it was contrary to Government policy.[55] Some also found it uncomfortable that Lord Bingham, who became Lord Chief Justice in 1996, spoke in favour of New Labour's controversial Bill to curb trial by jury.

An argument in favour of retaining the Law Lords in the legislature, to be repeated after the establishment of the Royal Commission on the House of Lords in 1999, was the great merit of having Law Lords available to offer legal advice or at least advice on legal matters. Certainly the quality of many of their speeches was commendable. Yet, for much of the century in family and criminal law, the Law Lords had been a force for reaction.[56] The inherent confusion of the legislative and the judicial was highlighted in the *Fire Brigades Union* case where so many Law Lords had spoken legislatively against the Government's proposed changes in the Criminal Injuries Compensation Scheme that it was difficult to find five Law Lords to sit judicially. Five were eventually found and they dutifully found the Home Secretary had exceeded his powers.[57]

In all of this the role of the Lord Chancellor appeared to be changing. From the 1970s, the Lord Chancellor's Office had become the Lord Chancellor's Department with responsibility for running all the courts. By the

---

[55] On this see generally, Alexander of Weedon *et al*, *The Judicial Functions of the House of Lords*, Written Evidence to the Royal Commission on the Reform of the House of Lords by a JUSTICE Working Party (1999) 6–7.

[56] Sometimes they were arguably wrong in law. The war crimes legislation was opposed by several Law Lords, including that distinguished international lawyer Lord Wilberforce, on the grounds of its being 'retrospective legislation', an argument questioned by leading international lawyers. It was the House of Commons, led by Margaret Thatcher and later by John Major, which undid the position of the Law Lords.

[57] Rozenberg (n 1 above) at 99–100.

mid 1980s the massive increase in legal aid had begun and the Department was forced to look for ways of capping expenditure as every spending department of government was forced to do. It was a process, however, alien to the legal profession and the judiciary. When Lord Hailsham began efforts to rein in the legal aid budget, the deference traditionally accorded to the head of the judiciary rapidly receded. It declined even further when Lord Mackay became Lord Chancellor in 1987. His Green Papers were seen by leading judges and practitioners as a sinister plot by the Treasury to bring market economics to the law by denying justice to the public and— as the rhetoric went—destroying the independence of the judiciary and the legal profession. (In fact, much of their motivation was pecuniary.) The Lord Chancellor was harangued politically and sued in the courts. The world seemed to be changing ever more rapidly, but that did not discourage Lord Mackay from offering the traditional defence of the office of Lord Chancellor.[58]

The Judges Themselves

What then distinguished the judges of the 1990s from their predecessors? Even if one had hard empirical evidence, it would no doubt be difficult to generalise about some one hundred High Court judges and forty appeal judges. If one were to take only the latter group, however, one would have seen a group in their late fifties to early seventies. They were likely to have been teenagers in the Second World War, and to have had their sense of England's role shaped more by Suez and ongoing economic decline than the notions of Empire which shaped the attitudes of judges forty years before. Their views of trade unions (except possibly ones in the legal profession) may well have been shaped by the Wilson years and *In Place of Strife*. Their view of the Welfare State, however, was likely to have been shaped by Gaitskell and Butler rather than Milton Friedman and Michael Portillo in his Thatcherite days. They leant towards being Europhiles and were more sympathetic to the liberal penal policies of a Roy Jenkins or a Leon Brittan than a Michael Howard or (as it transpired) a David Blunkett. They included some strong civil libertarians; they, after all, included a number

---

[58] It was 'extremely important for the working of our democratic institutions that there should be in the cabinet a person who represents in a particular way the system of justice . . . it is also helpful that there should be, at the head of the judiciary, someone who can be accountable to Parliament . . . it is also convenient that it should be linked with the speaker-ship of the House of Lords because of the very special nature of that House and in fact that I may act as Speaker and still participate in debates.' Cited D Woodhouse, *The Office of Lord Chancellor* (Oxford, 2001) 22.

whose provenance was South African. While one suspects most normally voted Tory, most were also likely to be 'wets', and the Conservatives knew it. As Sir Bernard Ingham said of the appointment of Sir Richard Scott to inquire into the sale of arms to Iraq, they have 'dredged up the wettest, most liberal judge, they could find.'[59] Even two Chairs of the Law Commission—Mr Justice Brooke and Mrs Justice Arden—had been labelled by the press as 'liberals', while one former Commissioner—now Mrs Justice Hale—had been labelled by the right-wing press as a 'feminist' opposed to marriage.[60]

At the same time the judges in this period operated in a different constitutional atmosphere. One of the results of consensus politics was that primacy appeared to lie with the Civil Service. The Permanent Secretaries appeared all powerful. Whereas judges stood confusingly outside the all-encompassing concept of parliamentary sovereignty, the Civil Service appeared to be included within the concept of responsible government, nominally reporting to dismissible Ministers. The arrival of Mrs Thatcher in 1979 meant the arrival of a Prime Minister who believed that the Civil Service was 'part of the problem'. After twelve years of battering by Mrs Thatcher, the Civil Service had an easier ride with Mr Major, although his policy of contracting out services and shrinking the Civil Service combined to sap power and morale from the executive branch. Parliament too had changed.

While the Labour Party, at least until John Major's rapid exit from the Exhange Rate Mechanism, was largely irrelevant, the Conservative Party had moved from being represented in the Commons by the old landed and professional classes to being composed of a much more Poujadist grouping. Poorly paid by professional standards, and with a lifestyle many regarded as unattractive, it was often assumed that the quality of MPs had dropped rapidly. It is scarcely surprising that, during the 1990s, the ever-expanding and expensive judiciary should appear increasingly significant as the power and size of the Civil Service declined and the nature of the Conservative Party was transformed from an establishment base to a bourgeois one. The transformation was underlined when one newspaper reported that Tory MPs were offended by the sight of Lord Justice Scott, having finished his report on arms sales to Iraq, riding to hounds in the hunting pink. It was all a long way from Sir Winston Churchill's justification of higher judicial

---

[59] *The Times*, 10 February 1996.
[60] She was cited in *This Week* (4 November 1995) as saying: '[w]e should be considering whether the legal institution of marriage continues to serve any useful purpose'. Lord Mackay was said to be 'a thoroughly decent man fallen among trendies.'

salaries in the 1950s by observing that 'one of Her Majesty's judges' had been observed 'waiting at an omnibus stop.'[61]

In the meantime some judges took to thinking about their roles in a broader way. An expansive thesis was advanced in speeches. Lord Woolf, in his Mann Lecture, likening the then current scene to the US Warren Court, said simply '[i]t is one of the strengths of the common law that it enables the courts to vary the extent of their intervention to reflect current needs, and by this means it helps to maintain the delicate balance of a democratic society.' He, however, went further and argued that Parliament could not abolish judicial review:

> If Parliament did the unthinkable, then I would say that the courts would also be required to act in a manner which would be without precedent. Some judges might choose to do so by saying that it was an irrebuttable presumption that Parliament could never intend such a result. I myself would consider there were advantages in making it clear that ultimately there are even limits on the supremacy of Parliament which it is the courts' inalienable responsibility to identify and uphold. They are limits of the most modest dimensions which I believe any democrat would accept.[62]

Coupled with Lord Browne-Wilkinson's comments about the need for the judges to control their own operations[63] and the apparent direction of human rights in the United Kingdom, the strength of the mood of the judges in the declining days of the Conservative period can be described as reaching back towards a Blackstonian role for the common law.[64] Lord Woolf himself shook off some of the protective colouration that English judges had

---

[61] Stevens (n 34 above) at 128. This was inappropriate for a group who were 'the envy and admiration of the world.'

[62] 'Our Parliamentary democracy is based on the rule of law. One of the twin principles upon which the rule of law depends is the supremacy of Parliament in its legislative capacity. The other principle is that the courts are the final arbiters as to the interpretation and application of the law. As both Parliament and the courts derive their authority from the rule of law so both are subject to it and cannot act in [a] manner which involves its repudiation . . . The courts will readily accept legislation which controls how it exercises its jurisdiction or which confers or modifies its existing statutory jurisdiction. I, however, see a distinction between such legislative action and that which seeks to undermine in a fundamental way the rule of law on which our unwritten constitution depends by removing or partially impairing the entire reviewing role of the High Court on judicial review, a role which in its origin is as ancient as the common law, pre-dates our present form of parliamentary democracy and the Bill of Rights.': H Woolf, 'Droit Public—English Style' [1995] *Public Law*, 57–8.

[63] N Browne-Wilkinson, 'The Independence of the Judiciary in the 1980s' [1992] Public Law 405. The judges, until the nineteenth-century reforms, did control their own courts. The logic of the utilitarian reforms was that the operation of the courts should be placed under the reformed Civil Service. Lord Hatherley's Judicature Commission suggested that there be a Ministry of Justice to perform this task. Such a solution was unacceptable to the judges, who lobbied for the alternative solution—hence the Lord Chancellor's Office (now Department).

[64] N Browne-Wilkinson, 'The Infiltration of a Bill of Rights' [1992] *Public Law* 405. See also S Sedley, 'Human Rights: A Twenty First Century Agenda' [1995] *Public Law* 386.

traditionally adopted. In discussing those cases where English law was held void because it conflicted with European Community law, he noted:

> [t]his can be explained by saying it was not Parliament's intention when passing the legislation in question to interfere with Community law. . . the fairytale is harmless, though in other jurisdictions the existence of a written constitution would be likely to make a more direct approach possible.[65]

There were increasing judicial hints that judges saw themselves—as least embryonically—as a separate branch of Government along the lines of the American judiciary. Through the 1980s and early 1990s, there were remarks that set the Conservative years apart from earlier decades. On a parallel theme, Lord Justice Sedley claimed that Dicey's concept of parliamentary sovereignty had given way to:

> a bi-polar sovereignty of the Crown in Parliament and the Crown in the courts, to each of which the crown's ministers are answerable—politically to Parliament, legally to the courts.

John Griffith could barely contain himself. He complained that Sedley:

> believes the country could be better managed and its citizens have greater freedom if the principles of the common law laid down by the judges (and to be developed and extended by them in the future) were given greater dominance . . . It is bold in the promotion of the judicial interest.[66]

The theme was perhaps most perceptively picked up by a High Court judge, Sir John Laws:

> The true distinction between judicial and elective power cannot be arrived at by a merely factual account of what the judges do or what governments or Parliament . . . do. The settlement is dynamic because, as our long history shows, it can change . . . As a matter of fundamental principle, it is my opinion that the survival and flowering of a democracy . . . requires that those who exercise democratic, political power must have limits set to what they may do: limits which they are not allowed to overstep . . . the doctrine of Parliamentary sovereignty cannot be vouched by Parliamentary legislation; a higher-order law confers it and must limit it.[67]

---

[65] Woolf (n 62 above) at 57–8.

[66] JAG Griffith, 'Judges and the Constitution' in R Rawlings (ed), *Law, Society and Economy: Centenary Essays for the London School of Economics* (Oxford, 1997) 289; JAG Griffith, 'The Common Law and the Political Constitution' (2001) 117 *Law Quarterly Review* 42; S Sedley, 'The Common Law and the Political Constitution: A Reply, *Law Quarterly Review*, 68.

[67] J Laws, 'Law and Democracy' [1995] *Public Law* 80; 'The Constitution: Morals and Rights [1996] *Public Law* 622; 'Is the High Court the Guardian of Fundamental Rights?' [1993] *Public Law* 59, 'Judicial Remedies and the Constitution' (1994) 57 *Modern Law Review* 213; and JAG Griffith, 'The Brave New World of Sir John Laws,' (2000) 63 *Modern Law Review* 159.

On the basis of these arguments, Sir John moved on to propound his theory of fundamental laws. Moreover, he could call up academic support in favour of this position. While even Lord Chancellor Mackay had endorsed Ronald Dworkin's argument that, in expanding the common law, judges were doing no more than relying on the fundamental principles on which the common law was based, that theory, when pushed into the public law arena, seemed more threatening to the traditionalists. What Dworkin appeared to be arguing was that any acceptable theory of a democratic model required protection of rights to balance the majority impulse. These fundamental rights were not subject to the will of the majority. The argument reflected the long-running argument in the United States about the justification, in democratic terms, of a Bill of Rights and an unelected federal judiciary. In this country it attracted support from the Institute for Public Policy Research and organisations like Charter 88, which normally had a more grass-roots approach. How far judges were influenced by this is not clear,[68] but the arguments they advanced were novel to the English common law tradition.

---

[68] Certainly this thinking has influenced others. See Institute for Public Policy Research, *Draft Constitution* (1991), 5–6.

5

Jurisprudence or Politics

The Formalist Tradition[1]

THE WOOLF-LAWS APPROACH to fundamental law was not merely alien to the Jowitt-Simonds formalist tradition, it flew in the face of three centuries of the English democratic tradition. That tradition had been slow to evolve and was not finally settled until the nineteenth century. It is important to emphasise the classical liberal element in this evolution, because the Liberal and then the Labour Parties have been the natural successors of the utilitarians, who were the force behind the nineteenth-century transformation of law and the legal system on the one hand and the flowering of parliamentary sovereignty on the other. Supporters of both Parties have sought to emphasise judicial restraint, and its logical corollary, the formalistic approach to language. The codification movement was thus a central utilitarian tenet, since utilitarianism inevitably emphasised the will of the majority. Indeed codification was integral to the rise of the modern State. In the United States this was highlighted by the Field Codes, while in England the criminal codifications in 1861 and the Sales of Goods Act in 1893 were prime examples. Codification had a more profound effect in British colonies—especially India—and in the United States, in the early development of State law in California and in other so-called code States.[2]

The judicial restraint aspect of English legal utilitarianism—emerging from Bentham's distrust of 'judge and co'—had, however, at least two other elements. First, after Halsbury's forays into appointing judges with links to the Conservative Party in the 1880s and 1890s and the first few years of this century, successive Liberal Lord Chancellors sought to make apolitical appointments. While Campbell-Bannerman's Lord Chancellor,

---

[1] J Steyn, 'Does Legal Formalism Hold Sway in England?' (1996) *Current Legal Problems* 43; J Goldsworthy, *The Sovereignty of Parliament* (Oxford, 1999) ch 8; J Rozenberg, *Trial of Strength: The Battle between Ministers and Judges over Who Makes the Law* (London, 1977) *passim*.

[2] M Lobban, *The Common Law and English Jurisprudence* (Oxford, 1991) ch 7 ('The Debate over Codification').

Loreburn, appointed appeal judges because of their politics, the High Court bench became less political, and this approach was confirmed after the appointment of Haldane as Lord Chancellor in 1912. The same Radical-Liberal-Labour tradition could be seen in Lord Gardiner's agenda in the 1960s. He saw no creative role for appeal courts, and therefore advocated the abolition of the second appeal to the House of Lords. Even his advocacy of the Law Commission, as we have seen, was premised on the assumption that 'lawyers' law' was unreformable by the courts, yet needed regular revision. A high priority was the remarkable nineteenth-century utilitarian goal, namely that contract law should be codified—a task one of Labour's stalwarts and an early Law Commissioner, Professor LCB Gower, was set and a project that was doomed to be abandoned. Ironically, but perhaps not surprisingly, it is now being resuscitated by the European Commission.

As academic law became more important, however, Labour academics added their views to the political assumptions. Sir Otto Kahn-Freund and Lord Wedderburn argued the case for keeping the courts out of labour law. Professor John Griffith provided the intellectual base for the formalistic approach to the common law and the judicial process. The law-is-the-law approach was essential, because otherwise judicial attitudes, predispositions, and prejudices took over and judges had bad attitudes: '[t]hese judges have by their education and training and the pursuit of their profession as barristers, acquired a strikingly homogeneous collection of attitudes, beliefs and principles, which to them represent the public interest.'[3] In short, judges were inevitably 'conservative and illiberal.'[4] Old Labour's position was clear.

While Labour saw the judges as unsuitable for decision-making because of their political views, and therefore sought to have them constrained by the formalist approach to the common law, the Conservative attitude was to be more flexible towards judicial creativity, providing the judicial role did not overtly conflict with the Diceyan concept of parliamentary sovereignty. It was Halsbury, Conservative Lord Chancellor between 1886 and 1892 and between 1895 and 1905, who was horrified to discover that the Australian Constitution allowed statutes to be declared unconstitutional. Dicey's icon of parliamentary sovereignty was the apparent intellectual base for the modern Conservative Party. Lord Birkenhead consolidated the Conservative position. Appeal judges were 'the handmaidens of the legislature.' That might be thought the role model for his successors from Dilhorne to Mackay. When one encounters, therefore, the Woolf and Laws approach,

[3] TC Hartley and JAG Griffith, *Government and the Law*, 2nd edn (London, 1981) 181.
[4] JAG Griffith, *The Politics of the Judiciary*, 4th edn (London, 1991) 275.

with an appeal to fundamental law, there is a clash with both the Labour and Conservative traditions. This similarity of approach can be seen by looking in the 1990s at the speeches of the then Labour Chancellor in waiting, Lord Irvine, as well as those of the last Conservative Lord Chancellor, Lord Mackay. It was scarcely surprising. The notion of all power flowing from the Queen in Parliament permeates the Constitution and politics. It explains so much in English society from the tendency to centralise to the obsessions with denying that any sovereignty has been surrendered to Brussels by EU legislation or to the judges by human rights legislation.

Lord Mackay set his face against a Bill of Rights—along with other members of the Conservative administration—on the ground that it would undermine parliamentary sovereignty, incidentally the same policy ground used by the Attlee administration from 1945 to 1951 to refuse incorporation of the European Convention. Lord Mackay was relatively calm about the judges' EU decisions, invalidating British statutes, which he argued were only one British statute read in the context of another British statute. He was, however, hostile to the Woolf thesis that Parliament is constrained by fundamental laws. Perhaps not surprisingly, however, it was Lord Irvine, then in opposition, who sounded the most serious warning notes. He reminded judges that judicial review was subject to 'the democratic imperative' and that 'courts are, in relative terms, ill-equipped to take decisions in place of the designated authority'.

> An interventionist approach to judicial review for error of law may, in part, undermine the *raison d'être* of the system of specialist administrative tribunals, which are intended by Parliament in most cases to replace, and not merely to supplement, the decision-making powers of the court.[5]

With respect to the central Government, the Irvine positions in opposition were even firmer:

> [t]he courts may not decide either on the validity or desirability of legislation . . . The legislative supremacy of Parliament is not merely a legal concept, a principle

---

[5]   A Irvine, 'Judges and Decision Makers: The Theory and Practice of Wednesbury Review' [1996] *Public Law* 59. There appears later to have been some rapprochement between Lord Irvine and Laws J. See especially Lord Irvine's introduction to Laws J's 1996 Mishcon Lecture. In his introduction, Lord Irvine ascribes the disagreement partly at least to his training in Moral Philosophy at Glasgow with its Kantian flavour and Sir John Laws' classical training as an Aristotelian. Irvine argues the need for 'a fuller communitarian critique of the classic liberal notion of the autonomous moral agent, on the basis that the individual can only be fully comprehended within the context of communities.' Irvine clearly favoured the European Convention on Human Rights, passed by Parliament, over an independent Bill of Rights with judges as arbiters of those rights. It may perhaps be asked why judges would not treat the former as a species of the latter. See also J Laws, 'The Limitation of Human Rights', [1998] *Public Law*, 254.

of the common law, recognised by the decision of the courts . . . It is Professor Hart's 'ultimate rule of recognition'.[6]

He added, 'The idea that an Act of Parliament could be held invalid by the judges became obsolete when the supremacy of Parliament was finally established by the Revolution of 1688.'[7] Lord Irvine therefore disassociated himself from Mr Justice Laws's views that, where fundamental human rights are involved, the *Wednesbury* test may be weakened.[8] He was clearly uncomfortable with the Pergau Dam case (1995):

> The soundness of a development in the context of an overseas aid statute requires evaluation and that should be for the Secretary of State not the court. . . . The courts should take care to abstain, under the mantle of construction, from elevating what is, in truth, a mere relevant consideration into a or the purpose of a statutory provision, thus curbing a valuable and legitimate facet of administrative autonomy.[9]

Lord Irvine conceded that under European Community law there was 'a species of fundamental law' and he attributed *Pepper v Hart* to the 'spillover effect' of EC law. With respect to Woolf and Laws, with whom Lord Irvine associated Mr Justice Sedley and Sir Robin (now Lord) Cooke, then President of the New Zealand Court of Appeal, Lord Irvine said:

> Of these suggestions four things must be said. First, they are contrary to the established laws and constitution of the United Kingdom and have been since 1688 . . . Secondly, many would regard as inconceivable, on the part of any Parliament which we can presently contemplate, any assault upon the basic tenets of democracy which might call for the invocation of the judicial power claimed . . . I have to wonder whether it is not extra-judicial romanticism to believe that judicial decisions could hold back what would, in substance, be a revolution . . .
>
> Thirdly, the danger with any extra-judicial claim of right to review the validity of any Act of Parliament is that to many it smacks of judicial supremacism. The role and significance of the judiciary in our society will be hugely enhanced if the European Convention on Human Rights is incorporated by Parliament into our law. . . The traditional objection to incorporation has been that it would confer on unelected judges powers which naturally belong to Parliament. The objection, entertained by many across the political spectrum, can only be strengthened by fears of judicial supremacism.
>
> Fourthly, it has to be made plain that those judges who lay claim to a judicial power to negate Parliamentary decisions, contrary to the established law and

---

[6] Irvine (n 5 above) at 61–62.
[7] 'The Judiciary: Public Controversy', *Hansard* HL Deb, vol 572, col 1255 (5 June 1996).
[8] Irvine (n 5 above) at 64–66.
[9] *Ibid* at 69. On this see reaction by D Pannick, 'Why Judges Cannot Avoid Politics' *The Times*, 7 November 1995.

uses of our country, make an exorbitant claim ... it is the constitutional imperative of judicial self-restraint which must inform decision-making in public law.[10]

When Lord Bingham was appointed Lord Chief Justice in 1996 by John Major,[11] on the advice of Lord Chancellor Mackay, his attitude to parliamentary sovereignty was reassuring to both Labour and Conservative Parties. At the 1994 Pilgrim Fathers' Lecture in Plymouth, he had said:

[i]f Parliament were clearly and unambiguously to enact, however improbably, that a defendant convicted of a prescribed crime should suffer mutilation, or branding, or exposure in a public pillory, there would be very little a judge could do about it—except resign.[12]

Moreover, Conservatives took heart from another stance of Lord Bingham suggesting caution about direct attacks on the Home Secretary for his penal policy. Bingham came from the more intellectual wing of the Bar and appeared sceptical about the robust Taylor views, based on the enthusiasm of the circuiteer. The Bingham view was that, while the Howard proposals were undesirable, they fell within the legitimate purview of the legislature—and that judicial observations should therefore be at least somewhat muted. As he put it, while he shared the concerns about Michael Howard's policy for mandatory sentencing and reducing judicial discretion, he did not share the concerns about the constitutional issues. 'As Parliament can prescribe a maximum penalty without infringing the constitutional independence of the judges, so it can prescribe a minimum.'[13]

In the long term, then, just as it was necessary to welcome judicial activism where appropriate, it was necessary to accept judicial restraint where appropriate, and the public arguments gradually developed about 'the least dangerous branch', just as Alexander Hamilton, the proponent of judicial review at the Constitutional Convention in Philadelphia, would have wished. Lord Goff observed of the role of politics and the judiciary,

---

[10] Irvine (n 5 above) at 76–78. See 'Judges' Claims Criticised by Labour Law Chief' *The Independent*, 17 October 1995; 'Labour Law Chief Attacks Judges' Supremacy Claim' *The Times*, 26 October 1995. 'I regard as equally unwise a number of recent extra-judicial statements by distinguished judges that in exceptional cases the courts may be entitled to hold invalid statutes duly passed by Parliament. This causes ordinary people not only to believe that judges may have got over and above themselves but that perhaps they are exercising a political function in judicial review cases instead of simply upholding the rule of law': Lord Irvine, *Hansard* HL Deb, vol 572, col 1255 (5 June 1996).
[11] 'Bingham to Succeed Taylor as Lord Chief Justice' *The Independent*, 17 May 1996; 'Shake-up in Top Law Jobs Offers Prospect of Radical Pairing' *The Times*, 17 May 1996.
[12] See T Bingham, 'Anglo-American Reflections', First Pilgrim Fathers' Lecture, Plymouth Law Society, 29 October 1994. Reprinted, T Bingham, *The Business of Judging: Selected Essays and Speeches* (Oxford, 2000) 239.
[13] 'Bingham Finds No Fault with Minimum Prison Sentences' *The Times*, 4 April 1996.

'although I am well aware of the existence of the boundary, I am never quite sure where to find it' and no doubt many judges shared that concern. In the *Fire Brigades Union* case, Lord Mustill noted that the attacks on the Home Secretary's powers 'push to the very boundaries of the distinction between court and parliament established in, and recognised ever since, the Bill of Rights, 1689.'[14] In addition to his constitutional arguments, Lord Mustill gradually spelled out an articulate and sophisticated view of judicial restraint. In *South Yorkshire Transport*[15] he set out to ensure that *Wednesbury* was not used as covert substantive due process. He dissented in *R v Brown*[16] believing that it was not the role of the courts to invent new crimes, in that case consenting adults indulging in sado-masochistic practices. In *White v Jones*[17] he took the cautious approach, justifying his refusal to hold a dilatory solicitor liable to a disappointed potential legatee, with an elegant blend of policy reasoning underlying his scepticism about the extension of *Hedley Byrne v Heller*.

In extrajudicial writing Lord Mustill distinguished 'liberal' from 'conservative' judicial work and noted, acerbically, 'this banality of discourse is encouraged by some judges who long to talk to the press and to appear on television.' He doubted whether judicial filling of gaps in the law 'is constitutionally desirable and whether the judges have the right qualifications to perform the task.' After labelling judicial styles classical, neo-classical, and romantic, he argued the pendulum theory of judicial creativity and restraint:

> If judicial law-making has come to seem too conventional, so that the growth of the law is stunted, a more free approach to the exploitation of legal materials becomes tolerated and even encouraged. But if this is seen as going too far, with judicial creativity too wild and unpredictable, informed opinion creates a force in the opposite direction, tending to impel judicial methods back towards the norm. The result is slow but repeated oscillation of judicial methods.[18]

The Public Debate

There is thus not one clash between the judges and the politicians, but a series of clashes. While it is fair to generalise about the views of the leading

---

[14] [1995] 2 AC 513. See also Lord Keith, who thought that to grant relief would 'represent an unwarrantable intrusion by the court into the political field and a usurpation of the function of parliament'. *R v Secretary of State for the Home Department, ex p Fire Brigades Union* [1995] 2 AC 513, 544.

[15] *South Yorkshire Transport Ltd v Monopolies and Mergers Commission* [1993] 1 WLR 23.

[16] [1994] 1 AC 212.

[17] [1995] 2 AC 207.

[18] MJ Mustill, 'What Do Judges Do?' (1996) 3 *Sartryck ur Juridisk Tidskrift* 622.

judges, as Mr Justice Holmes said, 'to generalise is to omit.' In certain constitutional areas, Lord Bingham urged caution. In a more general way, Lord Mustill articulated what is essential as judges moved more into the centre of the political arena, namely basic principles of judicial restraint. The judges being creative in traditional common law areas may well be commended; it may well be 'constitutional' for judges to develop a right to privacy;[19] judicial review may be vital to ensure fairness in society now that it seems that Parliament is increasingly ineffective in controlling executive discretion in individual cases; decisions on the EU and its form of supremacy have been handed to the judiciary by Parliament; and the incorporation of the European Convention added to the judges' responsibilities. At the same time, direct attacks on government sentencing policies were likely to justify complaints that the judges had moved over the line from the judicial to the political, if judges claimed some constitutional prerogative for such attacks. Judicial claims to be guardians of fundamental laws are likely to be met with understandable hostility as a breach of the traditions of parliamentary supremacy.

The Conservative Government was surely not without fault. Andrew Le Seuer has argued that the Major Government—and particularly Michael Howard, the Home Secretary—had gone out of its way to provoke the judicial-review dispute: '[t]he debate itself is a part of a government strategy for coping with judicial review.' He argued that some Government departments ignored their own legal advice in fighting judicial review cases, because it put the Conservative Government 'in the position of arguing the policies it knows will appeal to Archie Bunker and Essex Man, while the judges look wet and subversive.'[20] Certainly Michael Howard, the Home Secretary, and even Prime Minister John Major said things about judges which might be thought to violate *Erskine May's* injunction against 'reflections on a judge's character or motives' or 'language disrespectful' of the judiciary. After again losing in the High Court, the Home Secretary was heard to say of Mr Justice Dyson: '[t]he last time this particular judge decided against me, which was in a case which would have led to the release of a large number of immigrants, the Court of Appeal decided unanimously that he was wrong.'[21] Not very shocking; but deviating from the

---

[19] The power of the courts to do this was mooted by Lords Bingham and Hoffmann, but doubted by Lord Irvine: *Hansard* HL Deb, vol 572, col 1259 (5 June 1996). Lord Wilberforce, however, thought 'privacy is one of those areas where it may be appropriate for the judge to take a hand': *ibid*, col 1267.

[20] A Le Seuer, 'The Judicial Review Debate: From the Partnership to Friction' (1996) 31 *Government and Opposition* 8.

[21] 'Today', BBC Radio 4, 29 September 1995.

traditional norm, particularly as leading counsel for the Government had already advised against an appeal in that case.[22]

The temptations were clear. In defence of the judges, Ferdinand Mount argued that 'the Renaissance of judicial review was a healthy reaction, not a gratuitous interference. The judges have moved in to remedy the deficiencies of an over-mighty, over-whipped, single chamber parliament.'[23] *The Economist* claimed that the growth of judicial review had 'less to do with a new generation of supposedly activist judges eager to expand their power than with the vastly expanded reach of Government itself.'[24] At the same time, the main disputes over judicial review and Michael Howard's penal policy put the judges in a political position from which it was difficult to extricate themselves—at least in a way that allowed judicial independence and the separation of powers to grow intelligently. Indeed, it was the resignation of Lord Taylor that was the significant event in defusing the dispute.

Writing of the two most important cases in 1994, the *Pergau Dam* case and the *Fire Brigades* case, Alan Watkins said:

> [p]rogressive persons approve the courts' judgments because they disapprove of the two ministers' actions and of the Government generally. But what would Mr Robin Cook say if the courts prevented him, as Foreign Secretary, from donating money to what a Labour Cabinet considered a worthy cause?[25]

Others pointed out that whatever pleasure Labour was taking in the judges' activities in judicial review, they had not enjoyed the work of judges in *Laker*[26] and the *Grammar School*[27] cases. The problem was put in a slightly different way by Andrew Marr in his *Ruling Britannia*:

> Senior judges have enjoyed the popularity and power which judicial review and the rise of European law has given them; talking privately one senses that they are fully aware of their upward mobility in the British system. But it is not so long since the judiciary's name was mud after the Guildford Four and Birmingham Six miscarriages of justice. In future, where they seem out of touch, or silly, they will find themselves pilloried and criticised, by politicians as well as the media, more openly and harshly than they are accustomed to. In the fluid, ever-changing 'marketplace of authority' where the judiciary is hawking its judgments so happily, no authority is sacrosanct or forever, it has to be earned, and earned again, day after day, instance after instance. The more the judges overturn or challenge the deeds

---

[22] See also Leader, 'Judge Over Your Shoulder: Modern Courts and the Modern Politician' *The Times*, 17 October 1995.

[23] F Mount, 'From Major to Maurras' (1996) March *Prospect*, 31.

[24] 'Government v Judges' *Economist*, 16 December 1995, 22.

[25] *The Independent on Sunday*, 13 November 1994.

[26] *Laker Airways v Department of Trade* [1977] QB 643.

[27] *Secretary of State for Education and Science v Tameside Metropolitan Borough* [1977] AC 1014.

of elected politicians, the more they themselves will come to be judged in a similar way.[28]

One can see what Marr means. *The Spectator* unleashed Boris Johnson, the scourge of Brussels, in June 1995. Beginning with quotes from a Cabinet Minister that the judges 'are socially corrupt', he recorded the resentment among politicians that Nolan and Scott were 'now sitting in assize over the ministers and the entire political establishment.' Not only did Johnson take issue with the Woolf thesis, but pointed at Mr Justice Sedley, who had hailed 'a new culture of judicial assertiveness to compensate for and in places repair the dysfunction of the democratic process', as a former Marxist.[29] Johnson explained the change of attitude, and willingness to court 'the public opportunism that attaches to those who espouse one side of the political debate or the other' to what one QC allegedly described as 'a change in the balance of the legislature and the quality of the judiciary.' These very able barristers, who no longer bothered with becoming MPs:

> having been raised to the bench, and having made their pile as barristers . . . are trying to have their cake and eat it. They rejoice in the fancy new grounds for judicial review being imported from Europe . . . and . . . some of them relish the chance to engage in the political process. For these judges are no longer snaggle-toothed Wykehamists who think Gazza is a pop star. A new generation is coming up, and what especially enrages the Government is that their judgments tend to go in a liberal direction: if they are frustrated politicians, they sometimes seem to be frustrated Labour politicians.[30]

Sir Ivan Lawrence QC, MP, Tory backbencher and, at that time, Chair of the powerful House of Commons Home Affairs Committee, was the source of the remark that:

> we've opened up a whole field and made it impossible for the Government to make any decisions without being challenged . . . That alleged disaster in question is the process of judicial review, which is demonstrably transforming the British Constitution . . . What is the point of being Her Majesty's Secretary of State for Home Affairs, he must be asking himself, if he cannot decide whether or not Mohammed Fayed deserves a passport.

A few days later, Lord Taylor responded to the various allegations in his Mansion House speech:[31]

---

[28] A Marr, *Ruling Britannia* (London, 1995) 289–90.
[29] Sedley J had not endeared himself to Ministers by describing the Government's consultation paper on night flights at Heathrow as 'devious and deeply unattractive' and 'a farrago of equivocation': 'Air Transport 2: Noisy Flights' *Economist*, 11 November 1995, 37.
[30] B Johnson, 'The Long Arm of the Law' *Spectator*, 17 June 1995.
[31] 'Lord Mayor's Dinner to H M Judges', 5 July 1995.

In respect of Judicial Review, however, recent public and press criticism of the judiciary has moved beyond comment on the decisions reached and focuses increasingly on the legitimacy of the judges taking such decisions at all. If a judge strikes down the decision of a Minister, if a judge is appointed by the Government to investigate a matter of public concern, reports or is thought to be going to report adversely about individuals or groups within his terms of reference, cries are raised that he has got above himself. Phrases like 'power hungry' and 'frustrated politicians' are entering the commentators' lexicon. The suggestion seems to be that the senior judiciary have decided to mount a bloodless coup and to seize the commanding heights of the constitution.

. . . I have to assure you nothing could be further from the truth. The judges have no such ambition.

Three months later, Michael Howard gave a rabble-rousing speech at the Conservative Party conference and, as we saw, Lord Chief Justice Taylor at once responded with a vigorous rebuttal. Hugo Young argued that Taylor should not have done it, but was driven to it by Howard's decision to 'take discretion from the judges and hand it over, incrementally year on year, to the party conference . . . Since the Labour Party is terrified to do so, the LCJ steps forward as defender of the public interest.' Young went on, however, to castigate Lord Irvine who was 'to the civil law judges, what Michael Howard is, brutishly, to the criminal law judges . . . He seems to be getting ready for office by waving the judges off his future turf . . . What the judges, and the country will have to get used to is a more adversarial relationship between them and politicians, whoever is in power.'[32] With the Conservative Government anxious to evade part of the Nolan Report and individual Ministers working to rubbish the Scott Report, the newspapers had a field day: 'Judges vs. the Government' was a typical example.[33]

In its reporting *The Times* sensationalised the dispute, with one anonymous civil servant reported as saying that Ministers were 'gunning for judges' since they were 'seen as the last bastion of the liberal establishment.' A judge was alleged to have said the Government was running 'a hate campaign . . . to pour poison on the views of the judiciary.' A Conservative MP saw Mr Justice Sedley's finding of a procedural flaw in

---

[32] H Young: 'When Judges put Ministers in the Dock' *The Guardian*, 17 October 1995.
[33] 'It used to be easy to caricature the judges. They were reactionaries, they were Establishment, they never doubted the evidence of the police, they were so out of touch they didn't know who The Beatles were, and come hell or high water they would back a Conservative government . . . In Britain, governments have been winning a smaller share of the electorate, and party loyalties have been weakening steadily for 30 years or more. Assuming people want somebody they can look up to and trust, there is a vacuum that judges have been able to step into. The British judiciary has enhanced its capacity to do this by seeking to change, in the space of a few short years, virtually every negative element of the traditional judicial stereotype.' S Ward, *Independent*, 3 November 1993.

banning the visit of the Rev Moon as a 'further example of the contempt
with which some members of the judiciary seem to treat the views both
of this House and the general public.' Mr Howard's deputy, Ann
Widdecombe, was 'quite worried about the pronouncements of some of the
judges who appear to think that there is a policy role to be adopted by some
of the judiciary.'[34] As the judges not only exercised their powers that had
been dramatically increased by Britain's adhesion to the EU but increasingly assimilated continental and Commonwealth jurisprudence, clashes
with Dicey's vision of parliamentary sovereignty became inevitable. That in
turn meant clashes with an increasingly anti-European Conservative party.

Lord Hailsham, the former Chancellor, opined: 'I think there is a danger
at the moment of the judiciary entering into the field of the executive, but
vice versa there are signs of the executive encroaching on the judiciary.
They should both mind their steps.' Behind the scenes, however, one
Minister expressed delight about Michael Howard's sentencing proposals:
'[t]he judges will hate it. It'll be great. We're going to take them on . . . It
will be us against the judges and I have no doubt who the public will back.'
Lord Lester, a Liberal Democrat, described the Tory attacks as 'ignorant,
insolent and trumped up' and, sounding almost like Lord Goddard, added:
'we have some of the finest judges in the world and for ministers to suggest
they are partisan is a gross defamation.'[35]

The public embarrassment of the Major Government was aggravated
when the Conservative Party Chairman, Brian Mawhinney, leaked one of
the Lord Chancellor's Cabinet briefing papers to the political editor of *The
Daily Telegraph*, who was led to believe that the document was about to be
delivered as a speech by Lord Mackay. The document appeared to be a
warning to the judges to toe the line. The flap led to a formal press release
from the Lord Chancellor saying 'I would never warn the judiciary not to
overstep their powers by using judicial review to challenge ministerial decisions.' The situation was not helped, however, by Sir Ivan Lawrence QC,
MP, announcing that 'we shall statutorily have to restrict judicial review.'

So it went on. Lord Justice Rose predicted that tougher sentencing policies would lead to more murder—'what incentive does the rapist have to
leave his victim alive?' Lord Donaldson, the former Master of the Rolls,
was outspoken in his attacks on the Government's sentencing policy. *The
Sunday Times*, the most inflammatory newspaper in the Murdoch group,
said it all in an editorial entitled 'Howard Must Win':

> John Major and his ministers are at loggerheads with the judiciary as never
> before . . . Mr Howard is viewed by many judges as an ambitious, right-wing

[34] E Lightfoot and M Prescott, 'Too Big for Their Wigs?' *Sunday Times*, 5 November 1995.
[35] *Ibid.*

populist who shamelessly plays on people's instincts on law and order. Tory MPs who support his stand regard most judges as privileged occupants of an ivory tower who have long forgotten whatever they knew of life outside their comfortable security perimeter . . . Judges would be foolish to assume too high a degree of public respect . . . Much rests on the outcome of Howard v The Judges. This time, as Labour leaders recognise, it is in the public interest that Mr Howard wins.[36]

The Labour landslide of 1 May 1997 was, in some ways, a blessed relief.

Moral and Social Policies Creep in

It would be wrong, however to finish this analysis of the changing political positions of the judiciary in the 1980s and 1990s, without looking at the partial transference of moral issues from the parliamentary arena to the courts. While parliamentary legislation still lays down policies far more clearly than Congressional legislation in the United States, in the last twenty-five years there has been a noticeable tendency for the courts to be used to push moral and social policies forward. The clear line between the legislative and the judicial in these areas may be breaking down.

Parliament had passed the legislation on homosexuality, abortion and discrimination in the 1960s; and by the 1970s conservative groups were challenging the liberal establishment in the courts over pornography[37] and contraception.[38] On abortion, for instance, *Royal College of Nursing v Department of Health and Social Services*[39] was a landmark decision on new methods of abortion, thereby saving a 'messy' debate in Parliament. There has been increasing evidence that moral debates have migrated away from Parliament to the courts or to experts bodies, for instance, the Human Fertilisation and Embryology Authority. When local authorities renewed an interest in sterilisation of the mentally handicapped, the courts became involved and offered guidance of their own.[40] The courts have also been more willing to become engaged in moral issues such as turning off life support systems,[41] which an earlier generation of judges would have eschewed.

---

[36] *Sunday Times*, 10 March 1996.
[37] *R v Metropolitan Police Commissioner, ex p Blackburn* [1968] 2 QB 118 A-G *ex rel McWhirter v IBA* [1973] 2 QB 629; *R v Lemon, R v Gay News* [1979] 1 All ER 898; *R v IBA ex p Whitehouse* The Times, 14 April 1984.
[38] *Gillick v West Norfolk & Wisbech AHA* [1986] AC 112.
[39] [1981] 1 All ER 563.
[40] *re B* [1988] AC 199; *re EF* [1990] 2 AC 1.
[41] *Airedale NHS Trust v Bland* [1993] AC 789; *R v Human Fertilisation and Embryology Authority, ex p Blood* [1997] 2 All ER 687 (right to use deceased husband's sperm).

The courts also showed a willingness to reshape some aspects of the welfare state, taking on issues about how far local health authorities were entitled to take cost into account in paying for certain treatments or how far financial considerations could be taken into account by local authorities in closing nursing homes.[42] There have been some similar developments with schools as Government, while centralising power still further in Whitehall, has hollowed out local power centres—such as local education authorities and in effect allowed parents and school governors to use the courts to handle disputes.[43] The growth of judicial review knew few bounds.

It is arguable that the trend described above has its genesis in the 1970s. Not only was that the decade when the courts began making decisions outside the 'political' decisions described above in chapters three and four, but it was also the decade when Lord Scarman began to carve out a political role outside the courts. His report on the Brixton Riots has already been mentioned, but it was his Hamlyn lectures in 1974 which began the long road leading to the passing of the Human Rights Act. At the same time, the minority Labour government, attempted to implement controversial policies through delegated legislation, again leaving the courts to settle the issues. It was the Callaghan Government's efforts to prevent competition in the aviation industry and to undermine the grammar school system which had led to *Laker v Department of Trade and Industry*[44] and *Secretary of State for Education v Tameside Metropolitan Borough Council*.[45] Both expanded the *Wednesbury* boundaries.

In the 1970s it even became acceptable to use 'test cases'. Sometimes there were right-wing moral groups,[46] but environmental issues became important,[47] as did the funding of local government.[48] Even the Labour Party found itself using the courts against the Government[49]—a step that may have had its own impact on the left's traditional reluctance to pass decisions to the judges. As the 1980s gave way to the 1990s, pressure groups, especially single interest groups, began to use the courts. As local government declined in importance, and party debates in Parliament became even

---

[42] See for example, *R v Cambridgeshire Health Authority, ex p B* [1995] 1 WLR 898; *R v Gloucestershire County Council, ex p Barry* [1997] 2 All ER 1 (laundry services for the disabled).

[43] Eg *R v Governors of Haberdashers' Aske's Hatcham College Trust, ex p Tyrell* [1995] COD 399. And see M Hunt, 'Constitutionalism and the Contractualisation of Government in the United Kingdom' in M Taggart (ed), *The Practice of Administrative Law* (Oxford, 1997) 21.

[44] [1977] AC 1014.

[45] [1977] QB 643.

[46] *Gouriet v Union of Post Office Workers* [1978] AC 435.

[47] *Brent LBC v Environment Secretary* [1982] QB 593; *Nottinghamshire v Environment Secretary* [1986] AC 240.

[48] Eg *R v Secretary of State for Social Services, ex p AMA* [1986] 1 WLR 1.

[49] *R v Boundary Commission, ex p Foot* [1983] QB 600.

more closely circumscribed, animal rights and immigrant groups turned to the courts. Even here the European dimension was important. When those lobbying to overturn Sunday trading were prosecuted, they pleaded a 'eurodefence' when prosecuted for violation of the Shops Act 1950.[50] The Government was forced to act and a widening approach to the use of litigation for social purposes had become an accepted part of the legal scene.

Strangely enough, the transformation of the English judiciary over a twenty-five year period, during which they took cognisance of a far wider range of political and social matters, was achieved without the politicisation of the judiciary, at least in the sense the judiciary in France, Italy, Germany and Spain has become politicised. Even after Lord Mackay's decision to abandon the Kilmuir Rules limiting public remarks by judges, the judiciary on balance showed remarkable good sense about public appearances and public statements. In this regard the English judges do have a special relationship to politics, much closer to the Commonwealth model than the continental one. This has no doubt been aided by the fact that the British political elite, while undoubtedly guilty of sleeze, have lacked the more spectacular corruption of politicians in Belgium, Italy, Germany and France which has pushed examining magistrates into highly political inquiries.

Nevertheless the English judges have remained a part of the establishment, although less and less associated with Government. The closest links with government have come on security where the English courts made embarrassing decisions in the *Spycatcher* case[51] and similar cases. The other area where, for far longer than they should, the English judges deferred to the establishment view was in the matter of the police. While the judiciary liked to explain that it made mistakes because it was misled by the police, the truth is that the Guildford Four, the Birmingham Six, the Cardiff Three and the Tottenham Two were also strikes against the English judiciary who were too reluctant to question police evidence. It was partly a generational matter. With the retirement of Lord Lane as Lord Chief Justice, the strong tendency not to doubt the police receded. Administrative bodies to question convictions beyond the appeal process helped; the presence of three enlightened Chief Justices, Lords Taylor, Bingham and Woolf, has made the difference.

---

[50] *Torfaen Borough Council v B&Q* [1990] 1 All ER 129; *Stoke on Trent City Council v B&Q* [1984] 2 All ER 332; [1991] 4 All ER 221; *Kirklees MBC v Wickes Building Supplies Ltd* [1992] 3 All ER 717.
[51] *A-G v Guardian Newspapers* [1989] 2 FSR 23. See JAG Griffith, *Politics of the Judiciary*, 5th edn (London, 1997) 223–32.

6

Balance of Powers: the Independence of Individual Judges

H AVING REACHED 1997, which was to prove an important turning point in the constitutional history of the United Kingdom, it may be appropriate to pause to ask what roles the judges—individually and collectively—had at that point in time. How was the independence of the judiciary viewed?

An International Virus

Public interest in the concept of judicial independence seemed to be universal in the common law world at the end of the 1990s. For instance, the *Financial Times* of 11 February 1999 reported cases of attacks on judicial independence in Israel, Zimbabwe and Hong Kong. First: 'Israeli Judge Threatened' reported that ultra-Orthodox groups had called Mr Justice Barak a 'judicial dictator' and an anti-Semite and threatened his life because of his decisions in favour of a secular State. Second: 'Outburst by Mugabe may deter donors' reported that the President of Zimbabwe had called three of the five Supreme Court judges 'British agents' when they pointed out that the army had no legal right to arrest and torture journalists; their view was said by the President, to be 'an outrageous and deliberate act of impudence.' The third *Financial Times* heading that day was: 'Drive to resolve Hong Kong legal crisis' referring to the Chief Executive of Hong Kong Special Administrative Region (SAR) (C-H Tung) sending an emissary to Beijing to soothe feelings there about the first major decision of the Hong Kong Court of Final Appeal, which had replaced the Judicial Committee of the Privy Council at the time of the 1997 'handover'.

The Hong Kong Court of Final Appeal was composed primarily of Hong Kong judges, but including a judge from a panel of judges from common law countries. (The two UK judges on the panel were Lords Hoffmann and Nicholls.) Article 158 of the Basic Law was a compromise between the common law tradition that judges interpret the Constitution and the

Chinese tradition that interpretation lies with the State or the Party— specifically in this case the Standing Committee of the National People's Congress (NPCSC). The Basic Law appeared to leave judicial interpretation to the Final Court of Appeal and left to the NPCSC the overreaching power to interpret the Basic Law. The new court, led by its new Chief Justice, Andrew Li, began by appearing to capitulate entirely to Beijing. It decided in *Ma*[1] that the Provisional Legislative Council, which had been imposed by Beijing on the former colony and which many thought inconsistent with the Basic Law was, in fact, valid and that the courts of Hong Kong could not question the decisions of the National People's Congress in Beijing. Then, in an apparent volte-face, in the so-called right of abode cases,[2] where it might well have been appropriate for the court to consult the Beijing Committee on the Basic Law, the court chose to plough ahead and to grant what political critics felt was a overgenerous right to enter Hong Kong to those with a parental link. The court was vigorously attacked not only by those close to Beijing.

In London, the Foreign Office said that 'any move to restrict the independent judicial power of the Court of Final Appeal would be a serious matter of concern to us.'[3] At that point it looked as if Beijing was ready to pull back.[4] Thereafter the situation deteriorated.[5] Four Chinese 'experts' attending a meeting in Macau announced the judgment was 'unacceptable'. The Secretary for Justice in Hong Kong (Elsie Leung) visited Beijing hoping to cool the temperature. As a way of heading off a confrontation, the Hong Kong executive then asked the court to review its decision.[6] While locally there was concern about the facts of the case allowing legitimate and illegitimate children of Hong Kong residents to settle in Hong Kong, what agitated Beijing was the refusal of the Final Court of Appeal to refer the case to the Standing Committee of the National People's Congress in Beijing which has, in certain circumstances, the right to interpret the Basic Law. It also found incomprehensible the idea that the Hong Kong judiciary

---

[1] *HKSAR v Ma Wei Kwan David* [1997] 2 HKC 315.

[2] *Ng Ka Ling v Director of Immigration* [1999], HKC 425; 2 HKFAR 141 (1991).

[3] *Financial Times*, 10 February 1999.

[4] 'Beijing Pulls Back in Hong Kong Rift', *International Herald Tribune*, 10 February 1999.

[5] 'China insists Hong Kong rectify Court's Ruling', *International Herald Tribune*, 15 February 1999; 'China's disquiet with Court's powers rattles investors in Hong Kong' *Financial Times*, 16 February 1999.

[6] 'Hong Kong Court asked to clarify ruling' *Financial Times*, 25 February 1999. Yash Ghai, Professor of Constitutional Law at the University of Hong Kong was reported as saying 'this is close to government subversion of the court.' 'Hong Kong Asks Court to Explain Birth Ruling,' *International Herald Tribune*, 25 February 1999.

could strike down statutes passed in Beijing intended to apply in the SAR (the Special Administrative Region, namely Hong Kong).

While the Final Court of Appeal accepted that under British rule Hong Kong courts could not strike down UK legislation, it concluded that that had been changed by Article 19(2) of the Basic Law and the courts now 'have the jurisdiction we have stated to examine acts of the National People's Congress and its Standing Committee for [inconsistency] with the Basic Law.' Moreover, 'in the interpretation of a constitution such as the Basic Law a purposive approach is to be applied. The adoption of a purposive approach is necessary because a constitution states general principles and expresses purposes without condescending to particularity and definition of terms.'[7] The political reaction to the decision appeared at one point to be settled when the Final Court of Appeal issued a five-paragraph addendum to its basic decision. The statement conceded that the court could not 'question the authority of the National People's Congress or the Standing Committee,' while apparently not stepping back from its right to declare statutes invalid which violated the Basic Law.[8] The Hong Kong Government, however, later capitulated further and asked the Standing Committee to overrule the decision.[9] The defeat appeared complete.

With respect to the situation in Israel, the judicial activism of Mr Justice Barak, President of the Supreme Court, became a charged political issue in the 1999 General Election. There was particular hostility to the broad Barak interpretation of the 1992 'Basic Laws', which the Supreme Court had turned into a form of Bill of Rights. The adoption by the liberal majority on the Supreme Court of the test of 'the opinion of the enlightened public' as the basis of judicial discretion was branded by the right as elitist. The ultra-orthodox demanded legislation to 'outflank' the Supreme Court, including the establishment of a Constitutional Court on which the 'non-elitist' would be represented.[10] As we shall see, this threat became more real in 2001. In Zimbabwe, President Mugabe planned to solve his problem of

---

[7] *Cheung Lai Wah v Director of Immigration* [1997] HKLRD 1081; [1998] 1 HKLRD 772.
[8] While welcoming the fact that the Final Court of Appeal did not step back from its earlier judgment, Professor Ghai complained that 'It doesn't seem that the government has any understanding of the rule of law.' 'Hong Kong Bows to Power of China' *International Herald Tribune*, 27–28 February 1999.
[9] 'Bad Precedent in Hong Kong' (Editorial) *International Herald Tribune,* 22–23 May 1999. In *Lau Kong Yung v Director of Immigration* [1999] 2 HKC FAR 442, the Court of Final Appeal meekly admitted that the Government, not merely the court, had the right at any time to ask Beijing to interpret the Basic Law. For an interpretation of the actions of Chief Justice Andrew Li, see F Ching, *The Li Dynasty: Hong Kong Aristocrats,* (OUP, Hong Kong, 1999) ch 28. For a legal analysis of the issues see J Cottrell and Y Ghai, 'Between two systems of Law: The Judiciary in Hong Kong' in D O'Brian and P Russell (eds), *Judicial Independence in the Age of Democracy* (Virginia, 2001) 207.
[10] 'Israel's Barak' *Economist*, 10 April 1999.

judicial independence by appointing a commission of 300 persons to write a new Constitution.[11] When this proved difficult, President Mugabe merely drove out the Chief Justice and packed the court.

The Independence of Individual Judges in England

Contrasted with all this, it is acceptable, if not entirely accurate, to say that England has independence of the judiciary in the sense of independence of an individual judge. To take what are conventionally seen as the hallmarks of such independence—security of tenure, fiscal independence, impartiality and freedom from executive pressure—there is little doubt that, at its core, England qualifies under any reasonable standard of judicial independence with respect to individual judges. Even more than other countries, however, one has to look at the English scene historically and, at least to some extent, sociologically. Traditionally—and rightly—we look to the Act of Settlement of 1701 as the basis of the judicial independence, for by the Act judges were not to be dismissed without addresses by both Houses of Parliament.

The tenure of English judges since 1714 has been relatively peaceful, although among the Lord Chancellors, Lord Macclesfield in the eighteenth century and Lord Westbury in the nineteenth century, left under a cloud; and, as we saw above in chapter one, the judicial record was not as clear as some have assumed. The most notable recent example of problems among the regular judges was that of Sir John Donaldson, a High Court judge sitting as the President of the Industrial Relations Court. In December 1973, 187 Labour MPs called for his removal for 'political prejudice and partiality'. The move failed and, as we shall see, Donaldson ended as Master of the Rolls (President of the Civil Division of the Court of Appeal).

The fact that there were so few ripples to disturb the peace of judicial independence over three hundred years is mainly a tribute to the staid quality of the English judiciary and the political process which has protected it. Secondly, however, the advent of parliamentary supremacy, confirmed under George I and George II, and only marginally challenged under George III, meant a diminishing—and therefore less controversial—role for the judges. Moreover, with the arrival of a reformed and more democratic House of Commons after 1832, in whom virtually all legitimate power resided and which the rhetoric of parliamentary sovereignty protected, the creative role of the courts was increasingly limited by the political culture, as well as the galloping reforms engendered by utilitarianism. The utilitarian

---

[11] 'Apparitions in Zimbabwe' *Economist*, 3 April 1999.

view of the will of the majority was the mirror image of parliamentary sovereignty.

Judicial protection from politicians and political winds is, however, significantly by tradition. Judges have been 'eased out' from time to time. Certainly the introduction of a mandatory retirement age in 1959 helped, but the second Lord Hailsham, Lord Chancellor under Edward Heath and Margaret Thatcher, had to urge Lord Chief Justice Widgery[12] and Lord Denning[13] on their way. Judges also police their own. Early in 1998, Mr Justice Harman of the Chancery Division, much criticised by the legal press for arrogance, felt obliged to resign after a particularly damning condemnation by the Court of Appeal of his casualness and tardiness.[14] One must also remember the vast bulk of the full-time judiciary in England (now some 750, including some 550 circuit judges, the backbone of the professional judiciary), have no protection under the Act of Settlement[15] although they have limited protected status under other statutes, and the Lord Chancellor's Department handles dismissals with considerable natural justice.[16]

When analysing security of tenure, it must be remembered that the English increasingly use a probationary period before substantive appointment. The recorder and assistant recorder—both part-time appointments—are used as training grades, although they at least have term appointments. Appreciably more obvious was the old system of commissioners and the more recent system of Deputy High Court judges. That was patently a probationary system, preparatory to appointment to the High Court, with appointments on an ad hoc basis. For the man in the street these are an understandable and probably desirable arrangement to protect the quality of a judiciary which provides, through the courts, an important social service. The constitutional purist, however, would argue that such probationary arrangements are inconsistent with the Montreal Declaration on

---

[12] In fact Lord Denning delivered the message. G Lewis, *Lord Hailsham: A life* (London, 1997) 273.

[13] A Denning, *The Closing Chapter* (London, 1983) ch 1.

[14] Gibson LJ said 'conduct like this weakens public confidence in the whole judicial process. Left unchecked it will be ultimately subversive of the rule of law. Delays on this scale cannot and will not be tolerated. A situation like this must never occur again.' The Lord Chancellor announced that he shared the concerns of the judges in the Court of Appeal. 'Red Card for "worst judge in Britain"', *The Independent*, 14 February 1998.

[15] R Stevens, *The Independence of the Judiciary: The View from the Lord Chancellor's Office* (Oxford, 1993) 165.

[16] Nor should it be forgotten that the situation is similar in the US Federal System. 'Unprotected' bankruptcy judges and federal commissioners now exceed the number of federal district and appeal judges. In addition to the 850 federal judges with tenure, there are 770 bankruptcy judges and magistrates, 1400 administrative law judges and 2000 'presiding' administrative judges. None of these groups is constitutionally protected. J Resnik 'Judicial Independence and Article III' 353 (1999) *Southern California Law Review* 72.

the Independence of the Judiciary,[17] in legal terms no different from Singapore's probationary period for the High Court bench. While the recent House of Commons Home Affairs Committee's *Report on Judicial Appointments* did not think a five-year probationary period unreasonable and was willing to consider term appointments on the bench,[18] term appointments became the norm for English part-time judges after the Scottish courts ruled that the untenured position of sheriff-substitutes violated the Human Rights Act early in the New Labour Government.

Judicial independence is, in traditional studies, also closely associated with financial independence for the judges. There is no doubt an important element of public interest in this. An inadequately paid judiciary will be prone to temptation and the convention that the Government of the day accepts the advice of the Senior Salaries Review Body seems to have ensured an adequate, if not opulent, salary . If we look back to the seventeenth and eighteenth centuries, however, the great offices of State , including the judiciary, were an opportunity to accumulate wealth. Judges, often from modest circumstances, not infrequently ended as significant land owners and members of the aristocracy. Corfe Castle (Bankes) and Minster Lovell Hall (Coke) were the grand homes of judges from modest backgrounds. While judicial salaries were low, judges received a multitude of fees from various stages of litigation. They were free to sell the right to become 'court officials'; for instance, until well into the nineteenth century, the masterships, themselves lucrative, fetched very significant sums.

The system was put on a more rational basis under the influence of the utilitarians. High Court Judges' salaries were set at £5,500 in 1825—an immense sum for those days—reduced to £5,000 in 1832, the year of the Great Reform Act. Such salaries still enabled judges to compete in wealth with the great landowners. Indeed, economic historians report that during the nineteenth century Britain's economic fortunes meant that £5,000 became worth more not less. Yet when, in the 1870s, Gladstone talked of cutting salaries, he was greeted with cries of horror by the judges, who refused to discuss his reforming Judicature Bill while the threat existed. To Gladstone's suggestion that 'not only their salaries but also their pensions were extravagantly high,' Chief Justice Bovill of Common Pleas argued that 'since the judges' salaries were fixed everything, especially house rents, servants and horses have become very much more expensive.'[19] This interplay

[17] On this topic, see Kate Malleson, *The New Judiciary: The effects of the expansion and activism* (Aldershot, 1997) ch 5.
[18] House of Commons, Home Affairs Committee, *Judicial Appointments Procedures*, vol 1 (5 June 1996) paras 153–59, 176–81.
[19] Letter from Bovill to Selborne, 27 January 1873, Selborne Papers, vol 12 and see generally, D Duman, *The Judicial Bench in England 1727–1875* (London, 1982).

between the judges and government survived beyond the middle of the twentieth century and was settled only in the 1960s and 1970s when Governments came to accept—more or less automatically—the recommendations of the Senior Salaries' Review Body.

Independence, Objectivity and Impartiality

As already suggested, the English judges rank high on any international table of objectivity, particularly with respect to individual litigants. In the twentieth century, London has strengthened its reputation as the centre of commercial litigation primarily because of the judicial reputation for integrity, impartiality and technical competence. Impartiality can, however, be an ephemeral concept and despite the efforts of philosophers and psychologists, we still have only an amateur notion of what we mean by the concept.[20] Winston Churchill, as a Minister in a Liberal Government at the turn of the century, warned against allowing judges to decide cases where 'different classes' were concerned.[21] Even that most conventional of commercial judges, Lord Justice Scrutton, conceded in the 1930s that 'it is very difficult sometimes to be sure that you have put yourself in a thoroughly impartial position between two disputants, one of your own class and one not of your class.'[22]

As one seeks to reconcile these concerns with the reputation for impartiality in the broader sense of values, we need to remember that other constraints are at work which help to justify the judicial reputation for impartiality. English judges operate in a highly formalised doctrinal system, with a strong belief in law as a series of objective rules, which can be enforced impartially. Artificial as these claims may be, intellectually judges are traditionally thought to be both pushed towards objectivity and kept up to the mark by a functionally separate Bar, which itself has a reputation for independence and impartiality. This is, at least, the accepted position and it contains an important element of truth; although the sceptic might say

---

[20] The point was neatly illustrated by the French judge, Madame Haumont-Daumas, who tried Geoffrey Boycott, the well-known English cricket commentator, for assaulting his woman friend: 'It is true I have never heard of your Mr Boycott or even seen a game of cricket. It is like American baseball, isn't it? But for me it was better that way as it meant I was completely impartial.' S Pook, 'The Woman Who Hit Boycott for Six' *The Daily Telegraph*, 13 November 1998. The French judge's remarks are reminiscent of when Danckwerts J was put in charge of a dispute about doctors' pay in 1951. He concluded 'as I know nothing whatsoever about the matter, at any rate I come to it with an open mind.' Stevens (n 15 above) at 101.
[21] O Kahn-Freund, 'Labour Law' in M Ginsberg (ed), *Law and Opinion in England in the 20th Century* (London, 1959) at 232.
[22] TE Scrutton, 'The Work of the Commercial Courts', (1923) 1 *Cambridge Law Journal* 8.

that the interaction underlines the prejudices held by both bench and Bar. Where the judge has discretion, however, whether it be over sentencing, the interpretation of statutes or in restating the common law principles—the inevitably creative elements in the judicial process—the judges have more opportunity for allowing their views full rein.[23] As Lord Hailsham, a true Conservative Lord Chancellor (1979–87), observed of the judges: 'Unlike the keepers of the seraglio, they [the judges] do not have their political or social opinions carefully removed.'[24]

In the last quarter of the twentieth century, there was increasing scepticism about judicial impartiality and objectivity on the part of radical critics.[25] When the Bar was predominantly white, male, middle-aged, Oxbridge and public school educated, how could they possibly be impartial, was the cry. There is undoubtedly considerable confusion in the mind of judges (and the public and politicians) about what is meant by impartiality. The bulk of the public and politicians, however, are happy to accept the myth, significantly because there is a strong element of truth in the concept, even if it is not easily defined. It was clearly one of the reasons why judges have been so attractive as chairs of commissions or committees of inquiry and, more dubiously, commissions or committees to rethink delicate political issues.[26] Such judicial work is frowned on in the United States, with the Warren Commission into the assassination of President Kennedy being the exception and, in the view of most, no desirable precedent.

The English, however, have carried these judicial inquiries to remarkable lengths. In the 1950s, 1960s and 1970s, not merely inquiries into accidents, areas of probable law reform and criminal allegations, but all manner of disputes about union wage claims, disturbances in Northern Ireland and colonial misadventures were subjected to some form of judicial investigation. In a period when there was a vast array of Government commissions and committees, half of them being chaired by either judges or lawyers, the process was described by AP Herbert as 'Government by Radcliffery,' named after the Law Lord who chaired so many of these inquiries. It was a system of governance that suited England—and Britain—for much of the twentieth century; although the constitutional sceptic might take the view that it was, at best, an effective way of employing the well-paid, well-trained, but in policy work, increasingly under-employed, members of the bench. Since the British Constitution is organic, there was no conscious

[23] B Abel-Smith and R Stevens, *In Search of Justice: Society and the Legal System* (London, 1968), ch 6.
[24] Lewis, *Lord Hailsham* (n 12 above) at 27.
[25] See generally JAG Griffith, *The Politics of the Judiciary*, 5th edn (London, 1997).
[26] For Lord Bingham's concerns on this matter, see T Bingham, *The Business of Judging: Selected Essays and Speeches* (Oxford, 2000) 64.

decision to use the judges in this way, except possibly the Tribunals and Inquiries Act; still less was there any testing of the public's confidence in such a system.

While the judges stumbled on these roles by chance, in the name of impartiality, they sometimes left these inquiries with reputations sullied because their conclusions, or political views, were thought to be too clear or failed to agree with those of the Government. When Lord Devlin produced a report on riots in Nyasaland (Malawi), the then Prime Minister, Harold Macmillan, who disliked the conclusions, commented:

> I have since discovered that he is (a) *Irish*—no doubt with that Fenian blood that makes Irishmen anti-government on principle, (b) a *lapsed* Roman Catholic. His brother is a priest; his sister a nun . . . he was bitterly *disappointed* at my not having made him Lord Chief Justice.[27]

When in 1972, Lord Chief Justice Widgery was appointed to investigate 'Bloody Sunday' in Londonderry, his report was dismissed at the time by critics as a 'whitewash'.[28] That view was partially embraced by the Blair Government, which appointed another committee of inquiry, chaired by Lord Saville, a distinguished commercial judge, with two Commonwealth judges, to investigate 'new' evidence and draft a new report.[29]

In short the 'cost' to judicial impartiality was rarely considered as judges were parachuted in to consider delicate political and social crises.[30] The remarkable thing is that the judges so often did help to heal wounds, whether it was Lord Scarman on the Brixton race riots or Lord Taylor on the Hillsborough soccer disaster. While during the eleven Thatcher years, little use was made of the judges for inquiries, since Mrs Thatcher did not believe in 'shuffling off' responsibility to judges, with the Major years there was again spasmodic use of them. Lord Nolan failed to get the full support of the Conservative Government for his *Report on Standards in Public Life* but, as we saw, his treatment was generous when contrasted

---

[27] A Horne, *Harold Macmillan 1957–1986* (London, 1989) vol 2, 1957–86 at 180–1. For the delightful and penetrating study of the Devlin Report, see now B Simpson, 'The Devlin Commission (1959): Colonialism, Emergencies and the Rule of Law' *Oxford Journal of Legal Studies* 17 (2002) 22.

[28] K Boyle, T Hadden and P Hilliard, *Law and the State: The Case of Northern Ireland* (London, 1975) at 127.

[29] 'Bloody Sunday Inquiry Opens in Londonderry' *The Times*, 4 April 1998. The Saville inquiry was attacked in the *Daily Telegraph*, which described it as a 'mockery of the judicial inquiry system . . . the government . . . set up this unnecessary inquiry just to please the terrorists.' 'A shameful Inquiry' (Leader) *Daily Telegraph*, 20 May 1999.

[30] For instance, in his otherwise admirable book about the Scott Inquiry, Adam Tompkins scarcely considers the possible damage to the judiciary in using judges to inquire into delicate political issues. A Tompkins, *The Constitution after Scott: Government Unwrapped* (Oxford, 1998) *passim*.

with that accorded Vice-Chancellor Scott who reported on the Arms to Iraq affair.[31]

The Impact of the Balance of Powers on Judicial Independence

Looking at Scott, one is again reminded that there is much to be said for the US system of investigation of alleged political malpractice by the legislature itself, as was the norm in Britain until the 1920s. The investigation in the United States by Congressman Henry Gonzalez, Chair of the House Banking Committee, of arms sales to Iraq, may well have been more satisfactory than Scott.[32] For the UK, however, the allegation that the Government actively destabilised the Scott Report is the more constitutionally serious, apparently involving briefing against the Report. On balance, judicial naivety and political sidelining cannot possibly strengthen the judicial reputation for impartiality and whatever policy is supposed to justify the use of judges to chair committees and commissions. The executive, by such political attacks, runs the danger of destabilising the very reputation for impartiality that judges need if they are to perform both their judicial functions and the broader responsibilities they have acquired, almost in a fit of absence of mind, under the British Constitution.

When one looks at the actual operation of the separation of powers, there is a working relationship among the branches of Government which surprises Americans. Perhaps the concept was put most elegantly by Lord Simon of Glaisdale:

> What we had was not separation of powers but something far more subtle and far more valuable—a balance of powers. It is no use separating your executive if it has powers over the individual which are considered inordinate. The executive's powers should be balanced by that of the legislative and the adjudicature. That

---

[31] J Rozenberg, *Trial of Strength: The Battle Between the Ministers and Judges Over Who Makes the Law* (London, 1997) at 183–212; G Howe, 'A Judge's Long Contest with Reality' *The Spectator*, 27 January 1996; 'Procedure at the Scott Inquiry' [1996] *Public Law* 445. See also the views of John Major: 'Sir Richard (Scott) was an honest, highly intelligent and committed inquiry chairman, and he produced a thorough report, but it became clear when he began work that he did not have the grasp of the workings of government to put the issue at stake—the collapse of the Matrix Churchill trial—in context.' J Major, *The Autobiography* (London, 1999) 560.
[32] The distinction should not be overdrawn. The House and Senate Intelligence Committees had refused to be drawn into the investigation; the cause was taken up by Henry Gonzalez of the House Banking Committee, with a similar long-term lack of impact. See Tompkins, (n 30 above) at chs 6 and 7. An issue which goes beyond this book is how far the US Special Prosecutor drained away the responsibilities of Congressional Committees and could perhaps have taken on a role closer to that of the British judicial inquiry. The new Canadian Law Commission also appears to be taking on some of the responsibilities of judicial inquiries.

is threatened by advocacy of a system purely based on separation of powers. It is a balance of powers that will vouchsafe liberty of the subject and individual rights.[33]

In a system of responsible government, the different branches of Government interact constantly. Judges are regularly seconded to chair the Law Commission[34] and increasingly, since Parliament appears unable to find the time to legislate to implement the Commission's reports, the courts have themselves used these reports as the basis for developing the law.

In the 1920s the Law of Property Acts were drafted by committees chaired by judges and the same was true of the new Arbitration Act in the 1990s. Senior judges and Ministers meet regularly to discuss possible sources of conflict; and there are instances of powerful exchanges of view. During the Labour Government of 1945–51, Lord Chancellor Jowitt wrote to Lord Goddard, the Lord Chief Justice whom he had appointed, to the effect that he sincerely hoped 'that the judges will not be lenient to these bandits [who] carry arms [to] shoot at the police.' Conversely, the Attorney-General (Shawcross) wrote to the Lord Chief Justice complaining that the Court of Criminal Appeal had gone too far in restricting questions about how confessions had been obtained. The Lord Chief Justice agreed and said he would raise the complaint with his fellow judges.[35] Americans might well believe these to be examples of the executive inappropriately interfering with the judiciary, as President Roosevelt's relationship with Mr Justice Frankfurter and President Johnson's with Mr Justice Fortas have been regarded as suspect. In England such relationships are seen as ensuring the smooth running of 'the system'.

Such relationships exist within the acceptable levels of tolerance of the English concept of the balance of powers. One could argue that they reflect a more flexible—and not necessarily irrational—sense of separation of powers. A more egregious example of executive interference however, and one of the most recent, has already been alluded to. In the early 1970s, while the Industrial Relations Court under Sir John Donaldson was resorting to imprisonment to break the strike mentality in England, the Court of Appeal, under Lord Denning as Master of the Rolls, thought that imprisonment was not an appropriate way to settle industrial disputes. The Conservative Lord Chancellor, Lord Hailsham, direct as ever, was furious. He sent for Denning while he was presiding in the Court of Appeal. Denning refused to adjourn court to wait upon the Head of the Judiciary

---

[33] *Hansard* HL Deb, vol 609, col 719 (17 February 1999).
[34] The Swedish judiciary perform a similar function as does the *Section du Rapport* in the French *Conseil d'Etat*.
[35] Stevens (n 15 above) at 95.

(and Cabinet member). When they did meet, Hailsham accused Denning of deliberately directing certain cases to his court (he, after all, assigned cases in the Court of Appeal); Denning insisted he merely applied law to the facts.[36] There was, however, something rather unsatisfactory about the encounter, as least as far as the absence of executive influence over the judiciary is concerned.

Lord Donaldson and Lord Hailsham continued to have encounters that questioned any formal separation of powers and might be thought to be uncomfortable within the balance of powers. It emerged in 1983 that Lord Donaldson, by then Master of the Rolls, had been consulted by civil servants on 'how the judiciary could play a more constructive role in industrial relations.' Lord Hailsham defended such meetings as normal.[37] Two years later, however, when two judges had commented adversely in a judicial appeal on plans to abolish some forms of judicial review, Lord Hailsham, in a legislative debate, proudly announced that he had received letters of apology from the two judges: 'It is utterly improper in my judgment for a Court of Appeal judge or any other judge speaking on the Bench, to criticise matters passing through Parliament.'[38]

Lord Hailsham, however, extracted the proverbial pound of flesh from those who benefited from judicial independence. When Sir Harry Fisher in 1970 wished to retire from the High Court bench after only two years and go to the City, Hailsham was outraged. When Fisher suggested that the judicial office was not like marriage, Hailsham agreed and asserted that: 'it is more like ordination to the priesthood.' Hailsham was particularly concerned that if Fisher did not like the City, he might want to go back to the Bar. The Lord Chancellor made it clear that that was not allowed and he would do his best to prevent other judges giving him a right of audience. (The professional ethics of the Bar now formally prevent leaving the bench to return to the Bar.) Poor Fisher did not enjoy the City and had no choice but to end his days as head of an Oxford college.[39] In the future things may be different, since the Home Affairs Committee's *Report on Judicial Appointments* calls for the right to return to the Bar after service on the bench.[40]

How absolute, however, is judicial independence? Like academic freedom, it has to defer to judicial accountability, although it is a balance which has never been effectively analysed. To take the most extreme example, Lord Eldon's delays in the Chancery Court, said in 1820 to be close to

---

[36] Lewis (n 12 above) at 277–81 and Appendix 1.
[37] D Pannick, *Judges* (Oxford University Press, 1996) 184.
[38] *Ibid*, at 185.
[39] Lewis (n 12 above) at 275–76.
[40] K Malleson, *The New Judiciary* (Dartmouth, 1998) ch 4.

twenty years (see *Bleak House*), would not be acceptable in terms of judicial accountability today. No matter how strong judicial independence is, the situation is obviously a delicate one. When Lord Mackay, Lord Chancellor from 1987 to 1997, was faced with a situation, as he saw it, of inefficiency and considerable waste of public money in the Employment Appeals Tribunal he required the High Court judge then serving as President (Wood J), to follow certain administrative procedures to clear the backlog of cases. The judge resigned from the bench rather than accept the directive.[41] A debate in the House of Lords alleged a serious breach of judicial independence (Mackay had apparently invited Wood to 'consider his position'); the matter, however, petered out without any discussion of where independence ended and judicial accountability began. The potential conflict remains to be solved, but may well remain unsolved while the relationship of parliamentary sovereignty and judicial independence remains unclarified.

---

[41] *Ibid*, 50. The behaviour of Lord Mackay, in suggesting to Wood J. that 'he consider his position,' has led some to believe that Lord Mackay, normally the most temperate of men, had been provoked by Wood's reference to the Lord Chancellor's Scottish parsimony.

7

The Balance of Powers: The Judges as a Separate Branch of Government?

A S OF 1997, one could have said categorically that in England the judges were not a separate or co-equal branch of government. While the assertion is frequently made that judicial independence in the corporate sense exists, in the past it has existed primarily in the minds of some judges and a few liberal politicians to be produced at convenient moments in political and constitutional debate. The concept of parliamentary sovereignty, which reached its high water mark in the late Victorian period with the writings of Albert Venn Dicey, has ensured until now that separate branches of government, in the American sense, do not exist. While the power of judges has ebbed and flowed, the position in 1997 was very little different from 1897, when an introduction to the Constitution could explain that judges are subservient to Parliament, but it is a group with which Parliament does not like to interfere.

The US Parallels

Tracing the historical basis which led to the separate branches of government in the United States is difficult. At the Constitutional Convention, an urge to control legislation in the States was undoubtedly one reason. No doubt the separation was based partly on the writings of Montesquieu and Blackstone, but probably most significantly on the hostility to the Royal judges, a sentiment most obvious in New England, but clearly reflected in the Declaration of Independence. The emergence of the concept of the separation of powers in the eighteenth century is, as we shall see, murky. It is little wonder that the British ended up with a balance of powers rather than anything that met any rigorous test for the separation of powers. Nor has the concept either of the separation or the balance of powers been of particular interest to British scholars.[1] Yet clearly during the 1990s separation or balance was increasingly in the minds of British politicians. It also was of interest to some members of the Supreme Court of the United States.

Mr Justice Scalia in the *Independent Prosecutor* case looked to Article XXX of the 1780 Massachusetts Constitution:

> In the Government of this Commonwealth, the legislative department shall never exercise the executive and judicial powers, or either of them; the executive shall never exercise the legislative and judicial powers or either of them; the judicial shall never exercise the legislative and executive powers or either of them; to the end that it may be a government of laws, and not of men.[2]

It was an extreme position which did not prevail when the Federal Constitution was drafted in Philadelphia; despite Article III, checks and balances were the order of the day, as indeed, in reality, they must be in any political system. If, as some have argued, the US Supreme Court's concept of judicial review was inherited from the power of the Privy Council to strike down colonial acts, this too could be seen as a mixture of the executive and judicial.[3] Yet the three branches of government were set out clearly in the Constitution, no doubt under Hamilton's influence. The independent judiciary, however, owes its existence more to Madison, thwarted as he was in his other efforts to control the legislatures in the different States. The genesis of judicial independence in the United States was thus a catholic one. Moreover, it is important to remember that other colonies took a very different approach from Massachusetts. Jefferson in Virginia had rejected the 'honeyed' words of Blackstone. In New York the Constitution of 1777 provided for a final appeal court along the lines of the Judicial Committee of the Privy Council, composed of seven senators and the professional judges of the Supreme Court. There was also a Council of Revision which had, like the Privy Council, power to disallow legislation for 'unconstitutionality and impracticality.'[4] There was not, however, in any State, anything to compare with the merging of powers inherent in the English Lord Chancellor.

---

[1] See, however, MJC Vile, *Constitution and the Separation of Powers* (Oxford, 1967); W Gwyn, *The Meaning of the Separation of Powers* (Tulane, 1965); E Barendt 'Separation of Powers and Constitutional Government' [1995] *Public Law* 599; NW Barber, 'Prelude to the Separation of Powers' (2001) 60 *Cambridge Law Journal* 59.
[2] *Morrison v Olsen* 487 US 654, 697 (1988).
[3] JH Smith, *Appeals to the Privy Council from the American Colonies* (Columbia, New York, 1950).
[4] G Sergienko, '"A Body of Sound Practical Common Sense": Law Reform Through Lay Judges, Public Choice Theory, and the Transformation of American Law' (1997) 41 *American Journal of Legal History* 175; F Bergen, *The History of the New York Court of Appeals, 1847–1942* (Columbia, New York, 1985) ch 1.

The Lord Chancellor

The office of Lord Chancellor was pilloried by Gilbert and Sullivan as 'the embodiment' of 'everything that is excellent.'[5] On the other hand, the system was justified in 1943 by that powerful mandarin—and Permanent Secretary to the Lord Chancellor—Sir Claud Schuster:

> The advantages which accrue to the Cabinet from the presence of a colleague who is not only of a high judicial reputation, but who can represent to them the view of the judiciary; to the legislature from the presence in it of one who is both a judge and a minister; and to judiciary from the fact that its President is in close touch with current political affairs, is enormous. In a democracy, whose legislature may be advancing, or at least moving rapidly, and where the judiciary remains static, there is also a risk of collision between the two elements. Where the Constitution is written and the static condition of the judiciary is absolute, as in the United States, the danger of such a collision is very great. Even in England, with an unwritten Constitution and an unwritten common law unless there is some link or buffer (whichever term may be preferred) between the two elements the situation would be perilous.[6]

The Schuster statement is remarkably revealing both about the concept of the judicial role and the perception of judicial independence in England. It is the rationale for a system that reflects the immense power of parliamentary sovereignty in Britain. It justifies a system that has worked relatively smoothly in practice, and came to be challenged seriously only after 1997.

Such enthusiasm for the status quo, inevitable as it may be while parliamentary sovereignty looms so large, has not been shared by reformers over the last century. In the 1870s, as part of the great utilitarian reform of the courts, the judges had opposed the idea of a Ministry of Justice to handle the administrative powers being taken from the old court structure, and insisted that power be exercised by the Lord Chancellor. Hence the establishment in 1880 of the Lord Chancellor's Office (now Department). While, during the twentieth century, the judges tended to praise the arrangement, primarily because the Lord Chancellor was thought able to protect their independence against politicians, such enthusiasm was not shared by the

---

[5] WS Gilbert, *Iolanthe or the Peer and the Peri* (D'Oyly Carte, London, 1882) 9. Anglo-American legal historians can only delight in the information that the three gold chevrons which adorned the gown of Chief Justice Renquist during the Clinton impeachment hearings in the Senate in 1999 were added by the current Chief Justice of the United States in 1995 after he watched an amateur production of *Iolanthe* and was impressed by the Lord Chancellor's gown worn by the actor: Jeffrey Rozen, 'Recipient's Choice', *New Yorker*, 11 January 1999, p 28.

[6] Memorandum, 31 January 1943, (Lord Chancellor's Office papers, Public Records Office) 2/3630. R Stevens, *The Independence of the Judiciary: The View from the Lord Chancellor's Office* (Oxford, 1998) 3.

judiciary in the years after the Judicature Acts. John Duke, Attorney-General at the time of the Judicature Act 1873, was a great reformer who wished to merge the two branches of the profession and to codify English law, in addition to reforming the courts. After he succeeded to the Lord Chief Justiceship, as Lord Coleridge, his views changed. Making the Lord Chancellor head of the judiciary had been a great mistake. '. . . If I could have seen, as perhaps I ought, how the Judicature Acts would have worked, I would have resigned sooner than be party to it.' In particular, he regretted 'The enthroning of the Chancellor upon the neck of all of us.'[7]

As Attorney-General, Coleridge had favoured a Ministry of Justice; and the hope that the reformers had held in the 1870s for such a Ministry did not die. Lord Haldane, in the Report of his Committee on the Machinery of Government in 1918 called for a Ministry of Justice—although he still saw the need for a more restricted office of Lord Chancellor. The Chief Justice of the 1920s and 1930s, Lord Hewart, was paranoid, fearing that a plan to establish such a Ministry was under way.[8] There was talk of splitting the post of Lord Chancellor in the Labour Government of 1964–70, but Harold Wilson's Lord Chancellor, Lord Gardiner, was a conservative in professional matters, and nothing happened. In the early 1990s there was much talk by Liberal and Labour reformers that the Office should be split, and the matter was still on the agenda when the 1997 landslide occurred.

The Law Lords

In turn, however, as with the office of the Lord Chancellor, the position of the Lords of Appeal in Ordinary, the judges of the House of Lords, which also serves as the final court of appeal, inevitably undermines any basic concept of separation of powers. In the 1870s, the intention of the reformers, Lords Cairns and Selborne, had been to end the House of Lords as a judicial body, as well as reforming the Judicial Committee of the Privy Council.[9] In place of these two would be an aggrandised court of appeal, known as the Imperial Court of Appeal, sitting in the new Law Courts to be built in the Strand. A group of Tory right-wingers, led by Sir William Charley, although aided more thoughtfully by Lord Salisbury,[10] harassed

---

[7] EH Coleridge, *Life and Correspondence of John Duke, Lord Coleridge, Lord Chief Justice of England* (London, 1904) vol ii, 359. He also regretted the diminished role of the Lord Chief Justice.

[8] Stevens (n 6 above) at 37.

[9] R Stevens, *Law and Politics: The House of Lords as a Judicial Body, 1800–1976* (North Carolina, 1978) ch 2.

[10] He argued that judges should sit in the House of Lords as a legislative body 'since they often had to make law as judges they should be trained for it by sitting part of the time as

Disraeli's new administration after 1873 to restore the appeal to the Lords to protect the 'dignity' of the House. By the 1876 Appellate Jurisdiction Act, the House of Lords had its appellate power restored. Two judicial peers were created, to rise to four as the salaried judges of the Privy Council retired. In the 1880s, rather than being peers only during their service, Lords of Appeal were made life peers.

In theory the Law Lords are supposed to speak only on legal matters. That did not deter Lord Sumner in the 1920s from defending General Dyer for his role in the massacre at Amritsar, nor Lord Carson from opposing the Irish Treaty in 1922. Even closer to the legal, however, Lord Goddard and his successor as Chief Justice, Lord Parker, were strong advocates of hanging and flogging in the 1940s and 1950s.[11] Lord Merriman and other divorce judges held up liberalisation in divorce law and procedure in the following decades.[12] Perhaps the most dramatic political activities by the Law Lords, however, came in the late 1980s as Lord Mackay introduced Green Papers designed to make the courts and the profession more efficient and responsive to the needs of the public, primarily by introducing market reforms. The retired Law Lords behaved in a remarkable manner during the legislative debates.[13] No fewer than three—Lords Elwyn-Jones (a former Labour Lord Chancellor), Donaldson and Lane (then retiring as Lord Chief Justice)—implied that the Conservative Lord Chancellor (Mackay) was guilty of Nazi tendencies—and of course violating the independence of the judiciary. Lord Elwyn-Jones announced judges must be 'felt to be completely independent of the State' and 'there was a danger' of 'going down the American path.' Lord Hailsham, the then recently retired Conservative Lord Chancellor, expanded the notion of judicial independence far and wide. He regarded the Green Papers as 'an outrage.'[14] He defended:

> the most upright and most independent legal profession known to man . . . the judiciary remains the guardian of the liberties of the people . . . The independence

---

legislators.' Salisbury also argued that such a legislative experience also saved the judges 'from too technical and professional a spirit; and their decisions gain in breadth.' Letter, Salisbury to Selborne, 24 February 1873, (Selborne Papers: Letters, Vol XII, Lambeth Palace Library). Stevens (n 9 above) at 55.

[11] Stevens (n 9 above) at 362.

[12] Stevens (n 6 above) at 174–76.

[13] Some now argue that convention allows retired Law Lords to speak on political matters. Where the myth (or constitutional convention) came from is obscure. But see for instance Lord Lloyd's partially successful efforts to derail the Irvine efforts to curb the judges' right to decide on the rights of audience: 'Irvine Heads Off Clash with Judges Over Powers' *The Times*, 25 January 1999.

[14] *Hansard* HL Deb, vol 505, cols 1333–34 (7 April 1989). Ironically, Lord Irvine's plans for reform go far further than Lord Mackay's. M Zander, 'More Louis XIV than Cardinal Wolsey' [1998] *New Law Journal*, 28 July 1084.

of the judiciary depends more upon the independence and integrity of the legal profession than upon any other single factor.

The debates scarcely enhanced the reputation of the Law Lords or helped quieten the feeling that such debates undercut basic concepts—albeit based only on convention—of the balance of powers. It also failed to clarify the issue of whether the Law Lords really belonged in the upper House. They certainly had their uses, especially on select committees, but there was a high price to pay when, as in the Criminal Injuries Compensation Board case,[15] it was difficult to find a quorum to hear the appeal on the matter, since so many Law Lords had spoken in the legislative debates. Some critics—including *The Economist*,[16] the Institute of Public Policy Research[17] and, perhaps surprisingly, an increasing number of Conservative politicians[18]—thought their presence an anachronism. There clearly were some advantages of the existing arrangement:[19] some Law Lords have peculiar expertise in certain areas; their speeches sometimes stand out from their fellow peers in terms of perceptiveness; and they provide an important function in producing chairmen for Lords' committees, especially on EU legislation. In the circumstances the arrangement attracted the support of some commentators.[20] Overall, however, it was increasingly difficult to justify such an arcane arrangement, even under the balance of powers.

---

[15] *R v Home Secretary, ex p Fire Brigades Union* [1995] 2 AC 513.

[16] 'If the judiciary is to act as an effective check on overweening Government, it should be untainted by direct involvement either with the legislature or the executive' *The Economist*, 16 December 1995.

[17] *The Constitution of the United Kingdom* (IPPR, London, 1991).

[18] Eg John Patten, former Conservative Secretary of Education, 'Let's Reform the Lord Chancellor' *Daily Telegraph*, 10 July 1996; Lord Kingsland (Conservative Shadow Lord Chancellor), *The Law in Action*, BBC Radio 4, 4 February 1998.

[19] A recent example illustrates both the strengths and weaknesses of the link between legislators and judiciary. After the Omagh bombing in the summer of 1998, the Labour Government rushed through a Terrorism Bill to make membership in a proscribed organisation an offence. The plan was criticised in the legislative debates in the Lords by one of the Law Lords, Lord Lloyd, who had played a role as supervisor of the security services. The speech caused the Home Secretary embarrassment since Lloyd argued that such laws would be ineffective and, in any event, probably violated the European Convention on Human Rights. 'Law Lord attacks Bill on Terrorism' *Daily Telegraph*, 4 September 1998; 'The Roughest Justice' *Sunday Times*, 6 September 1998.

[20] 'The presence of the most senior members of the judiciary in Parliament enables the legislative process to draw on a tremendous and unique concentration of legal expertise.' J Rozenberg, *Trial of Strength: The Battle Between the Ministers and Judges Over Who Makes The Law* (London, 1997) 26.

The Appointment of Judges

Another of the issues in judicial independence in England is that the judges are chosen, as they are in most other common law countries although normally with the assistance of a Judicial Appointments Commission, by a politician, the Lord Chancellor. The English like to say that judicial appointments in their country are non-political, or even apolitical; and there are in fact no former MPs currently serving as judges. Europeans, however, find it difficult to comprehend how the system can be apolitical, when the final say for choosing most judges lies with an active politician, the Lord Chancellor, with appointments to the House of Lords and Court of Appeal made by the Prime Minister. Even the House of Commons Select Committee on Home Affairs has described the Prime Minister's involvement in senior judicial appointments as 'nothing short of naked political control.'[21] While civil servants in the Lord Chancellor's Department are influential and the Lord Chancellor consults the judicial heads of divisions, each Lord Chancellor boasts that the decisions are his and until 1997 each had rejected the idea of a Judicial Appointments Commission.

Yet in a sense the claims of the apolitical nature of the process are true. While the judiciary is chosen primarily from the English Bar, it is possible to argue that success and reputation at the Bar far outweigh other attributes in the selection process. (Whether success as an advocate should be the primary criterion for judicial appointment is a different matter.) Once again political convention provides more support than legal rules might. With a relatively small and cohesive Bar, there is an argument that 'the judges select themselves' as Sir George Coldstream, a former Permanent Secretary to the Lord Chancellor put it.[22] It is also true that the days when politics played an important role in getting on the bench have effectively gone. Lord Halsbury, at the end of the nineteenth century, was the last Lord Chancellor who blatantly appointed political supporters to the High Court bench; and after the 1920s, political service played little role in appointment to the House of Lords and Court of Appeal. Yet Mrs Thatcher rejected Lord Hailsham's report of the judges' preference and appointed Sir John Donaldson to be Master of the Rolls in the 1980s, and it was unlikely that she was unaware of Donaldson's work in the Tory cause in the Industrial Relations Court.[23] John Major preferred Tom Bingham as Chief Justice in preference to the judges' choice.

---

[21] House of Commons, Home Affairs Committee, *Judicial Appointments Procedure*, 1996, para 126.
[22] Interview with the author, October 1963.
[23] Stevens (n 6 above) at 172.

It is always difficult to define what is political. We should not forget that during the most radical Government in Britain's history (the Attlee Government of 1945–51) Lord Chancellor Jowitt refused to appoint divorced persons to the bench and, for a period, members of the Roman Catholic Church. While this latter was allegedly because they might have difficulty hearing divorce petitions on circuit, the real reason may well have been because he and the Home Secretary (Chuter Ede) were vigorously anti-Catholic.[24]

The Apparently Irreconcilable Concepts of Parliamentary Sovereignty and Judicial Independence

Parliamentary sovereignty, the wide jurisdiction of the Lord Chancellor, together with the appointment of judges by a politician and the dual roles of the Law Lords, have thus made it difficult to have an institutional concept of judicial independence, based on a notion of separate branches of government. That, however, has never discouraged the English judges from believing that there is such a concept as the independence of the judiciary in some kind of ethereal collective sense. In the same way that academics are inclined to see violations of academic freedom whenever they are faced with decisions they do not like, English judges tend to announce violations of judicial independence when events occur which they think undermine their dignity and, until recently, the English judges were big on dignity. That should not detract from the fact that there are occasions when such claims are legitimate. When, in the War Damage Act 1965, Parliament reversed the actual decision in *Burmah Oil v Lord Advocate*,[25] thereby saving the Government the need to pay damages, that was pronounced to be unconstitutional and a violation of judicial independence.[26] This legislative opposition, led by the Chief Justice, Lord Parker was powerful and justified; indeed in the United States such behaviour by the Government might well have qualified as an Act of Attainder.

In terms of judicial self-perception, the most significant claims of violations of judicial independence have been those relating to the fiscal independence of judges. The most spectacular example of this was during the economic crisis in the 1930s. As we saw in chapter two, in 1931, the

---

[24] *Ibid*, at 86–88.
[25] [1965] AC 75.
[26] L Blom-Cooper and G Drewry, *Final Appeal: A Study of the House of Lords in its Judicial Capacity* (Oxford, 1972) 366–74. Burmah Oil also held up the Wilson Government's acceptance of the European Convention on Human Rights. A Lester, 'Acceptance of the Strasbourg Jurisdiction: What Really Went on in Whitehall in 1965' [1998] *Public Law* 237.

National Recovery Act cut the salaries of public servants and the Order in Council implementing it cut judicial salaries although they were paid out of the Consolidated Fund. The judges were outraged. The insurrection was undignified and, in the traditional English way, ended in a compromise. A Bill was introduced saying that judges' salaries could not be cut (repealable, as is all British legislation). Yet the constitutional position of the judges remained confused and the interlocking relationship between the judges and responsible government, parliamentary sovereignty and Cabinet government murky.

For all the rhetoric and confusion, it is clear that judicial independence— at least for the judges as a class—is not a legal concept in England. At the same time, politically, its rhetoric is important in a body politic without a written Constitution, which relies on a congeries of statutes, delegated legislation, custom and convention for making the system work. Politically, the rhetoric normally does maintain a semblance of the separation of powers. The Schuster approach, however, underlined that in England there is no legal sense of the judges as a separate branch of government, although one must also remember that the 1930s were the high water mark of parliamentary sovereignty. In a decade which also saw the Scott-Donoughmore Committee on Ministers' Powers, Schuster's attitude was a restatement of the Diceyan concept of parliamentary sovereignty. The judges had a narrow delegated role.

Overview

While the reality of the judicial role has changed over the last five decades, the rhetoric has not. While the Lord Chancellor retains his triple roles and the Law Lords their dual ones, claims of separation of powers have to be treated sceptically. As long as the Diceyan concept of the supremacy of parliament survives, attenuated as it may have become, there can be no separate judicial branch of government.[27] Parliament not only provides the Government, in theory it provides the means of controlling the Government. Lord Hailsham, with his talk of 'elected dictatorship,' realised that the second of these functions has largely broken down. Backbenchers are now seen as cannon fodder rather than latter-day Hampdens. Parliamentary supremacy has largely given way to executive supremacy. That may explain why no observer of the Constitution could be unaware that in the last five decades, within the forbidding constraints of Dicey's

---

[27] As Lord Mustill, the Law Lord most articulate about judicial restraint, put it: 'it is the task of Parliament and the executive in tandem, not of the courts, to govern the country.' *R v Home Secretary, ex p Fire Brigades Union* [1995] 2 AC 513, 567.

dicta, the judges have developed a degree of flexibility which has given reformers the hope that there may be a serious rewriting of history.

If this were to come to pass, it was clear the judges would have to develop new strategies and rationales for the judicial process. *The Economist* opined in 1995: '[t]he best answer to current rows is a proper separation of powers in Britain.' The Lib-Lab think tank, the Institute for Public Policy Research, produced a version of a written Constitution which deconstructed the office of Lord Chancellor and established the judges as closer to the American system of a co-equal branch of government.[28] It was clear that politicians would have to think carefully how the increasingly powerful judges should be appointed and treated.

Whether the judges are capable of taking a strategic position is open to doubt. Lord Browne-Wilkinson has already put the case for the court system to be run by the judiciary, subject only to funds voted by Parliament.[29] This, in principle, would be similar to the situation in the United States where, for instance, Congress in 1998 questioned the federal judges on why they spend so much on judicial conferences ('boondoggles' said Senator Grassly, Republican of Iowa). Meanwhile Senator Cohen, Republican of Maine—later President Clinton's Secretary of Defence—called for a moratorium on building new courthouses and Senator John McCain, Republican of Arizona—who later challenged Governor George W Bush for the Republican nomination for President—called for an Inspector-General position within the Administrative Office of the Federal Courts. Gilbert Merritt, Chief Judge of the Sixth Circuit, was concerned about the 'very intense scrutiny' in Congress and ' "the generally negative attitude" towards the judiciary on Capitol Hill that borders on name-calling.' Congress has shown itself reluctant to increase the salaries of Federal Judges.[30] It all sounded faintly familiar. Fortunately, the Chair of the Judicial Budget Committee at the time was the talented and politically astute Richard Arnold, Chief Justice of the Eighth Circuit, who hides his prep-school provenance under an Arkansas accent. He purported to enjoy questions from Members of Congress:

---

[28] *The Constitution of the United Kingdom* (n 16 above).
[29] 'At first sight many would not regard the control of finance and administration as providing any threat to judicial independence. But if the matter is given more consideration, it is to my mind apparent that the control of the finance and the administration of the legal system is capable of preventing the performance of these very functions which the independence of the judiciary is intended to preserve, that is to say, the right of the individual to a speedy and fair trial of his claim before an independent judge.' N Browne-Wilkinson, 'The Independence of the Judiciary in the 1980s' [1988] *Public Law* 44, 45.
[30] RE Hirschon, 'Defence: Judges Deserve our Respect—and Salaries that support their Independence (2002) (May) *ABA Journal* 10.

[t]here's always been an inherent tension among the three branches of government. It is part of the constitutional plan . . . and there's certainly nothing wrong
with them questioning how we spend our money. That's part of their duty.[31]

Were Lord Browne-Wilkinson's and Lord Bingham's (his successor as senior Law Lord now, de facto, the senior judge in the legal system) Oxford
backgrounds ready for this? The arrival of New Labour was a good
moment to test the hypothesis.

---

[31] 'Court Spending under Review' (1996) *ABA Journal* February, 24.

8

New Labour in Power

The Lord Chancellorship

THE ARRIVAL OF the New Labour Government after the landslide in May 1997 set off a series of events that were to bring English legal culture to a point where a serious reanalysis of the role of the judiciary in public law was thought inevitable. The triggering events ranged from plans for reform of the House of Lords and the possibility of proportional representation for the House of Commons (it was imposed on the devolved parliaments of Scotland and Wales and throughout the UK in European elections) to the system of elected mayors and the incorporation of the European Convention on Human Rights into English law. As the Human Rights Act waited to be implemented, the chorus grew louder suggesting that having unelected judges interpreting a far-reaching and broadly drawn statute would pose a serious question of democratic legitimacy.[1]

The implications of this Act and the other constitutional changes were widespread. Could judges still be chosen in the secretive way that had produced generations of judges? Their work in private law was much admired and had helped make London a major centre for international commercial work, but their public law decisions, while increasingly important, were based on a role that was perhaps neither accountable nor transparent. Would the new political burdens on the judiciary in public law cases make it possible to continue to ignore the personal views of the judges, something that, at least since the First World War, the English had largely opted to do? Would the judges be able to continue their Houdini-like performances with political issues? Politicians and judges had warned that a wide range of activities from the Restrictive Practices Court and the Industrial Relations Court to the Human Rights Act and devolution were inappropriate for judicial decision-making because the issues they raised were political ones. Yet the

---

[1] K Ramsay, 'The Judges—Our New Oppressors' *Daily Telegraph*, 18 February 2000; 'Judges, Our New Rulers Editorial, *Daily Telegraph*, 13 July 2000; 'Rule of Judges', *The Economist*, 26 August 2000.

moment the legislation went through, the judges proudly announced that the issues they faced were legal not political. What was the future of the separation of powers, let alone the balance of powers?

New Labour's Lord Chancellor, Lord Irvine, has been appreciably more active in politics than most of the recent incumbents in his post, including his predecessor, Lord Mackay. Lord Irvine chaired a range of constitutional committees emerging from the Cabinet, from political pro-grammes (the Queen's speech) to constitutional issues such as devolution and the Bill of Rights.[2] His was an important voice in developing the political programme of the party. He joined actively in political debates.[3] In July 1998, *The Times* reported that Lord Richard was dismissed as Leader of the Lords by the Prime Minister, partly because he could not get on with Lord Irvine;[4] while Lord Jenkins, former Liberal Democratic leader in the Lords, complained that Lord Irvine exercised too much influence over the Prime Minister. The 1998 political trap which had the Conservative leader, William Hague, sacking his leader in the Lords, Lord Cranborne, because of a secret deal about hereditary peers, was reported to have been engineered by Lord Irvine.[5] It was Irvine who presided over the second sacking of Peter Mandelson. It was he who orchestrated the reform of the House of Lords.[6] Inevitably, in this atmos-phere, even though Lord Irvine occasionally sat as a judge, the public and the legal profession saw him less clearly as a member of the judiciary than most of his predecessors.[7] Nor did Lord Irvine's reluctance to spell

[2] See generally, D Woodhouse, *The Office of Lord Chancellor* (Oxford, 2001) ch 4.
[3] *Financial Times*, 7 December 1998.
[4] Lord Richard's wife shares that view. J Jones, *Labour of Love: The Partly-Political Diary of a Cabinet Minister's Wife* (London, 1999) *passim*.
[5] 'He is regarded as one of the most important men in Britain.' *Sunday Times*, 18 October 1998.
[6] For criticism of his activities in this area, see D Hurd, 'A Vessel Destined to Founder' *Financial Times*, 8 January 2002; F Johnson, 'Blair's First Crony Emerges Unscathed' *Daily Telegraph*, 25 January 2002. Irvine may well, however, have been correct in arguing that a dem-ocratically elected House of Lords would threaten the power of the House of Commons. By the spring of 2002, however, Lord Irvine had apparently lost the battle, perhaps evidence of his waning political influence. 'Cabinet Strife Behind U-Turn on Lords Reform' *Financial Times*, 14 May 2002.
[7] See, for instance, the Sunday newspaper magazine articles: I Hargreaves: 'Kingmaker: The Truth about Derry Irvine' *Observer, Sunday Review*, 11 October 1998, 6 ('not since Victorian times has any Lord Chancellor sought to take such political power') and T Rayment, 'Master of the Rolls', *Sunday Times Magazine*, 18 October 1998, 20. In the debates on the Scotland Bill, Lord Irvine agreed he would not sit on cases involving devolution: *Hansard* HL Deb vol 593, col 1984, (28 October 1998). On the other hand, it had been agreed that in such appeals involving Scotland at least two Scottish judges will be included in the Judicial Committee of the Privy Council. 'Extra Brief After 900 Years of Dispensing Justice' *Financial Times*, 3–4 April 1999. And see now, D Oliver, 'The Lord Chancellor, The Judicial Committee of the Privy Council and Devolution' [1999] *Public Law* 5.

out the kind of cases in which he was entitled to sit dispel the disquiet.[8]

Despite the overt politicisation of the office, the bulk of the legal establishment continued to argue in favour of the status quo. An apologia for the balance of powers—and especially for the Lord Chancellorship—was offered by Lord Woolf, then Master of the Rolls, shortly before becoming Lord Chief Justice:

> As a member of the Cabinet, he (the Lord Chancellor) can act as an advocate on behalf of the courts and the justice system. He can explain to his colleagues in the Cabinet the proper significance of a decision which they regard as being distasteful in consequence of an application for judicial review. He can, as a member of the Government, ensure that the courts are properly resourced. On the other hand, on behalf of the Government he can explain to the judiciary the realities of the political situation and the constraints on the resources which they must inevitably accept.
>
> As long as the Lord Chancellor is punctilious in keeping his separate roles distinct, the separation of powers is not undermined and the justice system benefits immeasurably. The justice system is better served by having the head of the judiciary at the centre of government than it would be by having its interests represented by a Minister of Justice who would lack these other roles.[9]

Lord Woolf was not alone in supporting the constitutionally amorphous role of the Lord Chancellor. Lord Bingham, former Chief Justice and now

---

[8] See, Written Answer from Lord Chancellor to Lord Lester, *Hansard* HL Deb, vol 614 , WA 163 (7 July 2000). 'The Lord Chancellor, in common with the Lords of Appeal in Ordinary, will bear in mind he might render himself ineligible to sit judicially if he were to express an opinion on a matter which might later be relevant to an appeal to the House.' See also *Hansard* HL Deb, vol 597, col 736 (17 February 1999). On when to sit Lord Irvine said: 'I am unwilling to lay down any detailed rules because it is ever a question of judgment combined with a need to ensure that no party to an appeal could reasonably believe or suspect that the Lord Chancellor might, because of his other roles, have an interest in a specific outcome.' The *Daily Telegraph*'s legal correspondent has, however, recently questioned his sitting in a case on an important issue in housing benefit. See J Rozenberg, 'When does a hotel become a house: Lord Irvine is to preside over a tenancy case. He says it is non-political, but it would affect government spending.' *Daily Telegraph*, 3 July 2001.

[9] H Woolf, 'Judicial Review—the tensions between the executive and the judiciary' (1998) 114 *Law Quarterly Review* 579. Lord Woolf has, however, remained steadfast in his view. At the annual Lord Mayor's banquet for the judiciary, he said any attempt to weaken the Lord Chancellorship would be a 'calamity', *Legal Week*, 19 July 2001. Of this concept, Lord Goodhart commented: 'To my mind it makes the Government and the judiciary sound too much like common members of a ruling elite—a group of platonic guardians or (what is perhaps much the same thing) a group of members of the Garrick Club . . .' *Hansard* HL Deb, vol 597, col 729, 17 February 1999. With New Labour the Garrick has replaced the Athenaeum as the centre of the Establishment. The Athenaeum now seems to be composed of physicians, surgeons and other tradesmen.

senior law lord, expressed similar views. He defended Lord Irvine's role as head of the judiciary and a cabinet minister, saying 'it enables him to act as guarantor of judges' integrity and independence. Since the Lord Chancellor, unlike other ministers, has no political ambition, he is well placed to argue the judges' case. For that reason his own independence has never been questioned and he is in a much better position than judges would be to protect—not the judges' interests—but the values of the legal system.'[10] Lord Irvine had implied that he was in favour of reform of the office of Lord Chancellor when he was in opposition. On his election to the Woolsack in 1997, any such temptations appeared to recede. Indeed, there has been no evidence that reform of the Lord Chancellorship had any support from his Lordship since his appointment in 1997. Rather the reverse is true. That has not prevented a segment of Labour backbenchers from suggesting that reform—ie some greater separation of powers at the top—is necessary. Rather more surprising, one of the current Law Lords, Lord Steyn, opined, just before the 1997 election that 'the proposition that a Cabinet Minister must be head of our judiciary in England is no longer sustainable on either constitutional or pragmatic grounds.' Steyn also argued that while the Lord Chancellor appeared to speak neutrally as head of the judiciary, 'the truth is different'[11] (and one can only speculate about what Lord Steyn, one of the majority of three in the first *Pinochet* case, would have thought if Lord Irvine had announced his intention of sitting in that case).

While the Law Lords were divided, some would have liked to see an end to membership in the legislative body. It was not altogether surprising, however, that in the summer of 1998 it was reported that plans for the reform of the House of Lords were in part being delayed because there was no agreement on what to do with the Law Lords or, for that matter, with the Anglican bishops.[12] Nevertheless, after the Royal Commission on the House of Lords, the Law Lords were left in place, with an anodyne statement about when they would not participate in legislative debates of a political nature. The 2001 draft House of Lords Reform Bill confirmed their continued presence, a presence which was reaffirmed by Lord Irvine's White Paper in 2002, shortly before he lost control over reform of the Lords.

The related issue was the selection of judges and particularly the establishment of a Judicial Appointments Commission. Lord Irvine at first embraced the idea of an Appointments Commission—it was, after all, part of Labour's policy at the time of the election[13]—then 'put it on a back burner'[14] then apparently abandoned it. Lord Irvine put great energy and resources into encouraging more women and minority applicants for the bench, although not with immediately dramatic results. The pressure for reform was, however, great. After various internal inquiries, Sir Leonard Peach produced a series of recommendations to ensure greater transparency in choosing judges and QCs.[15] Lord Irvine ultimately embraced the Peach proposals for Commissioners to supervise the appointments process although appointment of judges remains firmly in his hands. A substantive Judicial Appointments Committee remains, however, the policy of the Liberal Democrats and possibly of the Conservatives.

It was of course the dispute about human rights which appeared to differentiate New Labour from Old Conservative. Lord Mackay, the outgoing Conservative Lord Chancellor, opposed the incorporation of the European Convention on Human Rights on the ground that it would pass political decisions to the judges. Lord Irvine, while he accepted that proposition, also agreed that Labour had to do it, although there is evidence in the legislative debates that even he did not fully understand the constitutional revolution New Labour was effecting. The project had been John Smith's, not Lord Irvine's. The new legislation was a total reversal of Labour and Conservative views from the debates on the Restrictive Practices' Court when the Conservatives had pressed for and Labour had opposed judges being forced to make 'non-legal' decisions. It was not the only area where the parties appeared to have changed political clothes.

Human Rights

The separation of powers became an issue again in 1998 when the European Commission of Human Rights held, in a decision upheld by the European Court of Human Rights in 2000, that, in one part of Britain's 'dominions' (Guernsey), there was such lack of separation of powers as to be a violation of Article 6(1) of the European Convention on Human Rights, which provides that 'everyone is entitled to a fair and public hearing

---

[13] *A New Agenda for Democracy: Labour's proposals for constitutional reform* (Labour Party, London, 1997) 40.

[14] Lord Irvine opened up the appointments process. There are now advertisements for High Court judges. 'Justice—Now Seen To Be Advertised' *The Times*, 24 February 1998. See also G Drewry, 'Judicial Appointments' [1998] *Public Law* 1.

[15] *An Independent Scrutiny of the Appointment Process of Judges and Queen's Counsel in England and Wales*. A Report to the Lord Chancellor by Sir Leonard Peach (1999).

... by an independent and impartial tribunal. . .' In *McGonnell* the courts of Guernsey were found not to meet the standards set out in Article 6:

> The principal judicial officer who sat on the case, the Bailiff, was not only a senior member of the judiciary of the Island, but was also a senior member of the legislature—as President of the States of Deliberation—and, in addition, a senior member of the executive—as titular head of the administration presiding over a number of important committees. It is true, as the Government points out, that the Bailiff's other functions did not directly impinge on his judicial duties in the case and that the Bailiff spends most of his time in judicial functions, but the Commission considers that it is incompatible with the requisite appearance of independence and impartiality for a judge to have legislative and executive functions as substantial as those in the present case.[16]

Such a line of argument could not fail to raise questions about the traditional executive, legislative and judicial functions of the Lord Chancellor and the legislative and judicial functions of the Lords of Appeal in Ordinary. Indeed, in a debate on the implications for the Law Lords, Lord Patten—a Conservative—said that the dual role of the Law Lords 'flies in the face of Article 6.'[17] There was further support for that view when, in the Spring of 1999, the European Commission on Human Rights, by a vote of 14 to 5, found the UK had violated Article 6 when the Home Secretary had increased the sentence imposed on under-age children in the Bulger case.[18] Europe seemed to be saying that the casual British attitude to the separation of powers was no longer acceptable.

The Government itself, in early 1999, raised some of the issues which verged on structural changes in the separation of powers. As we have seen, the White Paper called for a Royal Commission on the House of Lords[19]

---

[16] *McGonnell v United Kingdom* (2000), 30 EHRR 289. See also Lord Lester *Hansard* HL Deb vol 597, cols 713–14 (17 February 1999) for support for the implications of *McGonnell*. See now also R Cornes, '*McGonnell v UK*, the Lord Chancellor and the Law Lords' [2000] *Public Law*, 166. For an attack on *McGonnell* and 'foreign lawyers', see Lord Waddington *Hansard* HL Deb, vol 597, col 718 (17 February 1999).

[17] Motion on Judicial Appointments, *Hansard* HL Deb, vol 597, col 1441 (1 March 1999).

[18] 'European Court Supports Bulger Killers' *Daily Telegraph*, 16 March 1999.

[19] *Modernising Parliament: Reforming the House of Lords*, (Cm 4183, 1999). See especially paras 19 and 20: 'The contemporary rationale for the Law Lords being life peers as opposed to ex officio members of the House is the major contribution they can make to the cross-bench element in the House ... The retired Law Lords play a particularly distinguished role in the examination of legislation, especially that with a highly technical or legal element. Most significant is their contribution to debates on the administration of justice, penal policy and civil liberties, where law and politics interact ... It is unusual, compared to most major democracies, to have judges sitting as members of the legislature in this way. It would therefore be legitimate to consider, when looking at fundamental reform of the purpose and nature of the House of Lords, whether the present arrangements should continue. But consideration would also have to be given to what this would do to the nature of Parliament as a whole, and how the supreme judicial authority could be reconstituted elsewhere in the system . . .'

which asked the Commission to decide whether the House of Lords should remain the final court of appeal with judges performing both judicial and legislative roles. The Commission was forbidden from considering the possibility of establishing a separate Constitutional Court, as had been suggested by Lords Goodhart and Lester during the debates on devolution for Scotland, where the legislation called for cases arising out of devolution to be heard by the amorphous Judicial Committee of the Privy Council.[20] These same debates had already allowed the Scottish judges to articulate the need for entrenching judicial independence in Scotland as part of the devolution process. Lord McClusky, one of the Scottish judges, made the point most powerfully, responding to the Lord Advocate's assertion that it was 'beyond belief' that the new Scottish First Minister would recommend to the Assembly the dismissal of High Court judges without cause:

> ... those views fly in the face of all experience. Leaving aside the numerous countries where the independence of the judiciary is a sick joke—and there are many of those—there have been recent and profoundly disturbing attempts to interfere with the independence of judges in mature democracies, including the United States and parts of Canada. Concerns have also been expressed about Australia. We would be totally naive to suppose that our new politicians in Scotland will be immune to such temptations—not least because criticism of judges' decisions are now the meat and drink of our daily newspapers, and populist politicians of whom we have always had our fair share in Scotland are likely to start calling for the removal of judges whose decisions have been criticized in the press, however unfounded the criticisms and however distorted the reporting of the decisions for which the judges have been responsible.[21]

It was such arguments that at least gave Lord Lester the opportunity to press for a Constitutional Judicial Commission to select judges for such cases, as well as being responsible for disciplining and dismissing them.[22] Lord McClusky had his view accepted; Lord Lester did not.

---

[20] See Scotland Bill debate *Hansard* HL Deb, vol 593 (28 October 1998); especially speeches of Lord Steel (col 1963), Lord Wilberforce (col 1965), Lord Lester (col 1968), Lord Goodhart (col 1973) and Lord Irvine (col 1984).
[21] *Hansard* HL Deb, vol 593, col 1968 et seq (28 October 1998); *ibid*, vol 594, col 50 (12 November 1998).
[22] *Ibid*, vol 594, col 41 (2 November 1998).

Pinochet

Nothing, however, so galvanised the issues relating to the independence of the judiciary and the separation of powers as the *Pinochet* case.[23] In October 1998, General Pinochet, the former dictator of Chile, was in the UK receiving medical attention when a Spanish judge issued an international warrant for his arrest to face charges in Spain relating to crimes against humanity (torture, hostage taking and murder). A Metropolitan Magistrate issued a provisional warrant for his arrest and two warrants were executed. One warrant was quashed (although the second one was not, allowing an appeal to the House of Lords) by a Divisional Court, presided over by Lord Bingham, the Lord Chief Justice, on the grounds primarily that the provisions of the Extradition Act 1989 had not been met and that the General was protected by sovereign immunity.[24]

The case then proceeded to the House of Lords where, somewhat to the surprise of the profession, in a five-judge panel, the majority (Nicholls, Steyn and Hoffmann) was not prepared to support immunity. In general terms it achieved this result by reading the Extradition Act more broadly and by constraining sovereign immunity more narrowly than the Divisional Court, in particular by assuming (if not articulating) that the international law of crimes against humanity took precedence over English law.[25] The opinion, handed down on 25 November 1998, was internationally controversial, although seen by many as a great victory for human rights.

The press went to work, together with the politicians, led by Lady Thatcher, who was an admirer of General Pinochet. It emerged that Lord Hoffmann had failed to disclose in public that he was the chair of the charitable wing of Amnesty International—the intervenor—and that his wife was employed full-time by that same human rights organisation. In an action unprecedented in modern times, although normal in the United States, there was a petition for rehearing. After two days of hearings, Lord Browne-Wilkinson, the presiding Law Lord announced that the case would have to be reheard, with the trenchant observation that 'Lord Hoffmann who did not disclose his links with Amnesty International was disqualified from sitting.'[26] This announcement was made on 17 December and at once the press began taking strong positions, many demanding or expecting that

---

[23] See generally, D Woodhouse (ed), *The Pinochet Case: a Legal and Constitutional Analysis* (Oxford, 2000); D Sugarman, 'The Pinochet Case: International Criminal Justice in the Gothic Style? (2001) *Modern Law Review*, 933.

[24] Woodhouse (n 23 above) at 4.

[25] *R v New Street Stipendiary Magistrate, ex p Pinochet Ugarte*, [1998] 4 All ER 897. The other two law lords were Lords Slynn and Lloyd.

[26] House of Lords, *Judicial Business: Consideration of the 11th Report from the Appeal Committee (Petition of Senator Augusto Pinochet Urgate)*. The other Law Lords hearing the

Lord Hoffmann would resign.[27] Various reports in the press suggested that the Lord Chancellor would not be unhappy if this occurred;[28] and Lord Irvine called for a register of the interests of judges.[29]

For students of judicial independence, conscious that the Act of Settlement 1701 had provided that judges could only be removed by a form of impeachment, these pressures were cause for concern. Lord Hoffmann was subject to more criticism when the full version of the petition for rehearing came down.[30] Lord Hutton, for instance, said that 'public confidence in the integrity of the administration of justice would be shaken if the decision stood.'[31] The Law Lords made it clear that Lord Hoffmann's interest was not a marginal one; although they were careful to say there was no evidence of bias on his part, but appearances were as bad as reality. The implications were immediately apparent. Within weeks, the Hong Kong Government, bowing to complaints from Beijing about the first major decision by the Hong Kong Court of Final Appeal, cited Pinochet/Hoffman as part of the justification for reopening the decision,[32] and there was soon concern about the dramatic increase in the English courts of efforts to get judges to recuse themselves because of conflicts of interest.[33] Even the Lord Chancellor was forced to recuse himself in one appeal after a barrister threatened to raise the *McGonnell* point—that his office violated Article 6 of the European Convention and he was therefore ineligible to sit.[34]

petition were Lords Goff, Nolan, Hope and Hutton. The decision was unanimous; see [1998] HLJ No 41 (QL).

[27] For example, 'Hoffmann Silence Dismays Judges' *The Guardian*, 29 December 1998.

[28] On the BBC 'Today' programme, Lord Irvine said that it was 'unprecedented' and 'in the highest degree unfortunate.' Lord Irvine refused to discuss Lord Hoffmann's 'culpability'— itself a chilling remark. '"Disrepute" Over Ruling on Pinochet' *The Guardian*, 29 December 1998. See also, 'Senior Law Lord Is Told To Make Sure Embarrassment Is Not Repeated' *The Guardian*, 18 December 1998. Lord Irvine was later quoted as saying Hoffmann should not resign: 'The Amnesty Lord Lies Low' *Evening Standard*, 24 March 1999.

[29] This probably reflected a serious misunderstanding of what the concerns were. A register of interests might easily record education, clubs, business or other interests and perhaps even political associations. A psychologist might argue that what really mattered were upbringing, family life and experience, social values and political experience. See now K Malleson, 'Safeguarding judicial impartiality' (2002) 22 *Legal Studies* 53.

[30] *R v Bow Street Metropolitan Stipendiary Magistrate, ex p Pinochet Ugarte (No 2)* [1999] 1 All ER 577.

[31] *Ibid*, at 599.

[32] 'Court Should Have Option To Reopen Cases' *Hong Kong Standard*, 27 February 1999.

[33] 'Judges Fight Back Against Challenges by Lawyers' *The Times*, 9 September 2001.

[34] The case concerned the representatives of a person who committed suicide in a police cell suing the police authority for negligence. D Pannick, 'Lord Chancellor Should Leave the Judging To the Pros' *The Times*, 12 March 2002. See also D Woodhouse, *The Office of Lord Chancellor* (Oxford, 2001) 127.

By mid-January 1999 the *Pinochet* case was before the Lords for the third time,[35] this time being heard by seven Law Lords. Some things were already clear. The bungling had caused acute embarrassment to a judiciary which liked to pride itself on the respect in which it was held in other countries. Moreover, whichever way the new hearing came out, it was a no-win situation for the formalistic traditions of English law.[36] The decision when it appeared, therefore, unsurprisingly, satisfied few. The few saw the reasoning of the majority of five as good legal craftsmanship.[37] They had held that the general might be extradited but only for acts of torture committed after 1988 when the British adhered to the International Convention against Torture. Most of the public probably agreed with *The Economist,* which found the reasoning 'muddled' and 'bizarre'. Cynics saw it as a somewhat desperate effort to save the reputation of the English judiciary[38] The political effect of the majority's decision was that with the number of extraditable crimes severely reduced, the case was effectively bounced back into the hands of the Home Secretary who, after deciding that extradition procedures might begin, eventually allowed General Pinochet to return to Chile under his general executive discretion.[39]

Whatever the viewpoint, however, no events could more obviously have underlined the element of judicial creativity and the importance of personal views in the final appeal court than the *Pinochet* cases. As the *Daily Telegraph* put it: 'One thing, however, is clear. If judges are asked to rule on

---

[35] 'The Law Lords and the General' *The Economist,* 19 December 1998, 18.

[36] 'If Pinochet appeal succeeds, it will be said that would demonstrate that the majority in the original panel of Law Lords was biased. If the appeal fails, it will be alleged that the new panel were showing Trade Union solidarity with their chums.' M Mears, 'Lawspeak' *New Law Journal,* 8 January 1999, 34.

[37] *R v Bow Street Metropolitan Stipendiary Magistrate, ex p Pinochet Ugarte (No 3)* [1999] 2 All ER 97. Until this decision it had been assumed, as the majority assumed in the first House of Lords case, that it was enough if the facts amounted to a crime in both the extraditing country and the requesting country at the time of the extradition. In future, extradition will exist only with respect to situations when such events were criminal in both requesting and extraditing countries at the time of the acts.

[38] 'Not Much to Celebrate' *The Economist,* 27 March 1999.

[39] '. . . yesterday's ruling was a masterpiece of buck-passing and damage limitation. The seven Law Lords avoided reversing the previous (and subsequently discredited) judgment by five of their colleagues, which in November denied the General state immunity. Yet they managed to rob the earlier decision of much of its force . . . Even so, yesterday's judgment can hardly be considered a triumph. The case has raised the judiciary's political profile, but not its reputation.' 'Back to Jack' (leader) *The Daily Telegraph,* 25 March 1999. *The Guardian* commented: 'It was always going to be difficult for this seven-member court to reverse the decision of the five Law Lords in the first hearing. To have done so would have underlined the random nature of justice . . . But the scope of the judgment yesterday was significantly narrowed, which ironically only illustrated the random nature of justice.': 'Pinochet Loses', *The Guardian,* 25 March 1999. See also 'Both Sides Celebrate a Victory' *The Times,* 25 March 1999. See now D Robertson, 'The House of Lords as a Political and Constitutional Court: Lessons from The Pinochet Case' in Woodhouse (n 23 above) at 17.

a highly political matter, they will behave in a political way.'[40] No case had so sorely tested the concept of judicial independence. Yet, especially on the right and in the legal profession, the urge to claim, in the face of the evidence, that judicial attitudes were irrelevant, even with the arrival of the Human Rights Act, was remarkable. Some of the attitudes were understandable. The right of the Tory Party was sympathetic to the General. Lord Tebbit announced that 'I rather wish we could get back to the old days when judges did not talk about the business of the administration of justice in public and did not give vent to so many views.'[41]

Within the profession, the Lord Chief Justice, Lord Bingham, warned judges that they 'should resist the temptation to seek reputations as liberals or "strict interpretationalists"' when the Human Rights Act came into force. He expressed the hope that the 'predictions that the legislation could lead to the risk of the judiciary becoming political would be seen to be false.'[42] Unfortunately, the aspirations of the Lord Chief Justice were somewhat undercut by the reports of his response when he heard of the choice of Lords Steyn and Hoffmann, both thought of as South African liberals, to sit in the first *Pinochet* hearing. Lord Bingham was alleged to have said: 'Well, that's two votes against.'[43] Whatever the truth of the report, the genie was out of the bottle. When the third hearing came on in January, the *Daily Telegraph*, the most staid of the broadsheets, ranked all seven Law Lords on the conservative-liberal continuum.[44] *The Times* saw the case, and especially the behaviour of Lord Hoffmann, as forerunners of the disaster that would overtake the judiciary when the Human Rights Act came into force.[45]

There were, if possible, even wider implications. The advertising of the creative role of the judiciary and the inevitable importance of personal views in such creativity was highly significant. Yet in a constitutional sense the spotlight was turned on judicial independence—even if commentators

---

[40] 'Back to Jack', *The Daily Telegraph*, 27 March 1999. And, in due course, the Home Secretary allowed the deportation proceedings to continue. 'UK gives the go-ahead to Pinochet extradition case' *The Financial Times*, 16 April 1999.

[41] Press Association, 'Pinochet Nightlead' 15 January 1999.

[42] 'Lord Chief Justice Issues Warning Over Human Rights Legislation' *The Daily Telegraph*, 11 January 1999.

[43] M Mears, *New Law Journal*, 8 January 1999, 34.

[44] Lord Browne-Wilkinson 'pragmatic but progressive'; Lord Goff, 'moderate'; Lord Hope, 'middle of the road'; Lord Hutton, 'the most conservative of the new panel'; Lord Saville, 'middle of the road to liberal'; Lord Millett, 'middle of the road'; Lord Phillips, 'the most liberal.' 'Seven May Be the General's Lucky Number' *The Daily Telegraph*, 18 January 1999. The difficulty of predicting judicial attitudes is well illustrated by the fact that of the two 'dissenters', Lord Goff opted for upholding the Divisional Court decision (thereby supporting the minority of two in the first House of Lords case), while Lord Millett opted for the majority in the first House of Lords case. See [1999] 2 All ER 97.

[45] K Ramsay, 'The Judges—Our New Oppressors' *Daily Telegraph*, 18 February 2000.

often missed that point—and on the role of a final appeal court. Those who might not be ready to endorse a Constitutional Court or even a Supreme Court could not fail to be embarrassed by the lottery which surrounded the panel system in the House of Lords. The link between the legislature and the final court of appeal came under fire. Even in England the separation of powers has some meaning, even if that meaning were more political than legal.

As *The Economist* warned, with the New Labour Government's constitutional changes, there would be 'a much wider array of cases' coming to the Lords:

> many of these will be highly contentious, and will bring the law lords into conflict with politicians . . . like all senior judges, they are in effect appointed by the Lord Chancellor, who is the government's senior law officer and sits in the Cabinet, after secret consultations among judges and top lawyers. This is an untenable method of selection for judges who will be ruling on issues of great public and political interest . . . by embarking on an ambitious programme of reform, the government has encouraged scrutiny of the murkier corners of the constitution and has raised the profile of judges. Having opened this Pandora's box, it will have to confront, probably sooner rather than later, the muddle at the very heart of the British constitution.[46]

The Economist wanted not only a separate court for constitutional cases, but the end of judges sitting in the House of Lords in its legislative capacity. Four days later, Lord Saville, apparently destined to spend his time as a Lord of Appeal redoing the Bloody Sunday Inquiry in Londonderry, put the issue bluntly:

> Convention has it that I should not speak or vote in politically controversial matters in the House of Lords. To a degree that is true, though the dividing line between what is and is not politically controversial is often very difficult to draw and is clearly getting more and more difficult to draw. Should I speak on the changes to Legal Aid, or the powers that the Lord Chancellor appears anxious to take over the organisation and rules of the legal profession? Should I speak on Human Rights or devolution? I have myself, at least temporarily, avoided the problem by not speaking on anything at all, but this is avoidance of the problem rather than a solution.[47]

---

[46] 'Judging the Judges' *The Economist*, 23 January 1999; R Stevens, 'The Case For Banishing M'Lud From the Lords' *The Times*, 22 December 1998.
[47] M Saville, Speech to the City Centre for International Trade and Arbitration (January 1999).

Human Rights and Judicial Power

In this context it is scarcely surprising that in a country so steeped in parliamentary sovereignty and from a party traditionally cautious about entrusting new matters to the judiciary, the Human Rights Act 1998, when it appeared, should be surrounded with cautionary caveats. Section 3(i) provided that 'as far as possible' primary and secondary legislation had to be read in a way that was compatible with Convention rights. Ministers, by section 19, were required to make 'a statement of compatibility' with the Convention when introducing legislation. The courts could not strike down incompatible legislation, but might give a declaration of incompatibility which would then lead to legislation or the Minister might change the legislation by executive order.

Some saw these as strong powers, but as the Bill was introduced, there was considerable downplaying of potential powers although not by the press. While *The Economist* announced that the Act represented the 'Rule of Judges,'[48] the tabloids claimed that school uniforms were dead; indeed they implied that gay sex and cross-dressing would be the norm in schools. Lord McClusky, the outspoken Scottish judge, announced that the Act would provide 'a field day for crackpots' and 'a pain in the neck for judges.'

Such critics counted without the traditional relationships between executive and judiciary, emphasised on this occasion as a 'partnership'. It was soon clear that training for the judges would counsel restraint. Jack Straw, the Home Secretary, said that the purpose of the judicial training was to explain how best to deal with 'sharp lawyers' who would make 'disruptive' points in hearings before 'busy' county court and Crown Court judges.[49] Lord Woolf, Master of the Rolls, and shortly to be Lord Chief Justice, said in an appeal:

> It was essential that counsel and those who instructed counsel took a responsible attitude as to when it was right to raise arguments based on the Human Rights Act 1998 and judges should be robust in resisting inappropriate attempts to introduce such arguments.

---

[48] 'Bringing Rights Home' *The Economist*, 26 August 2000. For relevant passages in *Hansard*, see J Wadham and H Mountfield, *Blackstone's Guide to the Human Rights Act 1998* (Blackstone, London, 2000).

[49] *Ibid*. See also his claim that judges would be 'sensible and realistic when dealing with Convention arguments,' (Leader) *The Daily Telegraph*, 13 July 2000. More recently Lord Irvine has announced that the 'prophets of doom' who said there would be a plethora of cases had been proved wrong. The number of Human Rights Act cases was small: 'the Act should be regarded as a co-operative endeavour between the Executive, Parliament and the judiciary to deliver a new rights-based culture.' 'Co-operation is key, say Irvine and Woolf' *New Law Journal*, 27 July 2001.

As the training went on, it was rumoured that two members of the Court of Appeal—Lords Justices Brooke and Sedley—had emphasised the need to interpret the Act cautiously. There was a suggestion that Lord Bingham had been moved from Lord Chief Justice to senior Law Lord in the summer of 2001 'to keep a lid on' the Human Rights Act.[50] This restraint was matched by a surprising lack of interest on the part of parliamentarians; it took almost two years to set up a Joint Committee on Human Rights.[51]

The Human Rights Act actually came into force in Scotland before it was operative in England. This posed interesting problems. It raised for instance the whole issue of the meaning of devolution under the Scotland Act. The Judicial Committee of the Privy Council—chosen rather than the House of Lords apparently as the result of misplaced Scottish sensitivities—found itself involved with Scottish criminal law which had gone no further than Edinburgh since the Act of Union of 1707. The Judicial Committee was faced with interpreting what was in effect a federal document, with responsibility for determining whether there had been a 'devolution issue'. In a pre-trial publicity case, for instance, the Scottish law lords, Lords Hope and Clyde, held that there was no doubt there was a devolution issue, while Lord Hoffmann had 'considerable doubt,' but in any event it was held that Article 6(1) had not been breached.[52] When convicted cannabis dealers appealed it was held that there was no devolution issue,[53] while confiscating property of convicted drug dealers was also held not to violate the Human Rights Act.[54] On the criminal side, the greatest publicity belonged to *Brown v Stott*, where the Scottish courts held that being forced to reveal the name of the driver of a car caught by speed cameras amounted to self-incrimination and was a violation of Article 6(1). That was rapidly overturned by the Privy Council.[55] Scotland also produced the first successful impact of the new Act, when the Court of Session struck down temporary Sheriff-Substitutes—part-time local judges—as being in violation of Article 6,[56] requiring independent and impartial tribunals, a decision that led rapidly to the Lord Chancellor's Department rethinking the tenure of Assistant Recorders.[57]

---

[50] J Griffith, 'The open conspiracy' *Times Literary Supplement*, 20 April 2001.
[51] J Wadham, 'The Human Rights Act: sufficient protection?' [2001] *New Law Journal*, 1411.
[52] *Montgomery v HM Advocate* [2001] 2 WLR 779.
[53] *Hoekstra v HM Advocate* [2001] 1 AC 716.
[54] *HM Advocate v McIntosh* 2001 SLT 304.
[55] [2001] 2 All ER 97.
[56] *Starrs v Ruxton* 2000 SLT 42 (1999).
[57] A O'Neill, 'Judicial Politics and the Judicial Committee: The Devolution Jurisprudence of the Privy Council, (2001) 63 *Modern Law Review* 603.

With respect to England, however, the Human Rights Act appeared to have little direct effect. As Lord Justice Auld put it: 'when we judges began to prepare for the implementation of the Human Rights Act, we feared that the courts would be overwhelmed by human rights challenges. It has not happened.'[58] Superficially that has indeed been true. There have of course been some decisions which caused excitement, for instance the admission to the country—later reversed—of Louis Farrakhan. Indeed most of the cases that caused excitement were rapidly overruled. For a while it looked as if the whole system of planning applications was likely to be toppled. In the *Alconbury* case the Divisional Court had held that the Department of the Environment, Transport and the Regions was not 'independent and impartial' under Article 6 when it was making planning decisions.[59] It therefore looked as if the planning process would be taken away from Ministers and power would pass to independent administrative bodies, whose decisions would be final. On appeal, the House of Lords, purporting to follow Strasbourg jurisprudence,[60] and probably in fact refining and improving it, saw nothing wrong with the existing system. As Lord Hoffmann put it, 'the Human Rights Act of 1998 was no doubt intended to strengthen the rule of law, but not to inaugurate the rule of lawyers.'[61] Extrajudicially Lord Hoffmann expressed the increasing scepticism that the Law Lords felt about Strasbourg jurisprudence. *Osman v UK*, invalidating police immunity, filled him 'with apprehension' and 'reinforced the doubts [he had] had for a long time about the suitability, at least for this country, of having questions of human rights determined by an international tribunal made up of judges from many countries.'[62]

So it went on. The courts upheld the kind of actions which many thought the Act might well invalidate, such as banning travel abroad by

---

[58] R Epstein, 'The Human Rights Act—will the law ever be the same again?' *New Law Journal*, 26 October 2001, 1558. See also F Klug and K Starmer, 'Incorporation through the "front door": the first year of the Human Rights Act' [2001] *Public Law* 654.

[59] *R ex p Alconbury Developments v Secretary of State for Environment* [2001] 2 All ER 929.

[60] Both Lords Hoffmann and Clyde appear to have given unjustified weight to Bratza J's concurring opinion in *Bryan v UK*, (1995) 21 EHRR 342, 354. I Loveland, 'Alconbury in the House of Lords' *New Law Journal*, 18 May 2001, 713.

[61] *New Law Journal* 18 May 2001, 713.

[62] L Hoffmann, 'Human Rights and the House of Lords' (1999) 62 *Modern Law Review* 159, 164. And see C Gearty, 'Unravelling Osman' (2001) 64 *Modern Law Review* 159. The *Osman* decision was partially rejected by the House of Lords in *Barrett v Enfield BC* [1999] 3 All ER 193). Lord Browne-Wilkinson, at 198–200 showed forcefully that *Osman* was irrational in terms of the English legal system. The European Court of Human Rights was forced to modify its position in *Z v UK*, (2002) 34 EHRR 3.

persons suspected, but not convicted, of football hooliganism[63] and anti-social banning orders.[64] The City of London was disappointed that the Act had not curbed the activities of the Financial Services Authority.[65] The courts refused an injunction to prevent publicity about a footballer's sexual exploits, in the cause of section 10's protection of freedom of expression.[66] Indeed, the leading case where the Act had been applied was *Wilson v First County Trust*, where part of the Consumer Credit Act 1974 had been found in breach of Article 6.[67] The attitude of the practising profession was summed up in an article entitled 'Dead end?' in *Legal Week*. The *Alconbury* case was assumed to be evidence that the Human Rights Act would never have much of an effect on the English legal system.[68]

As so often in the legal system—whether the 1966 Practice Direction allowing the House of Lords to overrule its own earlier decisions of *Pepper v Hart* on the introduction of legislative material to interpret statutes—much of the impact of the Human Rights Act has been psychological. In particular Lord Steyn, who has established himself as the most influential Law Lord in this as in other areas, took a powerful approach to public law. For instance in *R v Home Secretary, ex p Pierson*[69] he said:

> Parliament does not legislate in a vacuum. Parliament legislates for a European liberal democracy based upon the principles and traditions of the common law . . . and . . . unless there is the clearest provision to the contrary, Parliament must be presumed not to legislate contrary to the rule of law.

While, at the moment, the Steyn approach appears to conflict with the approach of other Law Lords, the next decade will determine how far the Law Lords will be prepared to redraw statutes in the light of the Human Rights Act.

---

[63] *Gough v Chief Constable of Derbyshire* [2001] 4 All ER 289. 'Travel Ban on Suspected Hooligans Upheld' *The Daily Telegraph*, 14 July 2001; 'Football hooligans and human rights' *New Law Journal*, 26 October 2001, 1562.

[64] *R (ex p McCann) v Crown Court at Manchester* [2001] 4 All ER 264.

[65] R Money-Kyrle, 'Forum' *Legal Week*, 20 September 2001.

[66] *A v B* [2002] 1 All ER 449.

[67] J Harvey, 'HRA "flood" is more of a trickle' *Legal Week*, 11 October 2001. But see also *R (ex p H) v Mental Health Review Tribunal* [2001] EWCA Civ 415, holding the burden of proof in Mental Health Act incompatible with Article 5.

[68] J Bowman, *Legal Week*, 24 May 2001. In *Ashdown v Telegraph Group* [2001] 4 All ER 666, the court agreed there might be situations where the Human Rights Act could impact the Copyright Acts. For scepticism about whether the Human Rights Act could apply to anti-avoidance devices in taxation, see *R v Dimsey (No 2)* [2001] 4 All ER 786.

[69] [1998] AC 539, 575.

It was in this bold spirit that Lord Steyn approached the interaction between the Human Rights Act and the *Wednesbury* principle, essentially the test of unreasonableness for judicial review. It is arguable that in *R v Home Secretary, ex p Daly*,[70] all the Law Lords accepted a test of proportionality—imported from EU and continental jurisprudence—in human rights cases to justify the balancing test that the courts had been applying to weigh such rights against 'good government'. More importantly, however, Lord Steyn then reintroduced the test of proportionality into the *Wednesbury* situation:

> First, the doctrine of proportionality may require the reviewing court to assess the balance which the decision-maker has struck, not merely whether it is within the range of rational or reasonable decisions. Secondly, the proportionality test may go further than the traditional grounds of review, in as much as it may require attention to be directed to the relative weights accorded to interests and considerations . . .[71]

The sceptic might even see the slippery slope of substantive due process.[72]

New Labour and New Millennium

The landslide victory of New Labour under Tony Blair in May 1997 found the overt hostility between judges and Government less obvious than it had been under John Major. This was significantly because Lord Bingham, as Chief Justice, was of a more cerebral and less confrontational disposition than Lord Taylor, but also because, as we saw, he took a more conventional view of parliamentary sovereignty. Lord Woolf, who had just taken over as Master of the Rolls, did not repeat his flirtation with fundamental laws,

---

[70] [2001] 2 WLR 1622.
[71] Lord Steyn had taken a similar view in *Alconbury*. 'Trying to keep the *Wednesbury* principle and proportionality in separate compartments seems to me unnecessary and confusing.' [2001] 2 All ER 929, 976. P Plowden and K Kerrigan, 'Judicial Review—a new test?' [2001] *New Law Journal*, 1291. For Lord Mustill's views on the slippery slope of proportionality, margin of appreciation and irrationality, see MJ Mustill, 'Margins: A Right to be Wrong?' (Blackstone Lecture, Oxford, 4 May 2000) *Law Quarterly Review* (forthcoming).
[72] And see Lord Steyn dissenting in *R v Lambert* [2001] 3 All ER 577, arguing that the Human Rights Act should have retroactive effect. In fact the issue of retroactivity is fascinating. In their efforts to anglicise the European Convention on Human Rights, the judges have claimed that these rights were already protected by English law, yet perhaps illogically, they have held that the Human Rights Act does not operate retroactively. This came to a head at the end of 2001, when the 'Guinness Four' were victorious in the European Court of Human Rights, which held that their earlier conviction in the English courts violated the European Convention. The Court of Appeal in effect refused to follow or implement the Strasbourg ruling. 'Guinness Four Lose Court of Appeal Case' *The Financial Times*, 22/23 December 2001.

but instead made an articulate defence of the British system of balance of powers rather than the separation of powers, in particular defending, as we saw, the role of the Lord Chancellor in much the same terms as Lord Schuster had done sixty years earlier. The context of the judiciary could, however, once again change, as a powerful Prime Minister faced a weak and divided opposition, especially after the Conservative debacle in the 2001 election deprived the country of an effective opposition. Lord Irvine had earlier sought to prevent any conflict between judiciary and executive with the observation that: 'I regard as unwise observations off the bench by eminent judges that the courts have reacted to the increase in the powers claimed by government by being more active themselves', and adding for good measure that 'this has become all the more important at a time of one-party government. It suggests to ordinary people a judicial invasion of the legislature's turf.'[73]

Nor was there any evidence that judges were abandoning their new creative role; far from it. The judicial willingness to be bold in public law cases was shown in the *Shah* case where the House of Lords, led by Lords Hoffmann and Steyn, effectively created a new 'social group' under the Geneva Protocol on Refugees in order to protect Pakistani women against the possibility of 'gender related violence' if they were deported back to their country of origin.[74] In the interpretation of statutes Lord Steyn remarked in a tax case that:

> during the last 30 years there has been a shift away from the literalist approach to progressive methods of construction. When there is no obvious meaning of a statutory provision the modern emphasis is on a contextual approach designed to identify the purpose of a statute and give effect to it.[75]

The new judicial attitude to the common law was put by Lord Browne-Wilkinson in *Kleinwort Benson v Lincoln City Council*:[76]

> The theoretical position has been that judges do not make law or change law: they discover and declare the law which is thought the same. According to this theory, when an earlier decision is overruled the law is not changed; its true nature is disclosed, having existed in that form all along ... In truth judges make and change law. The whole of the common law is judge-made and only by judicial changes in the law is the common law kept relevant in a changed world.

---

[73] *Hansard* HL Deb, vol 597, col 710 *et seq* (17 February 1999); and see *ibid*, vol 572, col 1255 (5 June 1996).
[74] *Islam v Home Secretary*, an appeal from *R v Immigration Appeal Tribunal, ex p Shah* [1999] 2 AC 629.
[75] *IRC v McGuckian* [1997] 3 All ER 817.
[76] [1998] 4 All ER 513.

As to the personal impact of the judges, Lord Browne-Wilkinson could not have been clearer:

> The features of current judicial reasoning are therefore as follows: First, the actual decision is based on moral, not legal factors. Second, these moral reasons are not normally articulated in the judgment. Third, the morality applied in any given case is the morality of the individual judge.[77]

The spirit of Jowitt and Simonds was truly dead.[78]

---

[77] N Browne-Wilkinson, 'The Impact of Judicial Reasoning' in B Markesinis (ed), *The Impact of the Human Rights Bill on English Law* (Oxford, 1998) 21.

[78] For recent creative decisions see, for example, *Re A* [2000] 4 All ER 961 (Court of Appeal intervened to allow operation on conjoined twins against wishes of parents); *Arthur JS Hall v Simons* [2000] 3 All ER 673 (House of Lords ending barristers' immunity from negligence in litigation); *R (ex p Pretty) v DPP* [2002] 1 All ER 1 (House of Lords upholding right of DPP to refuse immunity to person assisting in suicide); *White v White* [2000] 2 FLR 981 (House of Lords moved towards a presumption of equal division of assets in divorce).

9

The Second Coming

T HE GENERAL ELECTION in the early summer of 2001 may
have marked yet another milestone in British constitutional history.[1] The second landslide in favour of New Labour left the Conservatives with a bleak future and suggestions that, in any forthcoming
General Election, the Liberal Democrats might become the official opposition. For New Labour the implications were remarkable. The party was
returned with effectively the same lop-sided majority. With a Cabinet dominated by the Prime Minister, or possibly the Prime Minister and the Chancellor of the Exchequer, it was seen by many as a further nail in the coffin
of parliamentary government. Compared with Dicey's time, parliamentary
sovereignty had come to mean Cabinet or executive supremacy or perhaps
prime ministerial sovereignty. Was the presidential style of government,
adopted probably unconsciously by Tony Blair, to become the basis of the
Constitution?

Reprise

The election success was taking place amid a remarkable series of constitutional developments which had first been pressed by Blair's deceased
predecessor as Labour leader, John Smith. Within the first two years after
their landslide victory in 1997, as we saw, New Labour had established
devolved Parliaments for Scotland and Wales, had reinstituted the Parliament in Stormont, had introduced proportional representation for all but
UK national elections, (although the Jenkins Committee had recommended
a form of it), had completed the first stages of reform of the House of
Lords, had produced a Freedom of Information Bill, and had incorporated
the European Convention on Human Rights into English law by the
Human Rights Act. The directly elected mayor had arrived in London and
was available elsewhere.

---

[1] D Butler and D Kavanagh, *The British General Election, 2001* (London, 2002).

In so many of these changes the courts were destined to play a significant role. The Judicial Committee of the Privy Council, despite its amateur system of selecting panels, was nominated as the arbiter of disputes between Westminster and the Scottish Parliament. The judges, by the Human Rights Act, could not strike down Westminster statutes (although they could Scottish ones). They had, however, the right to request fast track legislation to remedy breaches which was, in its own way, a more powerful solution. As the then senior Law Lord, Lord Browne-Wilkinson put it:

> The incorporation of the European Convention on Human Rights into English law will have a major impact on the methodology and reasoning of the judges. In large part the Convention is a code of the moral principles which underlie the common law . . . As these cases come before the courts in Convention cases the courts will be required to give moral answers to moral questions. Moral attitudes which have previously been the actual but unarticulated reasoning lying behind judicial decisions will become the very stuff of decisions on Convention points. The silent true reason for decisions will have become the stated *ratio decidendi*.[2]

Almost everything seemed 'up for grabs'. The Royal Commission on the House of Lords, while not radical in composition, was invited to consider whether the Law Lords should continue to be involved as legislators. While the evidence of both Labour and Conservative parties was in favour of their continued membership of the Lords, the Liberal Democratic Party, and particularly the Liberal lawyers, Lords Goodhart and Lester, argued for a separate Constitutional Court. It was not an argument that was totally out of bounds. After the *Pinochet case*, the *Daily Telegraph* commented 'we now seem to have a supreme court, just not a very competent one.' That newspaper also saw the implications of that case: 'This can only strengthen calls for greater public scrutiny over the way in which judges are appointed, most likely leading, in the present climate, to greater politicization.' *The Guardian* looked at it rather differently, calling for a new look at the Law Lords, demanding a more open appointments' process and a commitment to human rights on the part of appointees.

Lord Lester argued that during his time at the Bar the judges had become a third branch of Government. The parallel with the United States was obvious. While many would question his position, it was becoming

---

[2]   N Browne-Wilkinson, 'The Impact on Judicial Reasoning,' in B Markesinis (ed), *The Impact of the Human Rights Bill on English Law* (Oxford, 1998) 21, 22. With this should be contrasted David Robertson's view, arguing that the Law Lords 'are in many ways, just another branch of the British administrative class' sharing their 'professional expectations which are largely inchoate, and which are quite unsuited as the basis of creative law making which shapes our lives. Many have sought a description of judicial ideology, but the truth about their attitudes, in some sense, is that they are not ideological enough': D Robertson, *Judicial Discretion in the House of Lords* (Oxford, 1998) 400–1.

increasingly difficult for the judiciary, and particularly the Law Lords, to fulfil all the complex roles they had come to play and were being invited to play within the Constitution. Increasingly, active Law Lords—most recently Lords Saville and Steyn—had consciously chosen not to participate in legislative debates. In 2000 no serving English Law Lord participated in a legislative debate. In 2001 only Lord Scott (he of 'Arms to Iraq') spoke on the issue of hunting. He is a master of foxhounds. Some would not regard that as a non-contentious matter.

There was also a sense in which judges were finding their role as chairs of public commissions and committees increasingly hazardous. Lord Saville was invited, together with two Commonwealth judges, to revisit the Bloody Sunday events in Londonderry nearly thirty years after the Widgery Report. While this was intended to be basically a factual inquiry and therefore one that, in theory, judges should be well equipped to undertake, the Committee was vigorously attacked by the *Daily Telegraph* for being created at all: 'a mockery of the judicial inquiry system . . . this government . . . set up this unnecessary inquiry just to please the terrorists.'[3] The length and expense of the inquiry, projected at five years and reported to be costing up to £200 million, led one of the Commonwealth judges to abandon the enterprise, fearing he might die on the job.

Perhaps the writing was on the wall for the wide-ranging judicial inquiry. The report by Lord Phillips on BSE cost some £30 million and lasted more than three years. While it was generally agreed to be a 'good' report, its time and cost were used to justify not using a judicial inquiry after the foot-and-mouth outbreak in 2001. Instead, various committees were set up: a committee to investigate the Government's handling of the crisis; a scientific committee, based on the Royal Society, to examine the veterinary issues; and a commission to look at the future of agriculture and farming methods. In addition, the outbreak was being examined by the National Audit Office and the Parliamentary Public Accounts Committee.[4] The multi-targeted approach was at once attacked by the opposition which alleged a cover up in the absence of a full judicial inquiry. Judicial review was sought to force the Government to have an 'independent' inquiry;[5] and

---

[3] When Lord Saville ruled that British troops called as witnesses in the Bloody Sunday inquiry would be denied anonymity, the *Daily Telegraph* published an editorial entitled 'Resign Lord Saville' after the English Court of Appeal, led by Lord Woolf, had overruled the Tribunal. L Blom-Cooper, 'Tribunals under Inquiry,' [2000] *Public Law* 1.

[4] 'Search For Lessons From Foot and Mouth,' *Daily Telegraph*, 10 August 2001.

[5] 'Triple Foot and Mouth Inquiry Provokes Claims of Cover Up,' *Daily Telegraph*, 10 August 2001. At first instance, at least, this failed, the judge holding that the remedy was 'at the ballot box.' This decision was upheld on appeal. Both Conservatives and Liberal Democrats were incensed that these were not going to be public inquiries. There was also criticism of the composition of the three Government inquiries. Particular ire was directed at the inquiry to look

the European Parliament threatened a public inquiry.[6] While the excuse for not having such an inquiry in England was time and money, protection of the constitutional position of the judges would have been equally justified.

Perhaps more open to attack in a constitutional sense was Mr Justice Macpherson's inquiry into the Stephen Lawrence murder—a tragic racist murder poorly investigated by the Metropolitan Police. Observers felt that the judge—and his lay Committee—did a good job analysing the facts and the police handling of the case. It was generally felt, however, that as the Committee moved on to analysing policies and making normative statements about the future, judges were in no better position than others to claim expertise. In particular the press cast doubt on the wisdom of unspecific allegations of institutional racism in the Metropolitan Police and on suggestions which appeared further to restrain free speech.[7] The *Daily Telegraph*—and others—were convinced that the Macpherson Report was partially responsible for a growth in violent crime in London.[8]

The matters were highly charged and some of the claims unfair, but the attacks underlined the view that the judges might be coming to the end of their useful life as chairs of committees which go beyond the primarily factual and analytical. Certainly Mr Justice Macpherson's later behaviour suggested an inability to handle the political fallout from the report. The judge justified his use of the phrase 'institutional racism' by saying that 'all we did was refine it. It was first used by a black activist in 1975.' The activist was Stokely Carmichael, at the time noted for his racist views. Mr Justice Macpherson went on to claim a 'right-wing vendetta' and announced he would 'now refuse to grant any more media interviews,' a somewhat odd remark for a judge who had shown little sympathy for the police officers whom the report criticised. As he put it: 'they were given a pretty rough time. They deserved it.'[9]

It was perhaps inevitable that the Lord Chancellor, as the embodiment of the judicial, the legislative and the executive should be the focus of much of

at the government's handling of the epidemic. Dr Iain Anderson, an employee of the Labour Party until 1997 and thereafter a Special Assistant at 10 Downing Street, was named Chair. 'Focus,' *Sunday Telegraph*, 12 August 2001.

[6] 'Judged by Europe,' (leader) *Daily Telegraph*, 16 January 2002. While an EU Committee ultimately appeared in the UK, it turned out to be a Brussels boondoggle.

[7] Eg Charles Moore, 'Everyone Deserved Better' *Daily Telegraph*, 2 March 1999; 'Handcuffing the Police' *Daily Telegraph*, 24 April 1999.

[8] See, for instance, T Utley, 'Bring Back Stop and Search, For the Sake of All of Us' *Daily Telegraph*, 4 January 2002: 'The New Year's Day shooting of an Asian teenager for her mobile phone was a direct result of the Macpherson Report.' By March 2002, *The Voice*, the leading black newspaper, was calling for the return of stop and search because of the growth of gun culture.

[9] 'Macpherson Fury at Right-wing Vendetta' *Independent*, 28 April 2001; M Mears, 'Lawspeak' [2001] *New Law Journal* 4 May.

the tension flowing from the political positions articulated by New Labour. Lord Irvine was more willing to be confrontational than his predecessor Lord Mackay and not always as politically circumspect.[10] Moreover he was far more powerful politically. The *Daily Telegraph* dubbed him 'first crony.' He was close to Prime Minister Blair and perhaps some of the attacks on the Lord Chancellor were in effect attacks on the Prime Minister who, like Margaret Thatcher, was thought to have a presidential style. Lord Irvine chaired significant Cabinet Committees, not merely those relating to law, but also those charged with the extensive programme of constitutional reform.[11] He was effective in hand-to-hand political encounters. Lord Irvine was therefore in a delicate position, made more difficult by the inexorable growth in the cost of legal aid, despite the Mackay reforms. As the Lord Chancellor produced the Access to Justice Bill, he was vilified by the legal profession (although this time not by the Law Lords) more vigorously than Lord Mackay had been. By 2001, however, it was clear that the Access to Justice Act had both legitimised the conditional fee—a rather muddled English version of the American contingent fee—and had privatised legal aid with respect to many types of action. It was a remarkable revolution, little understood outside the legal profession.

The judges (especially the retired Law Lords) reserved their hostility for Lord Irvine's plans to remove from the judiciary the power to determine rights of audience. Irvine's was not an easy political road. He was a partisan politician in reforming the House of Lords and was seen by some as an over-mighty subject; yet he had on other occasions, when not attempting to reform his spending department or the body of which he was Speaker, to appear as head of the judiciary. In this last capacity he frequently sounded conservative—indeed reactionary where his own office was concerned—while his leader, Tony Blair, was castigating persons with conservative inclinations. He cautiously made judicial appointments more transparent.[12] While admitting that the Human Rights Act would transfer some political issues to the judges, he appeared opposed to a Supreme Court, although that opposition may be weakening if that goal could be achieved without

[10] Nor was Irvine as successful as other Cabinet members in spinning stories. His encounter with expensive wallpaper was oft -told.
[11] D Egan, *Irvine: Politically Correct?* (London, 1999).
[12] See the Peach Report: *An Independent Scrutiny of the Appointment Processes of Judges and Queen's Counsel in England and Wales: a Report to the Lord Chancellor by Sir Leonard Peach (1999)*. R Rice, 'Former Star of the Bar Papers Over the Last Cracks in His Image' *The Financial Times*, 7 December 1998. Lord Irvine flirted again with the idea—in an interview on Woman's Hour—and in a speech to the Ethnic Minority Lawyers Conference: 'Public May Get Say in Who Sits As A Judge' *The Times*, 22 March 1999.

tampering with the office of Lord Chancellor.[13] He opposed reform of the Lord Chancellorship and taking the Law Lords out of the legislature, as well as appearing to endorse his right to determine the panels for hearing specific cases.

The Lord Chancellor's role—together with that of the Law Lords—had been supported by the 2000 Report of the Royal Commission on the House of Lords[14] but it may have been undermined by the *McGonnell* decision in Strasbourg.[15] A combination of New Labour, the political and personal views of the Lord Chancellor and the Cerberus-like nature of his office meant that Lord Irvine's tenure as Lord Chancellor was accompanied by a low rumble of controversy, aggravated shortly before the 2001 election by a Labour fundraising dinner, organised by the Lord Chancellor, where some thought inappropriate pressure had been put on members of the legal profession who inevitably looked to the Lord Chancellor for promotion.[16] An increasingly broad spectrum of opinion had come to believe the Lord Chancellorship could not continue in its present form.

Despite the murmurings of many in Parliament and the profession, Lord Irvine's close relationship with the Prime Minister ensured that he survived as Lord Chancellor after the second Labour landslide in 2001, when many of his colleagues were demoted. In fairness, however, although Lord Irvine

---

[13] Lord Irvine believed the case for a Supreme Court has not yet been fully made out. Speech by the Lord Chancellor to the Third Worldwide Common Law Judiciary Conference 5 July 1999, 19. (cited by Lord Steyn: 'The Case for a Supreme Court', (2002) 118 *Law Quarterly Review* 382).

[14] Royal Commission on the House of Lords, *A House for the Future* Cm 4534 (2000), ch 9. But as Lord Steyn pointed out: 'The anomaly of the Lord Chancellor sitting in the Appellate Committee and the creation of a Supreme Court, were subjects beyond the terms of reference of the Royal Commission. The curiously truncated nature of the enquiry avoided the searchlight being turned on the Lord Chancellor's judicial role and the merits of the idea of creating a Supreme Court.' Steyn: (n 13 above).

[15] Lord Steyn has now added his powerful voice to those believing that *McGonnell* applies to the Lord Chancellor. See Steyn (n 13 above) at 19: 'The very grounds on which the Lord Chancellor seeks to justify his sitting on the Appellate Committee demonstrate that on principled and pragmatic grounds the practice is no longer defensible. The sooner it ceases the better. By gracefully accepting the inevitable, the Lord Chancellor, a principal architect of the Human Rights Act 1998, will render another great service to our law. If he does not do so, it can only be a matter of time until the issue arises whether his participation in a committee deprived it of the character of an independent tribunal under Article 6 of the European Convention. Such a case will cause embarrassment and damage to our highest court and our legal system. It should be unnecessary. But it may have to be faced.'

[16] 'Tories Accuse Irvine in Fund Row' *The Daily Telegraph*, 19 February 2001; 'I Did Nothing Wrong, Says Irvine' *The Times*, 22 February 2001; 'Lords Denounce Irvine over His "arrogance,"' *The Daily Telegraph*, 22 February 2001; Bruce Anderson, 'Being Derry Irvine Means Never Having to Say You're Sorry,' *The Spectator*, 24 February 2001. See also Peter Riddell, 'Lord Chancellor's Deviousness Could Haunt New Labour' *The Times*, 14 November 2001, alleging that Lord Irvine, 'with all the smarmy charm of a confidence trickster' had deceived Parliament over the timetable for implementing the Freedom of Information Act.

was conservative in many areas, he had achieved remarkable changes. He had put his weight behind Lord Woolf's plans to modernise and cheapen litigation by making the judges somewhat closer to case managers. He had cut the cost of legal aid by the misnamed Access to Justice Act, he had helped push through the Human Rights Act and, rather reluctantly, by the summer of 2001, he had agreed to implement the Peach Report. This latter required him to appoint Commissioners for Judicial Appointments, who would offer advice and ensure openness in the choosing of judges. He was not, however, prepared to give up the right to select judges.[17] Nor did he hesitate to use his power, in 2001, to move Lord Bingham, the cerebral and independent Chief Justice to be the senior Law Lord, replacing him with Lord Woolf, an establishment figure with a reputation of being more emollient and thus perhaps more willing to adapt to the Lord Chancellor's whims.[18]

Lord Irvine's influence with the Prime Minister was also assumed to be behind the failure of the Home Office to be given control over the Courts Service, which remained with the Lord Chancellor's Department after the 2001 election.[19] As always with New Labour, it was difficult to distinguish fact from spin. What was clear was that responsibility for human rights, freedom of information, data protection, Church and State, the Monarchy, the Channel Islands and the Isle of Man were taken from the Home Office and given to the Lord Chancellor's Department. Lord Irvine and Lord Williams became responsible for Lords' reform and Lord Irvine also took over from the Prime Minister the Chairmanship of the Constitutional Reform Policy Committee. No wonder many of the senior judges were

[17] For an excellent analysis of the current situation, together with the latest statistics on women and ethnic minority judges, see T Legg, 'Judges for the New Century' [2001] *Public Law* 62; see also, B Hale, 'Equality and the Judiciary: Why should we want more woman judges?' [2001] *Public Law* 484.

[18] For a criticism of these moves, see J Griffith, *Times Literary Supplement*, 20 April 2001, 16. Some sense of the increasing importance of the senior Law Lord—a title first given in the 1980s—can be gleaned from the most recent report of the Review Body on Senior Salaries. He is treated as the President of the final court of appeal and given a salary equal to the Lord Chief Justice of Northen Ireland, the Lord President of the Court of Session and the Master of the Rolls: 'The Senior Law Lord's role is beyond that of the other Lords of Appeal in Ordinary—relates primarily to the efficient management of the judicial business of the Lords and Judicial Committee of the Privy Council including the minimalization of possible delays. This role can be critically important in cases of extreme personal sensitivity such as appeals agains the death sentence to the Privy Council from a Caribbean jurisdiction ... The Senior Law Lord's role involves determining the allocation of Lords of Appeal in Ordinary—including retired Law Lords still eligible to sit—to hear specific cases. From time to time this may involve consultation with the Lord Chancellor over cases that the latter has indicated an intention to hear himself ...' Review Body on Senior Salaries, *Twenty-Fourth Report on Senior Salaries*, vol 2 (Cm 5389–11 2002). If a Supreme Court is established, the title of Lord Chief Justice should logically fall on the President of that court.

[19] J Rozenberg, 'When Does a Hotel Become a House?' *Daily Telegraph*, 3 July 2001.

enthusiastic supporters of the office of Lord Chancellor.[20] It did not pay to tangle with Derry Irvine; but Johan Steyn and David Blunkett were prepared to risk it.

The Lord Chancellor, the Supreme Court and the Judges

Nobody has pointed out the impossibility of the Lord Chancellors' roles more forcefully then Lord Steyn. Lord Woolf, as we saw, offered an apologia for the complex nuances of the job. Lord Irvine, not surprisingly, thought the office essential for the working of the British Constitution. The Lord Chancellor's representative in the House of Commons repeated the mantra in December 2001:

> the office is unusual in the way that it combines different roles, but it is also unusually useful, because through it the judiciary has a representative in the Cabinet and the Cabinet has a representative in the judiciary. As such, we believe that the Lord Chancellor is well placed mutually to represent the views of each branch of our constitution to the other.[21]

Lord Irvine was, however, about to meet his intellectual Waterloo. In what was close to an unprecedented attack on the constitutional flaws of the office of Lord Chancellor, Lord Steyn in the Neill Lecture at Oxford in March 2002 made it clear that the only thing that stood between ending the Law Lords sitting in the House of Lords legislatively and the establishment of a proper Supreme Court was Lord Irvine's insistence that he continue to sit as a judge:

> . . . nowhere outside Britain, even in democracies with the weakest forms of separation of powers, is the independence of the judiciary potentially compromised in the eyes of citizens by relegating the status of the highest court to the position of a subordinate part of the legislature. And nowhere outside Britain is the independence of the judiciary potentially compromised in the eyes of citizens by permitting a serving politician to sit as a judge at any level, let alone in the highest court which fulfils constitutional functions.
>
> The major obstacle to creating a Supreme Court is the privilege of the Lord Chancellor of sitting in the Appellate Committee of the House of Lords. I will argue . . . the Lord Chancellor's participation in the judicial business in the highest court no longer serves a useful purpose and is contrary to the public interest. The privilege of serving Law Lords to participate in legislative business is no longer defensible. This is an obstacle of a lesser order: in reality it only exists to

---

[20] For the Lord Chancellor's efforts to gain control of administrative tribunals, currently run by the Department of Trade and Industry, see 'Cabinet Battle Looming For Control of Tribunals' *The Times*, 2 July 2001.
[21] *Hansard* HC Deb, vol 475, col 155 (4 December 2001).

this day to keep afloat the Lord Chancellor's anomalous privilege of sitting in the Appellate Committee.[22]

Lord Steyn then argued convincingly for an end of the Law Lords in the legislature and for the Lord Chancellor to sit judicially.

Lord Steyn demolished the traditional argument, which can be traced back to Shuster, explaining the great benefits that flowed from having a judge in the Cabinet and a Cabinet member as head of the judiciary:

> This is the scaffolding which is said to support the Lord Chancellor's judicial role. At the outset one may ask how the Lord Chancellor's minimal sittings in the Appellate Committee can be said to promote these ends. The answer is apparently that the fact that the Lord Chancellor occasionally sits in the Appellate Committee increases his stature with his cabinet colleagues and among the judges. Presumably the former know, and the judges certainly know, that the Lord Chancellor can rarely sit and only in relatively unimportant private law cases. It would be surprising if either side was particularly impressed with his judicial role. The very foundation of the argument is built on sand. But on wider grounds the argument is specious. The proposition that the Lord Chancellor represents the judiciary in the Cabinet reveals the fragility of the argument. The judiciary does not need a 'representative' in the Cabinet. In no other constitutional democracy does the judiciary have a 'representative' in the Cabinet. In any event, in respect of all matters discussed in Cabinet, including all aspects of policies in regard to civil and criminal justice, the Lord Chancellor is subject to collective responsibility. He cannot therefore act as a representative of the judiciary. The implied suggestion that the Lord Chancellor can act as an impartial arbiter between the Cabinet and the judiciary is constitutionally unsound and practically unattainable.[23]

Into Lord Steyn's judicial sights also came a parliamentary answer that Lord Irvine had given about what cases he was entitled to sit in and who controlled the composition of panels.[24] In both situations the Lord

---

[22] Steyn (n 13 above) at 4–5. Nor would Steyn have any truck with the idea, floated by the Lord Chancellor's office, that Strasbourg would allow the Lord Chancellor's privileges for historical reasons: 'Standing back from these developments, one may legitimately ask what message would be sent across Europe if the European Court made a drastic exception to the principle of separation of functions between the executive and the judiciary in favour of the historical anomaly of the Lord Chancellor's position in Britain. Why should it not then be acceptable to have a Minister of Justice in the highest court of an Eastern European Country? It seems to me probably that the European Court will want to apply minimum standards of judicial independence consistently across Europe.'
[23] *Ibid*, at 16–17. The Steyn assumption is that the Lord Chancellor would drop his right to sit as a judge, but all his other functions would continue. While arguing that he should give up his judicial function, Diana Woodhouse has argued that all the functions should go. 'The Office of Lord Chancellor: time to abandon the judicial role—the rest will follow' (2002) 22 *Legal Studies* 128.
[24] *Hansard* HL Deb, vol 613, col 77–78 (22 June 1999).

Chancellor took the divine right position, which Cardinal Wolsey would have understood.[25] The claim to control panels must have come as some surprise to the senior Law Lord, Lord Bingham, who had twice publicly announced that he controlled them. The Steyn judicial assault sounded as if it were signalling the end of the Lord Chancellor as a practising judge. That possibility, however, underestimated the resilience and pugilistic nature of Derry Irvine.

The vigorous response was not long in coming. In a press conference in April 2002, Lord Irvine pulled few punches. As to the argument that his sitting as a judge prevented the establishment of a Supreme Court, the Lord Chancellor was dismissive:

> We've heard this argument now umpteen times. It doesn't get better by repetition—in fact it becomes rather wearisome . . . (Lord Steyn's) is a hand which has been fully dealt. You could wish that he would find another pack to play with . . .
>
> He's not a political scientist, he knows nothing about the internal workings of Government—or very little—and all I can say is that all my predecessors have maintained the importance of the office.[26]

The Lord Chancellor was not impressed by Lord Steyn's obsession with the separation of powers, dismissing 'his very rigid view of the separation of powers, in turn influenced by his experience in South Africa where the rule of law had broken down.'[27] Irvine reduced the Steyn argument for a Supreme Court to a demand for a 'grand new architectural venture.' That

---

[25] 'One might have thought that there would be crystallized conventions governing the participation of the Lord Chancellor in judicial business of the Appellate Committee. When this point was probed during 1999 in questions in the House of Lords the Lord Chancellor confirmed expressly that there are *no* such conventions and in particular he rejected the idea that he should follow the advice of the Senior Law Lord or Law Lords collectively about his sitting. He asserts an absolute right in his unfettered discretion to decide when to sit. The Senior Law Lord and individual Law Lords are not so privileged: they must bow to the collective will. The Lord Chancellor also asserted that he '*delegates* to the Senior Law Lord the day-to-day management of judicial business, including the composition of committees.' He therefore asserts a right to intervene. A concession that the senior Law Lord, and the Law Lords, are in control, would have breached the fragile edifice. It is, however, an astonishing proposition that a member of the executive claims to this day to have the right to decide who among the Law Lords should sit on a particular case. It is, however, by no means a theoretical point. If the Lord Chancellor has the legal power to dictate in a given case the composition of the highest court in the land, he will be entitled to exercise it and nobody will in practice know when the power has been exercised directly or indirectly. Not much legal certainty and transparency there.': Steyn (n 13 above) at 8–9.
[26] J Eaglesham, 'Lord Chancellor Shows He Is Not Afraid To Fight Fire with Ire, *Financial Times*, 15 April 2002.
[27] J Rozenberg, 'I Saved Judges From Blunkett Says Lord Irvine' *Daily Telegraph*, 15 April 2002.

'the Lord Chancellor, because of his desire to continue sitting, is preventing the judges from having a new building—that's just nonsense.'[28]

The Lord Chancellor was equally contemptuous of the Steyn argument that the judges could look after themselves and did not need the guiding hand of the Lord Chancellor. He was insistent that without his views the Home Secretary would have seized control of the court system after the 2001 election. Besides which, Irvine argued, at the time of the Royal Commission on the House of Lords the Judges' Council had insisted that the Lord Chancellor's position should remain intact. In its evidence it had said that the judges had:

> no doubt that this dual role has historically proved invaluable in maintaining the independence of the judiciary in England and Wales and we have considerable anxiety that any other arrangement would result, in time, in the encroachment of executive government into the proper sphere of judicial independence essential in a democratic society.'[29] There were, however additional practical battles where the judiciary was clearly united.

The battle lines were becoming clearer, although it was unclear how far the judiciary was prepared to support Lord Steyn.

The Human Rights Act meets Bruiser Blunkett

During the first Labour Cabinet, the Home Secretary had been Jack Straw, a barrister, who talked of partnerships with the judiciary with respect to the Human Rights Act. With the reshuffle in 2001, following the second landslide, Jack Straw moved to the Foreign Office, and David Blunkett moved from Education, where he had a reputation for toughness, to the Home Office. Whereas Straw's views were shaped by the chattering classes of North London who appreciated the finer points of rights based jurisprudence, David Blunkett came out of Sheffield local politics where the incorporation of the European Convention on Human Rights into English law was, perhaps, less discussed, and there was more concern with duties than with rights.[30] There was another sub-plot, as there almost invariably was in New Labour politics. Members of the Cabinet casting around for 'Anyone

---

[28] Eaglesham (n 26 above).
[29] F Gibb, 'Strong Seas But a Sure Touch at the Helm,' *The Times*, 16 April 2002.
[30] When Lord Donaldson, retired Master of the Rolls, disagreed with Home Secretary Blunkett about human rights on the *Today* programme, the Home Secretary accused Donaldson of 'patronising' a 'council house boy': *The Spectator*, 29 December 2001, 47. Lord Donaldson was later helpful to the Home Secretary in the House of Lords debates.

but Gordon (Brown)' to succeed Tony Blair should he step down, were increasingly advocating David Blunkett. It was a heady brew.[31]

By the summer of 2001, it looked as if David Blunkett was heading for a clash with the judges over an issue that had been familiar to Michael Howard—sentencing policy. The skirmishing was familiar. In July, the Home Secretary announced a new look at sentencing, announcing that:

> How criminals are punished—and how we ensure they don't offend again—is too important to be left to the judges and politicians alone . . . I want to hear what people think: not just those who have a traditional role or official interest in the criminal justice system, but those who have a right to be involved and to be consulted—the public who are so often the victims.

In particular, Blunkett felt that the courts had not been giving sufficiently severe sentences to sex offenders, and a penal code along continental lines was proposed.[32] When the Home Secretary complained that 'the public, the police and victims are frustrated and angered by a system that fails to deliver sentences that ensure public safety and help to cut crime,' the Lord Chief Justice responded by saying to judges 'don't send people to prison unless it is really necessary.' Lord Woolf attributed the lack of confidence in the legal system not to the judges but to overcrowding in the prisons.[33]

At this point the agenda changed. In *R (ex p Fazi) v Home Secretary*, Mr Justice Collins[34] held that four detainees at the Oakington Detention Centre in Cambridgeshire were illegally held. Although they were legally held by English immigration law, the 'administrative convenience' argument was held to violate Article 5 of the European Convention incorporated into the Human Rights Act, since the holding was not proportionate to the need. The newspapers reported—although the remarks do not appear in the official judgment—that Mr Justice Collins had described the situation at Oakington as a 'disgrace' and added that to call Oakington a detention centre was 'euphemistic and misleading.' *The Daily Mail* added fuel to the flames by suggesting that those detained might now sue for £110m for unlawful detention.[35] David Blunkett was reported to be experiencing 'deep anger'

---

[31] J Naughtie, *The Rivals: The Intimate Story of a Political Marriage*, (London, 2001) *passim*.

[32] 'Blunkett Heads For Clash with Judges' *The Daily Telegraph*, 6 July 2001; 'Blunkett Seeks Support For Sentencing Reform' *ibid*, 30 August 2001.

[33] His position was liberal and consistent. 'Stop Jailing So Many, Says Lord Woolf', *The Times*, 29 January 2001; 'Chief Justice Attacks Prison As Straw Plans To Jail More' *The Daily Telegraph*, 1 February 2001; 'Put Fewer Offenders In Jail' *The Times*, 30 January 2001; 'Judges Told To Cut Jail Sentences By Up To a Half' *The Times*, 26 October 2001.

[34] Some of Collins J's judgments had upset Michael Howard: F Gill, 'Judge Dismayed Tory Ministers,' *The Times*, 8 September 2001.

[35] 'Yesterday a judge decided that under laws forged in Europe, asylum seekers, given private rooms, satellite TV, and a gym had their human rights infringed. What's more, they can now

and discovered that 'elected politicians now seem to come second to judges because of the Human Rights Act.'[36] The Home Secretary was about to be given a powerful new weapon. Three days later the World Trade Center and part of the Pentagon were destroyed and the war on terrorism began.

The Home Secretary thereafter made a series of statements contrasting the democratically elected and transparent Parliament with the non-democratic and non-transparent judiciary.[37] The Prime Minister was reported as backing the Home Secretary with regard to his plan to repeal part of the Human Rights Act in order to allow an effective anti-terrorism bill.[38] Two weeks later, Blunkett introduced a second package of anti-terrorist measures with 'his strongest warning yet to judges and human rights lawyers not to undermine them.' He was still furious about the Oakington decision, and demanded that judicial review be curbed.[39] In an Op Ed piece in *The Times*, the Home Secretary refused to accept that there was a dichotomy between democracy and 'fundamental freedoms based on the primacy of the individual':

> This is a false dichotomy but it raises important questions. The freedom of every individual depends on stability, order and the maintenance of democratic practices. Freedom springs not from abstract legal process but from political action. After all, British democracy was not created by lawyers and judges. It was created through the struggle and the political engagement of the people . . .
>
> It is crucial that (the judiciary) protect our rights by recognizing that at certain moments in history, the majority must be protected from the minority—not just the minority from the majority. This is such a time.[40]

As the political conferences approached, the Labour Home Secretary found himself rehearsing all the reasons the Conservatives had advanced for not incorporating the European Convention on Human Rights. The new Act appeared to be in danger.

At Labour's truncated conference at Brighton, David Blunkett repeated his refrain, paying particular attention to judicial review, which had become 'a lawyer's charter.' As he put it, 'it is justice we seek, not just the primacy of jurisprudence.'[41] The courts, in short, were paying too

---

sue for £110m. The world HAS truly gone mad' *The Daily Mail*, 8 September 2001. See also, 'Asylum Seekers: the Headache Gets Worse' *The Daily Telegraph*, 8 September, 2001

[36] *The Daily Mail*, 8 September 2001; 'Blunkett Despair At £110m Asylum Ruling,' *The Times*, 8 September 2001.

[37] 'On the Record' BBC 1, 23 September 2001.

[38] 'Security Comes Before Human Rights Act, says Blunkett' *The Daily Telegraph*, 24 September 2001

[39] 'Blunkett Brings In Tougher Anti-terror Measures' *The Guardian*, 6 October 2001.

[40] D Blunkett, 'At Times Like These, the Majority Must Be Protected From the Minority' *The Times*, 4 October 2001.

[41] 'Blunkett Attacks Judiciary In Fight Over Terrorism' *The Daily Telegraph*, 4 October 2001.

much attention to the rights of minorities. No one was spared. Some civil liberties lawyers were accused of inadvertently stirring up racial hatred,[42] while the *Guardian* editorialised: 'with a crude attack on judges and a populist history of freedom which ignored the role of the courts, Mr Blunkett did little to enhance his reputation.'[43] In particular, the *Guardian* was appalled by the 'vitriolic attack on judicial review.' Lord Woolf, before he was Chief Justice had opined that judges, if presented with parliamentary efforts to curb judicial review, might be entitled to ignore them. He was, by the autumn of 2001, appreciably more circumspect: 'I hope, in taking action against those who are attacking our system, we don't lose sight of the importance of maintaining the system . . . The Human Rights Act is a very useful check to see whether the Government's getting it correct.'[44] *The Daily Telegraph* found itself, surprisingly, in sympathy with the *Guardian*, and taking Lord Woolf's earlier threats at face value: 'Short of repealing the Geneva Convention and the European Convention on Human Rights, (Blunkett) will not be able to wrest control of our frontiers from the judiciary. Indeed, even if he did abrogate those treaties, it is more than likely that the judges would disregard him and carry on as before.'[45]

Blunkett, however, was not easily intimidated. When the anti-terrorism Bill was outlined, the Home Secretary explained that it would 'strike a balance between respecting our civil liberties and ensuring they are not exploited.' In particular, the judges were to lose control of deportation orders made on national security grounds, and Article 5 of the European Convention, incorporated into the Human Rights Act would be suspended under the provisions of Article 15.[46] *The Daily Telegraph*, which saw little good either in European treaties or judicial activism, had a field day:

---

[42] 'Civil Liberties Groups Accused of Jeopardizing Citizens' Safety' *The Financial Times*, 4 October 2001
[43] 'Restraining Blunkett' *The Guardian*, 4 October 2001.
[44] 'Lord Woolf warns on human rights' *New Law Journal*, 5 October 2001. Interestingly, Lord Woolf then found himself embroiled in a situation where he appeared to be advocating the incarceration of paedophiles without trial. 'Judge Sparks Row with Plan On Paedophiles,' *The Financial Times*, 27 December 2001; 'Lord Chief Justice Defends "Custody" Call' *The Daily Telegraph*, 30 December 2001. When, in the spring of 2002, David Blunkett issued a series of initiatives designed to curb crime, these were criticised by Lord Woolf ('You can have initiative after initiative to reform the criminal justice system but if you don't touch the basic problems you will never achieve public confidence'). Francis Gibb of *The Times* commented 'Although courteously delivered, Lord Woolf's speech reflects mounting criticism among judges . . . about the spate of headline grabbing anti-crime measures announced by the Home Office, Lord Chancellor's Department and government law officers.' 'Blair's Crime Crackdown Won't Work Says Law Chief' *The Times*, 17 May 2002.
[45] 'A Thumb on the Scales' (Leader) *The Daily Telegraph*, 16 October 2001.
[46] 'Blunkett Seeks Powers To Remove Terrorist Suspects' *The Daily Telegraph*, 16 October 2001.

Such treaties and laws based on them, create what is, in effect, a politicized judiciary. The politicization is not along party lines—our judges are scrupulous. It is rather the impression in Britain of a Continental form of law that invites judges to interpret individual cases in the light of political generalizations about what is right and wrong. The judges seem to have decided these principles do not allow deportations . . . The objection to this is not so much that our judges are biased or inept, but that such decisions ought to be made by people whom we can call to account. When they are made by people outside the political process, elections become devalued and voters become disillusioned. It is quite understandable that many judges today, worried by the tendency of successive governments of both parties to arrogate more and more power to themselves, try to use human rights provisions to dig their heels in. But it is quite wrong if Parliament is in the position where it cannot really pass laws.[47]

As the government talked about suspending Article 7 so that any new legislation against anthrax hoaxes might be used retrospectively,[48] David Blunkett gave a speech to the Institute for the Study of Civil Society.[49] It was a clarion call for a return to Dicey, relying on Michael Beloff and Sir William Wade as authorities for the proposition that judicial activism had gone too far. 'We must address this issue and bring sense back into the system for it to deliver all that is required by the public it serves and for the democracy it serves.' For good measure he also suggested that the criminal justice system 'is geared more towards protecting the perpetrators of crime rather than the victims of crime' and that the courts were not well run. 'Expecting people to be good leaders and managers because they are clever lawyers is foolish and flies in the face of everything the business world knows.' He looked for help from lawyers if they were a 'profession' and not merely 'a trade.'

The judges no doubt noticed the climate. As Mr Dooley, an American cartoon character from the 1930s, noted: 'th' judges read th' election returns.' Just at this moment, the Court of Appeal chose to overrule the Oakington decision, partly by rationalising European human rights precedents to justify the detentions on the ground that it was 'not an unreasonable price to pay.'[50] Lord Phillips, the Master of the Rolls, presided in the decision, but he was also involved, with Lord Chancellor Irvine, in producing a report designed to curb the number of judicial review cases and to encourage their settlement.[51] Perhaps the most remarkable manifestation of

[47] 'A Law Unto Themselves' Leader, *The Daily Telegraph*, 22 October 2001.
[48] 'Anthrax Hoax Law May Breach Human Rights' *The Daily Telegraph*, 22 October 2001.
[49] 25 October 2001.
[50] R English, 'Acorns of wisdom from Oakington' *New Law Journal*, 9 November 2001, 1629. The case is currently on appeal to the House of Lords.
[51] 'Judicial Review Will Face New Pre-action Protocol' Legal Week, 8 November 2001, 2.

an olive branch from the judiciary occurred in *Home Secretary v Rehman*[52] a House of Lords decision argued in May 2001, but decided in October of that year. There in holding that deportations from the UK for matters of national security did not have to be limited to threats to the UK, Lord Hoffmann added a telling paragraph:[53]

> I wrote this speech some three months before the recent events in New York and Washington. They are reminders that, in matters of national security, the cost of failure can be high. This seems to me to underline the need for the judicial arm of government to respect the decision of ministers of the Crown on the question of whether support for terrorist activities in a foreign country constitutes a threat to national security. It is not only that the executive has access to special information and expertise in these matters. It is also that such decisions, with serious potential results for the community, require a legitimacy which can be conferred only by entrusting them to persons responsible to the community through the democratic process. If the people are to accept the consequences of such decisions, they must be made by persons whom the people have elected and whom they can remove.

The Institute for Civil Society speech, however, was still reverberating. With a sense of recent history, Blunkett was reported as believing that fifty years earlier the judges were not sufficiently active, but 'I feel just as strongly about the swing in the opposite direction.' The judges had become too powerful—and were not draconian enough in criminal cases.[54] It later emerged that Lord Chancellor Irvine had asked the Home Secretary to cut the reference to the judges as 'too powerful' and Blunkett had refused. Lord Irvine was reported as being 'furious' and the relationship between the Lord Chancellor and Home Secretary sank to such a low that the Attorney-General had to intervene. Meanwhile in response to Blunkett's complaint that the judges had 'established judicial review as an almost boundless jurisdiction over almost every kind of governmental activity,' Lord Chief Justice Woolf in a public lecture replied: 'If one is in a position of power, it is sometimes easy to get things wrong . . . The Human Rights Act is the brake which encourages proper consideration of the interest of individuals, albeit it may be a little inconvenient to do that.'[55]

David Blunkett was not intimidated. He continued his assaults on the judiciary, insisting that he would not let the judges use the Human Rights Act to overrule the House of Commons. 'The law will be made by those who are held to account for both making it and changing it . . . Get that

---

[52] [2002] 1 All ER 122.
[53] *Ibid*, at 142.
[54] 'Blunkett Hints At Curbing Power of Judges' *The Daily Telegraph*, 26 October 2001.
[55] 'Irvine "furious" with Blunkett Over Speech' *The Times*, 31 October 2001.

right and our democracy will be alive.'[56] He continued to rail against 'airy-fairy civil libertarians,' and to belittle the legal profession.[57] The Bar Council retorted that 'the first sign that judicial review is working is that politicians are squealing about it,' while the Chairman of the Bar Council called it 'an authoritarian government.'[58] Meanwhile the left-wing QC, Michael Mansfield, observed: 'No one wishes to see a politically active judicial system, but given the majorities that recent governments have had, it is vital to have a counter-balance.'[59]

The Home Secretary went ahead with his Anti-Terrorism, Crime and Security Bill, derogating from Article 5 of the European Convention of Human Rights to allow suspected terrorists to be detained without trial.[60] The Bill was railroaded through Parliament and, while the Lords eventually forced the abandonment of race hatred crimes, the Bill curbing the Human Rights Act became law in December.[61] *The Economist* reported that 'some of (Blunkett's) remarks have sent shivers through the judiciary by making open criticism of judgments that have gone against the Home Office.'[62] Blunkett's assault, however, continued. When Mr Justice Sullivan found unlawful the Government's system of fining lorry drivers found to have illegal immigrants aboard—albeit unknowingly—under Article 6 of the European Convention, Blunkett exploded again.[63]

What was perhaps most remarkable was that no leader of New Labour, which had engineered the assault on parliamentary sovereignty which the Human Rights Act represented, was prepared to articulate an accepted revised philosophy. Lord Irvine who defended having the Lord Chancellor also sit in the Cabinet, so that he might protect the judges, said not a word. As *The Economist* concluded, 'David Blunkett has added to the overall impression that this is a government that does as it pleases and brooks no criticism.'[64] By the end of 2001 an observer might well adopt the view of the Special Rapporteur of the United Nations Commission on Human Rights: 'any government who makes itself immune to an independent judicial

[56] 'Rein In the Judges, Says Blunkett' *The Daily Telegraph*, 9 November 2001.

[57] A Miles, 'Is the Home Secretary Really Above the Law?' *The Times*, 14 November 2001.

[58] 'New Bar Chairman attacks Blunkett's menacing noises' *New Law Journal*, 21 December 2001, 1875.

[59] 'Judgment Day' *Legal Week*, 15 November 2001, 12.

[60] M Zander, 'The Anti-Terrorism Bill—What Happened?' '*New Law Journal*, 21 December 2001. 1880.

[61] Eg J Wadham and S Chakrabarti, 'Infinite detention without trial' *New Law Journal*, 26 October 2001, 1564; 'Editorial,' *New Law Journal*, 16 November 2001, 1681; 'Peers Inflict String of Defeats On Terror Bill' *The Financial Times*, 7 December 2001; 'Peers Cut Terrorist Bill Down To Size' *The Daily Telegraph*, 7 December 2001.

[62] 'Labour's Taliban Tendency' *The Economist*, 17 November 2001.

[63] 'Blunkett Fury As Judge Says Lorry Asylum Fines Are Illegal' *The Times* 6 December 2001.

[64] 'Labour's Taliban Tendency' *The Economist*, 17 November 2001.

review of whether its actions are lawful or unlawful is potentially despotic.'[65] During the autumn the odd shadow boxing continued with the Lord Chief Justice demanding heavier sentences for mobile phone robbers while urging judges not to imprison unnecessarily; meanwhile, the Home Secretary wanted the judges to be tougher on crime but have fewer people in prison. Perhaps fortunately for the judges, with the Terrorism Act secure, David Blunkett turned his attention to immigration, cannabis, the police and even sentencing reform.[66]

---

[65] [1994] *Commonwealth Law Bulletin*, July 958.
[66] There had, however, been a slow change in the Home Secretary's rhetoric during the autumn. Early on, the whole Human Rights Act seemed threatened. Behind the scenes, however, human rights groups were able to persuade Blunkett that the Act also protected the majority from the minority and the most basic human right is the right to be protected against internal or external aggression.

10

The Future

THE ENGLISH CONSTITUTION has grown organically. For those seeking principled changes the process of picking one's way through the 'wilderness of single instances' is at best a frustrating one. Pendulums oscillate violently. The Labour Government which incorporated the European Convention of Human Rights also produced David Blunkett. Rhetoric lives longer than reality. Just as many acts are done in the name of the Queen without her knowledge, parliamentary sovereignty is still a potent symbol to the right wing of the Conservative Party in its thinking about Europe. In the same way, parliamentary sovereignty is a symbol to the left wing of the Labour Party which clings to notions of parliamentary control long after many powers have migrated to Prime Minister, Brussels and the judiciary. So too the judiciary suffers from its pendulum effect in its style, aggravated by its reluctance to leave its mythological hideouts, whether they be judicial independence or denying the inevitable policy element in judicial decisions. At their core, both in politics and law, convenient myths have their meaning. In the day-to-day world, however, they make intelligent discussion of the role of judges, in what passes for the British Constitution, difficult.

Lord Irvine's insistence that parliamentary sovereignty has not been impaired by New Labour's constitutional reforms is understandable. While many who would regard themselves as reformers see the judges as the incipient third branch of Government, with Britain appearing to be on the edge of a written Constitution by which the democratic deficit might be judged, this is still far from reality. Rank and file MPs of all parties are not about to abandon parliamentary sovereignty. They feel as strongly about that as if they were eighteenth-century Whigs—although their power is appreciably less and their independence not apparently cherished by New Labour. Their confusion about their position, however, is so great that they failed to realise that by championing an elected second chamber they were weakening still further the power of the House of Commons. Nor have they fully understood that when one party has a handsome majority, parliamentary sovereignty, while on rare occasions it may give elected MPs real power, is actually a delegation of effective total power to the executive. Modern party control, the declining importance of private members' Bills, the growing ineffectiveness of the parliamentary question, have all weakened older concepts of parliamentary sovereignty or supremacy.

There has, of course, been a sea change in the role of the judges. The Privy Council now has to decide whether the Scottish legislative Assembly has violated the letter (and, if the judges seek to be constitutional lawyers, the spirit) of the Scotland Act. As a result of Britain's status in the EU, de facto judges may hold parliamentary legislation inoperative. The incorporation of the European Convention on Human Rights has meant that judges have been given the right to flag violations of the Human Rights Act after hearings which required the judges to make difficult moral and political judgments in delicate areas. The changes are not the same, however, as a constitutional court or the end of parliamentary sovereignty. The Human Rights Act was fundamentally different from the US Constitution's notion of judicial review of legislation or the power of the German Constitutional Court; it was even a considerable distance from the Supreme Court of Israel which, under its President, Mr Justice Barak, had taken the British system, which it had inherited in 1948, and turned it into something akin to the American model based on the Basic laws of 1992.

In determining where the story will end, it is important to remember that even with devolution, and some 'hollowing-out' of Government, Britain continues to be blessed with legislation which normally speaks clearly, authoritatively and finally on difficult social issues. That is an inevitable result of Government control of legislation and drafting. In the United States such social issues often lead to a murky half-life as the result of the tri-partite system of Government, the absence of serious party discipline, federalism, and perhaps a different political and social ethos. Thus, in the UK, issues have been spelled out clearly in such matters as abortion, the limits of ethical research, race discrimination, the death penalty, and gun control. That does not mean that the courts have not been increasingly involved on the periphery; but it has meant that many of the policy issues have been clearly settled publicly in a democratic forum. That could, of course, change. The Jenkins Committee recommended a form of modified proportional representation, in place of first past the post, in Westminster elections. This could lead to coalitions as the norm. If the legislature were to produce compromise legislation then, even without the direct right to strike down legislation, courts could find themselves in a far more significant position in interpreting vague wording, based on compromise policies. There is also talk of greater use of referendums. If introduced, and even if not as destructive as the California

Initiatives,[1] the courts might find even more political issues moving in their direction.

Yet most political observers have noted a greater centralisation in England in the last twenty-five years. Centralisation has been the norm in England since 1832, but it tends to come in waves. The great liberal reforms from the 1850s up to the mid 1870s centralised the courts and the civil service. The growth of the Welfare State between 1906 and the First World War put immense power in certain Government departments. A different form of centralisation occurred with the Labour Government of 1945–51, with nationalisation of basic industries, the implementation of the Beveridge proposals including the National Health Service and centralised control over the economy.

The centralisation which has occurred over the last twenty-five years has taken a different form. While there has been privatisation and a freeing of economic controls, even Mrs Thatcher was responsible for dramatically increasing central control.[2] This can be seen in controls over primary and secondary education, where teachers were thought to have far too much input and over universities, who were regarded as failing to make sufficiently useful contributions to the economy and business. Under the Conservative Government local government was abolished in London and capped elsewhere. The Civil Service was put under greater political pressure and control over the police and the courts was centralised. While under New Labour this centralisation was superficially reversed, with devolution to Scotland and Wales and an elected Mayor in London, the tradition of control from Whitehall continued. When centres of power outside Government control did not respond sufficiently fast, they were superseded—for instance important planning decisions may be taken away from local government. Inevitably, such centralisation—even with aberrations like devolution and human rights—has affected and probably changed the nature of—and has certainly affected the power of—parliamentary sovereignty.

To look a little further and to turn the clock back to 1960, another factor becomes clear: the judges have grown more important because others have become less so. Local government, which at one time had a certain independence, is now patently under the control of Whitehall. The Civil Service which for so long, under the guidance of Sir Humphries, largely operated the power inherent in parliamentary supremacy, is less powerful. Mrs Thatcher saw the Civil Service as 'part of the problem' and brought it, in many ways, to heel. New Labour has chosen to undermine it by vastly

---

[1]   P Schrag, *Paradise Lost* (University of California, 1998) *passim*.
[2]   S Jenkins, *Accountable to None: The Tory Nationalization of Britain* (London, 1995).

increasing the number of special advisers. The older universities once had great influence in Whitehall and Westminster. They were undermined by Mrs Thatcher and diluted by Mr Major. Under New Labour, they were increasingly starved of funds and micro-managed into subservience. The unions, which brought down both a Conservative and Labour government in the 1970s, are but a shadow of their former selves. The Church, which in the 1960s could hold up divorce reform, changes in the criminal law and even commercial television is now virtually irrelevant in an almost totally secular society. The armed forces have shrunk dramatically and their political voice has been stilled.

In the early twenty-first century there are still some centres of power. Under New Labour, industry—the CBI, the FBI and the Institute of Directors—remains important, perhaps, in what we are told is an enterprise society, increasingly so. The City of London likewise has become more central under New Labour and the Bank of England's Monetary Policy Committee has achieved an element of independence which has it controlling the bank rate. The other major centre of power is the press. With the arrival of the popular press at the end of Victoria's reign, the press was always important but that importance was limited. No politician wanted to offend the press and the Establishment was concerned with the leaders in *The Morning Post* and *The Times*. The popular press seemed to take on fresh significance in the 1990s when *The Sun* claimed to have won the 1992 election for the Conservatives. New Labour, however, turned seeking support from the press into an obsession. 'Spinning' the news began to compete for attention with parliamentary involvement.

All these developments inevitably had an impact on the context of parliamentary sovereignty. With the decline in the Church, Civil Service, universities and other aspects of the old order, inevitably the judges would appear as more significant. Industry, commerce and the press are now the competitors to compete with parliamentary power. It is this context that in the rapidly changing scene the judiciary has to be evaluated.[3]

---

[3]   The nature of the bench has changed in another way. Between 1950 and 2000 the size of the Court of Appeal has tripled, the High Court quadrupled and the circuit courts are some seven times as large as the old county courts. The membership in the Privy Council, given automatically to members of the Court of Appeal, is increasingly composed of judges. The High Court judges, automatically given knighthoods, represent an increasing percentage of that honour. The senior salaries review body is increasingly involved with the judiciary as the numbers of judges increase inexorably and the number of civil servants and senior officers in the armed forces decline. If the public feels there is a growth in 'judgeocracy', the feeling is understandable.

The Issues

The question is, should there be a 'real' separation of powers and a more meaningful concept of judicial independence? It is a vital moment to be asking this question, for the Blair administration is fulfilling its commitment to reform of the Constitution. Nevertheless, to transform the Constitution so that there is a more realistic separation of powers would require a significant rethinking of political philosophy and the abandonment of various fundamental conventions and myths which operate, in some ways, quite satisfactorily in practice. In an era, however, when the Human Rights Act is an accomplished fact and proportional representation is in the air, reformers will inevitably envisage the Americanisation of the separation of powers.

Over the last thirty years there is little doubt that the role, power and self-perception of the judiciary has changed. Perhaps nothing changed the judges more than the long period of Conservative rule between 1979 and 1997. For the first decade there was effectively no political opposition—for Labour was split and then drifted leftward and into the political wilderness. The decline in the concept of an opposition coincided with the realisation of the declining importance of the House of Commons. Lord Hailsham caught the atmosphere with his phrase 'elected dictatorship' to describe the relationship of legislature and executive. The Government made laws; backbench MPs were there to provide the votes. The declining independence of MPs, even the decreasing importance and increasing triviality of question time, inevitably appeared to leave a vacuum, particularly with respect to controlling the executive. It was into the vacuum thus created—accentuated by the decline in other institutions that had previously enforced norms—that the judges stepped, as some of them even hinted that they would help 'remedy the democratic deficit'.[4]

Skirmishing over powers tends to lead to conflict. The conflict between the judges and the Conservative Government became most public in the battles between Lord Taylor, the late Lord Chief Justice, and Michael Howard, the last Conservative Home Secretary, primarily concerning penal policy. It was not a dignified dispute. The interesting question now is, what will be the long-term impact of the 1997 and 2001 Labour landslides? With a massive, and, at this stage, docile majority of Labour members in the House of Commons, and with an apparently chronically weak opposition, will the judges once again feel they are faced with the task of keeping some sense of balance in the Constitution? By the late autumn of 2001, with Home Secretary Blunkett in a militant mood, the answer is probably 'Yes'.

---

[4] J Griffith, 'Who will referee the refs?' *Times Literary Supplement*, 25 September 1998.

Since the Prime Minister, with the war on terror in full flow, refused to protect the transference of the protection of rights to the judges made by the
Human Rights Act, then the answer is almost certainly 'Yes'.

As the second term of the Labour administration gathered steam after
2001, there was certainly the potential for further conflict. Jack Straw,
Home Secretary from 1997 to 2001, shared many of the assumptions of his
much derided predecessor, Michael Howard. He called for longer sentences
and demanded toughness on crime. As we have seen, however, Lord Bingham
was less willing than his predecessor, Lord Taylor, to pick fights and perhaps more sympathetic to the policies: he approved of a relaxation in the
rules of evidence and was willing to see restrictions on the use of juries,
although he opposed, in the legislative debates, the changes in evidence in
rape cases and was opposed to mandatory sentences for murder. With Lord
Woolf replacing Lord Bingham as Chief Justice in 2001 his position is less
clear and his inclination would probably be more sympathetic to
Government wishes. As revealed in the Queen's Speech in June 2001 these
changes would be extensive, including allowing previous convictions as evidence, curbing double jeopardy and weakening the independence of juries.
The contentious issue of whether judges or Ministers set tariffs for imprisonment remained. When David Blunkett became Home Secretary in 2001,
his tone of 'toughness on crime' was brasher than Jack Straw's and turned
out to be a prelude to a bout of judge bashing. To the cynic, Michael
Howard began to look like a liberal. While Lord Woolf was expected to
avoid conflict with the executive, some of the judiciary might not be so
circumspect.

It would be wrong, however, to think of these developments as some
sudden kind of judicial putsch. For thirty-five years the atmosphere has
made it inevitable that judges would have more influence in the day-to-day
involvement in the political issues of the nation. In the 1950s, 1960s, and
1970s, Parliament, by legislation, in effect instructed the judges to return
to matters relating to competition and labour relations. By the 1960s the
judges had moved to renew judicial review of administrative decisions.
From the mid 1960s onwards, following the freeing of stare decisis by the
Lords, the appeal judges have been more willing to reclaim their traditional role of pushing forward the boundaries of the common law.[5] The

---

[5] *Kleinwort Benson Ltd v Lincoln CC* [1999] 2 AC 349. The decision overruled the long-
standing principle that money paid under a mistake of law could not be recovered. Relying on
a report of the Law Commission and comparative law, Lord Goff concluded (at 375): 'I can
see no good reason for postponing the matter for legislation, especially when we do not know
whether or, if so, when Parliament may legislate'. F Bennion argues that the reasoning of the
Law Lords in this case threatens the rule of law: F Bennion, 'A naked usurpation?' *New Law
Journal*, 19 March 1999, 421.

decline of competing centres of power has made natural evolution appear as a putsch.

The English are somewhat reluctant to come to grips with the implications of a judiciary increasingly involved with what, in other societies, would be regarded as political issues. The cult of parliamentary sovereignty hangs so heavily in the air that the reality of recent transfers of powers to the judges and others is shrouded in its mythology. The idea of a Judicial Appointments Commission worries some, although an Advisory Committee is already here. They share a Hamiltonian willingness to leave the final choice to a wise elder (the Lord Chancellor); and they remain nervous about any further openness in the process. Many appear to be especially uncomfortable with any system which would allow judges to be questioned either about their political or personal views or their suitability to be judges.[6] Lord Neill, until recently Chair of the Committee on Standards in Public Life, expressed the establishment shock:

> This is a disastrous way of appointing the judiciary. We can carry openness to its full length—I believe that openness is one of the great seven principles of public life; I proclaim that—but there must be limits to it. The limit comes when we try to interrogate potential judges.[7]

Lord Irvine and Lord Bingham are similarly offended. They are distressed by the American system of Senatorial review of Presidential judicial appointments, which they associate with the Bork and Thomas hearings, although the typical hearings before the Senate Judiciary Committee provide a more healthy airing of views. If the House of Lords continues in its present form, then their concerns are probably justified. If, however, there is a Constitutional or Supreme Court, it will need to choose judges not merely from the Court of Appeal and it will be legitimate to question such persons on their views of moral and political issues.

England together with Scotland and Northern Ireland is apparently moving down the route of a substantive Judicial Appointments Committee. This was the direction of the IPPR draft Constitution in 1991, the Justice *Report of the Future of the Judiciary* in 1993 and, most importantly, the Peach

---

[6] 'Top Judge Says US Style Vetting Will Harm Bench' *The Times*, 18 December 2000. Lord Browne-Wilkinson said: 'I myself would never have become a judge if there was any question that I would have to go through the kind of performance that Judge Bork or Clarence Thomas had to go through'. For a vigorous restatement of the status quo, see S Kentridge, 'The Highest Court: Selecting the Judges' (Sir David Williams Lecture, Centre for Public Law University of Cambridge, 10 May 2002) *Cambridge Law Journal* (forthcoming). For another colonial defence of the status quo, including the functions of the Lord Chancellor, the House of Lords as the final appeal court and the legislative role of the law lords see Lord Cooke of Thorndon, 'The Law Lords: An Endangered Heritage' (Chancery Bar Association Summer Lecture, Lincon's Inn, 11 June 2002).

[7] *Hansard* HL Deb, vol 597, col 1446 (1 March 1999).

Report in 1997. Yet it may be that all these reports were headed in the wrong direction. Judges choosing judges is the antithesis of democracy. In all major common law countries—the US, Canada, Australia and South Africa—the executive chooses the judiciary, although sometimes with advice from a Judicial Appointments Commission. To hand over the appointment of judges to a commission might well ensure bland appointments. The courts do have important political powers and responsibilities, whether the rubric is separation of powers or balance of powers. The choice of judges is too important to be left to a quango. Quaint as it may sound in this egalitarian era, Hamilton may well have been right.[8] At the very least, if there is to be a Constitutional or Supreme Court, its judges must be chosen by elected officials and subject to examination by a democratic body.

Leaving the power of appointment with the executive at a time of rapidly increasing judicial power makes it even more important that there be transparency about the persons whom it is prepared to appoint. A recent Permanent Secretary to the Lord Chancellor, Sir Thomas Legg, opined that, as more 'political' jurisdiction was given to the judges, the point would be reached—sooner or later—when the public would legitimately think that the political views of the judges were important in deciding who should be appointed. He has also suggested that, if the Lord Chancellor were to continue to appoint judges, they might be subject to confirmation by a committee of a reformed House of Lords.[9] The solution would be similar to that used for appointments to the Constitutional Court of South Africa.[10] The Conservatives have had interesting responses to the problem. A former Conservative spokesman on constitutional affairs (Liam Fox) called for the questioning of judges on their views, while the former leader of the Conservative Party, William Hague, took that concern to its logical conclusion by calling for a House of Commons' veto on senior judicial appointments.[11] By early 2002, Iain Duncan Smith, the new Conservative leader,

---

[8] Cited by Lord Bingham in the Justice Annual Lecture, 2001: 'Promising this, I proceed to lay down as a rule that one man of discernment is better fitted to analyse and estimate the peculiar qualities adapted to particular office than a body of men of equal or perhaps even superior discernment. The role and undivided responsibility of one man will naturally beget a livelier sense of duty and a more exact regard to regulation. He will, on this account, feel himself under stronger obligations, and more interested to investigate with care the qualities requisite to the stations to be filled, and to prefer with impartiality the persons who may have the fairest pretentions to them'. Justice, *Bulletin*, Autumn 2001, 9.

[9] *The Daily Telegraph*, 19 January 1998.

[10] Kate Malleson, 'Assessing the Performance of the South African Judicial Service Commission' (1999) 116 *South African Law Journal* 36.

[11] 'Judiciary Needs Greater Scrutiny' *The Times*, 15 April 1999 (Fox); *The Times*, 25 February 1998 (Hague). The dubious role of the European Parliament in the selection of Nicholas Bratza QC as the British judge on the European Court of Human Rights was not an encouraging precedent for such a system. (Labour MEPs attacked his appointment because, as a

appeared to demand the questioning of nominated senior figures (possibly including judges) by a parliamentary committee. Twice, in the Lords, the Shadow Conservative Lord Chancellor, Lord Kingsland, has called for nominated Law Lords to appear before a joint committee of the Lords and Commons.

The judges may well have to take note of the sudden public concern about the personal and political views of the Bank of England's Monetary Policy Committee to which, in 1997, Gordon Brown, the Chancellor of the Exchequer, delegated power over the bank rate. It may well be that the judges, like the bankers and economists, cannot expect to move into the political arena without being at least subject to the public inspection suffered by Monetary Policy Committee members (thus far ignored by Chancellor of the Exchequer, Gordon Brown). While the judges' ability to absorb political issues and claim that they are merely legal is considerable, the limit of that ability may have been reached. While the *Pinochet* case and the Human Rights Act caused further debate on the politics of the judiciary,[12] Lord Irvine announced he could see no need for public or political involvement in judicial appointments, even with respect to the Lords of Appeal in Ordinary—the judges in the House of Lords—who have always been outside the regular judicial structure and have become de facto a Supreme Court, with an increasingly political case load.[13] As a politician who has rightly refused to give up his right to appoint judges, this was an

barrister, he had represented the Thatcher Government.) Indeed allowing the European Parliament to select judges from a panel submitted by a country (rather than the previous system which allowed a country directly to nominate a judge) has not patently improved the quality of that court's judiciary.

[12] *The Times* was concerned generally with the highly political nature of the *Pinochet* case and specifically with the failure of Lord Hoffmann to recuse himself: 'Lord Hoffmann's political background has thus become part of the tangled web that the *Pinochet* case has woven round questions of sovereignty, Parliament and the law. This affair has huge consequences, not only for international law but as a pointer to the ways in which the role of the judiciary will change once the Human Rights Act enters into force next year. In this country, unlike the United States, a judge's political views have been accepted as his private business. Because the Act will greatly enlarge the powers of the courts, that is unlikely to continue. Judges trained in a tradition which requires them to interpret laws on the basis of precedent, but not to challenge them, will be called to judge the compatibility of Acts of Parliament with the broadbrush European Convention on Human Rights which the Act incorporates. They will be confronted, in the Lord Chancellor's words, with legal choices which offer immense scope for political and philosophical disagreement. The political views of individual judges are bound to come under scrutiny. At the least, more sensitivity about resigning from cases will be required than Lord Hoffmann has shown. That will not be all. The more power shifts from Parliament to the courts, the stronger will be demands for public vetting of judicial appointments—and that could further politicise the judiciary. This is the least of Mr Straw's worries today; but the *Pinochet* case illuminates legal minefields ahead'.: 'Straw and the Law' (Leader), *The Times*, 8 December 1998.

[13] 'I don't think you should pigeonhole people and demand to know their values in order to decide whether to appoint them. In relation to Pinochet you could ask [candidates]: "do you

ultimately untenable position and it may reflect Lord Steyn's point that the Chancellor's position represents more an urge to protect his own office rather than an ideal political solution. In short, the need for a fundamental rethink of the Constitution remains essential. Some of the wilder claims for reform have been abandoned. It may well be, however, that the flirtation by some of the Liberal Democrats in the early 1990s with an importation of the separation of powers may have been not only unrealistic but unhelpful.[14]

The Judiciary

This book has recorded the various changes in the outlook of the judges. When contrasted with Jowitt and Simonds, Lord Browne-Wilkinson, senior Law Lord until 2000, typifies the change in the judicial world. In developing the common law he addressed the creative role of the judges and the personal element in legal rationalisation inevitable in every decision. He has discussed the creative role in interpreting statutes and contracts. He has made it clear that the Human Rights Act requires moral and social choices. As if to underline the change of approach that Browne-Wilkinson embodied, as 2001 drew to a close, the House of Lords decided cases which emphasised the public roles it was by then occupying, so very different from the 1950s. In the *Pretty* case the House of Lords discussed the most intimate details of assisted suicide, in the end concluding that the Director of Public Prosecutions was entitled to refuse to give an undertaking that the husband would not be prosecuted if he assisted in the voluntary euthanasia of his wife.[15] It also reinstated judgment against Dame Shirley Porter for gerrymandering while leader of the Westminster Council, describing her behaviour as 'disgraceful', 'dishonest' and 'corrupt'. Whereas the Court of Appeal had allowed her appeal apparently because that was the way politicians behaved, Lord Scott (of Arms to Iraq fame) warned of the dangers of political corruption which 'feeds upon democratic institutions from within'.[16] *Pretty* and Shirley Porter provided further illustrations, if any were needed, that at least some of the moral and political issues, traditionally dealt with by the House of Commons, had migrated to the courts.

---

share the values of the three in the majority or the two in the minority?" I see no advantage to be gained from that. Judges should be appointed on their merits as lawyers'.: 'Former Star of the Bar Papers Over the Last Cracks In His Image'. *The Financial Times*, 7 December 1998.

[14] Indeed, Lord Lester has recently made clear he no longer supports a separation of powers in the American sense. See House of Lords Debate on the Separation of Powers, *Hansard* HL Deb, vol 597, col 710 *et seq* (17 February 1999).

[15] *R (ex p Pretty) v DPP* [2002] 1 All ER 1.

[16] '"Homes For Votes" Brings Down Porter' *The Financial Times*, 14 December 2001.

The political landscape and constitutional development have facilitated such changes. There has been what may well be seen as a revolution in the self-perception of the judiciary, although without the benefit which the American Constitution enjoys of a sophisticated literature on judicial restraint and judicial activism, analysing the inherent conflict between judicial powers and the democratic model. While certainly the judges began modestly aggrandizing their positions and styles in the 1960s and 1970s, the change became more obvious when consensus politics began to evaporate after 1979. The judges took on greater prominence after the collapse of serious opposition in the early 1980s. The more presidential style of Mrs Thatcher and the declining importance of Parliament and other institutions were factors in making judges, as protectors of the Constitution, more important. While the House of Commons regained some initiatives under John Major's ill-fated administration, the massive Labour landslides in 1997 and 2001 meant that Tony Blair was able to emulate Mrs Thatcher's presidential style. The judges could be needed again as a counter-weight to the elected dictatorship, for as Lord Bingham, the senior Law Lord, has put it: 'the courts tend to be most assertive, active and creative when political organs of the state are least effective'.[17]

The massive Labour landslide in 2001, so the political commentators tell us, may mean ten further years of Labour rule. The public spectacle of the Conservative efforts to find a replacement for William Hague may well have confirmed that prediction. Their choice of Iain Duncan Smith was thought by many to be as ill-fated as Labour's choice of Michael Foot after the 1979 defeat. The House of Lords will presumably now be totally reformed and will perhaps acquire additional influence owing to the declining importance of the House of Commons and the arrival of an elected element. Regional government could well come to England together with further devolution. Additional investment in health and education could mean a greater role for the private sector. While such changes may well come with Labour, the different political landscape could have implications for the reform—or some would see even possible abolition—of the Monarchy,[18] the absorption of Northern Ireland in Eire[19] and perhaps even, if the Scots can wean themselves away from the Barnett formula and overrepresentation in the British Cabinet, the total independence of Scotland.[20] Having started a constitutional revolution without a clear vision of the ultimate purpose

---

[17] J Rozenberg, 'Lords Need Common Touch' *The Daily Telegraph*, 17 April 2001.
[18] The problem is that the proposed alternatives to Monarchy leave much to be desired.
[19] See P Mandelson, 'The Future of Ireland' *GQ*, January 2002.
[20] For which the Supreme Court of Canada has now produced an excellent precedent. *Reference re Secession of Quebec* [1998] 2 SCR 217. See WJ Newman, *The Quebec Secession Reference* (York University, Ontario, 1999).

or goals, virtually anything is possible. What is already clear is that it is becoming slowly more accurate to describe Britain as a constitutional democracy rather than a parliamentary democracy.

In this atmosphere the judges are likely to have far more power and will have to develop appropriate political strategies. It is here that judicial restraint and judicial activism become most significant. As English judges—and those who observe them—consider the alternatives, history and comparative studies may shed light. Some overseas observers look forward to the English judges becoming much more activist and more powerful in the Constitution. With so much constitutional change and so little sense of what New Labour's goals for the Constitution are, with the power of the House of Commons in decline, together with that of the Civil Service as it becomes diluted with political advisers, some greater role for the judiciary is probably inevitable. Yet this may be the very moment when the judiciary may find it is most in need of caution and humility.

Certainly it is a time when, having admitted their policy-making role, especially in the final court of appeal, judges need to be reminded of the virtues of judicial restraint. During the period of high formalism, there was no need for this; indeed the judges needed to be taught the virtues of judicial activism. In the United States, there is a sophisticated literature ranging from Black and Rostow through Hart to Wechler and Bickel, justifying Hamilton's claim of the 'least dangerous branch'. There is, however, in the House of Lords, especially among judges like Lords Hoffmann and Steyn, an evolving sense of the jurisprudential and political role of the judiciary. As the power of the judiciary becomes more obvious, a literature and understanding of the judicial role will become essential.

Strangely enough, a restatement of the constitutional advantages of a balance of powers, and particularly the benefits of a subsidiary role for the courts in a system of responsible government or parliamentary democracy has come from an unlikely source. Bruce Ackerman of Yale, an iconoclastic American constitutional lawyer, has produced what is de facto, an apologia for the balance of powers and a limited role for the judiciary in responsible government an article in the *Harvard Law Review*.[21] The paucity of English rationalisation for the modern role of the judiciary in a system of responsible government gives this work considerable significance. The work may even stimulate a domestic literature.

---

[21] B Ackerman, 'The New Separation of Powers' (2000) 113 *Harvard Law Review* 633. Calling for 'constrained parliamentarianism' Ackerman argues that a range of issues, from democracy itself to human rights are better served by responsible government and a constitutional court, as a checking court, than they are by an independently elected president and a Supreme Court. He argues that the parliamentary model would have handled the impeachment of President Clinton far more effectively than the US system. See B Ackerman, 'Revolution on a Human Scale' (1999) 108 *Yale Law Journal* 2279 at 2340–47.

Parables from Abroad

Lawyers tend to admire a courageous bench and there is much to admire, whether it is the bench in Zimbabwe standing up to President Mugabe—until he packed it in a move worthy of James II[22]—or the revival of the judiciary in Malaysia,[23] which has begun forcing Prime Minister Mahathir to abide by the rule of law in that country; and we can only applaud the courage of the South African courts in ordering the State to provide drugs for Aids victims despite the iconoclastic medical views of President Mbeki.[24] Yet as one moves from the courageous to the politically wise, it is easy to see how a jurisdiction, based on the English model of judiciary, can get itself into trouble and judicial courage can easily turn to judicial humiliation. Such, as we have seen, was the case in Hong Kong.[25] Yet history is littered with examples of judicial hubris ending in judicial tears. When, in the Federalist period at the beginning of the nineteenth century, American state judges (like their Federal brethren led by Chief Justice Marshall) were believed by the electors to have become too powerful, the winds of Jacksonian Democracy blew, ending with the New York State Constitutional Convention of 1846, providing for the election of judges in that State. It was a trend that swept the nation, and one which still strikes fear into the heart of the English judiciary, and is distasteful to the English of most political stripes.

Yet there is a far more recent cautionary tale. The judicial activism of the Supreme Court of Israel is well known. We have already seen that it led to a totally restructured Judicial Appointment Committee which contains politicians. In the 1990s, however, especially under the leadership of

[22] Mugabe forced out the Chief Justice (see AR Gubbay, 'Judicial Independence in Zimbabwe' *New Law Journal*, 9 March 2001, 357) and then packed the bench, with the new tame Chief Justice picking panels favourable to Mugabe. See also 'Mugabe Regime Prepares to Axe White Judges' *Guardian*, 5 June 2000; and also 'Mugabe's Judges Back Seizure of White Farms' *The Daily Telegraph*, 3 October 2001. The new Chief Justice, Godfrey Chidyausiku, then expanded the Supreme Court from 5 to 8, adding Mugabe supporters. 'Harare Court Reverses Farms Ruling', *The Financial Times*, 3 October 2001.
[23] 'Judicial Bravery Startles Malaysia' *International Herald Tribune*, 2 July 2001. The change came with the new Chief Justice, Mohammed Dsaiddin Abdullah. See also 'Mahathir's Anniversary Blues' *The Economist*, 14 July 2001.
[24] 'Pretoria Court Orders Treatment For HIV Babies' *The Financial Times*, 16 December 2001. This decision has now been provisionally approved by the Consitutional Court and forced the Government into a more responsible position.
[25] The ongoing saga of the Hong Kong Final Court of Appeals included another right of abode case. On this occasion, the National People's Congress in Beijing did not intervene. Martin Lee SC, QC, leader of the Democratic Party, attributed the non-intervention to the Beijing leadership's increased self-confidence. 'What if they don't feel confident any more? We are at the mercy of Beijing through the chief puppet (Mr Tung). That is the worrying thing'. 'One Country, How Many Systems?' *The Economist*, 4 August 2001. See also, 'Hong Kong Reasserts Authority' *International Herald Tribune*, 21/22 July 2001.

Mr Justice Barak, President of the Supreme Court, the two Basic Laws of 1992 were translated into something akin to a written Constitution. As Justice Barak put it: 'Everything is justiciable'. It was a powerful aphrodisiac. The Barak court became involved in challenges to acts of torture by the security forces and deporting political prisoners, as well as ruling on the highly contentious privileges of orthodox Jews. In all of these the Barak court was seen as favouring the liberal solution. The rhetoric overheated and early in 2001 a resolution was accepted by the Knesset that there should be a Constitutional Court to hear appeals from the Supreme Court. It would be composed of three judges of the Supreme Court, two Rabbinical appeal court judges, one Sharia court judge, one judge from the new immigrant groups and four academics, none of whom might be a lawyer, but could be a sociologist, historian, political scientist or philosopher. While the resolution may not become law, it is attractive to the Orthodox groups, the Arab parties (there is currently no Arab on the Supreme Court) and immigrant groups who tend to be militant conservatives.[26] These parables—if so they be—may have been absorbed by the English judges.

The Need for a Supreme Court

By far and away the most dramatic extension of judicial power by New Labour was the incorporation of the European Convention on Human Rights by the Human Rights Act. As with devolution cases, the Human Rights Act, even during a period when it is being construed narrowly, is a powerful reminder that the House of Lords is not only a Supreme Court but a Constitutional Court. How should this be recognised? Within the last decade the previous generation of Lords of Appeal shied away from a separate building, emphasised they are not regular judges and lobbied to remain in the legislature. As New Labour began the second stage of reform of the House of Lords, Lord Irvine defended the retention of the Law Lords in a partially elected House on the ground that 'in this country we have never applied the doctrine of the separation of powers because we are pragmatists, not purists'.[27] The Bingham-Steyn case for a Supreme Court, well

---

[26] S Shetreet, 'The Critical Challenge of Judicial Independence in Israel' in PH Russell and DM O'Brien (eds), *Judicial Independence in the Age of Democracy* (Virginia, 2001) 233. See also S Shetreet, *Between Three Branches of Government: The Balance of Rights in the Matter of Religion* (The Floershinider Institute for Policy Studies, Jerusalem, 2000) *passim*.
[27] *Hansard* HL Deb, vol 632, cols 299–302 (8 November 2001); cf Lord Irvine's announcement that the British Constitution 'is based firmly in the separation of powers': *Hansard* HL Deb, vol 572, col 1254 (5 June 1996).

resourced with a building of its own, seems unanswerable.[28] While there may be a case for putting retired Law Lords in the legislative manifestation of the House of Lords, the idea of having active judges sitting in what is, at best, to be a partially elected House is unacceptable, even under the balance of powers.

So, too, the use of judges for other than factual committees of inquiry should be curtailed or abandoned. In the case of Nolan and Scott, as well as in the case of Dame Elizabeth Filkin, the Parliamentary Commissioner, the Houses of Parliament have made it clear that they are not interested in outsiders reviewing their ethics or practices. The corollary of that is that they must be prepared to sanction themselves, as they did in the Marconi and Hoare inquiries and as does Congress in the United States. For the general public this may be less than satisfactory, but it is constitutionally inappropriate for judges (or civil servants) to be used and then abused. As Lord Woolf said in 1996, such enquiries represent 'a role the judiciary do not seek but has been thrust upon them'.[29] The problem for Government is who to use apart from the judges for commissions and inquiries. New Labour's favourites in the rebranding of Britain—successful entrepreneurs (known to the Victorians as the nouveaux riches), luvvies (as members of the entertainment industries had become known), journalists and footballers—in general turned out to have defects not normally present in judges, dull as the judiciary may otherwise be.

Even with a Supreme Court, there are still other issues to be solved. The future of the Judicial Committee of the Privy Council will largely solve itself when, as seems inevitable, General Medical Council and other professional matters are handed to the High Court, and when New Zealand terminates appeals as its Government says it will—and when the West Indian nations complete their proposed Court of Appeal. Will Scotland and Northern Ireland accept whatever replaces the House of Lords as a final court for devolution and other matters? If there is a Supreme Court for the whole UK, it will require legislation not only in Westminster but in Edinburgh and Stormont. What will happen to the House of Lords' panel system? A 'serious' final court of appeal, ultimately and inevitably, needs to sit *in banc*. The Bingham argument that having *in banc* hearings would advertise political and policy differences and encourage hearings on the appointment of Law Lords is an argument comprehensible only by the establishment mind. It is these diverse views that make the panel system a

---

[28] R Cornes, 'Time for a home of their own?' *New Law Journal*, 18 January 2002, 63; See T Bingham, 'A New Supreme Court for the United Kingdom' (Constitution Unit Lecture, UCL, 1 May 2002).

[29] *Hansard* HL Deb, vol 572, col 1272 (5 June, 1996).

lottery, especially where policy issues are most obvious in an appeal.[30] To achieve *in banc* hearings, however, would require the curbing of the orality of proceedings before such final court. That would mean a clash with the powerful vested interest of the Bar which would oppose more of the appeal process being handled on paper. It would also mean that the new Supreme Court would have to have control over its docket. The Supreme Court, or its appeal committee, would have to be the arbiter of which cases would be heard. While New Labour likes to claim a willingness to address hard issues, it is also sufficiently image-conscious that it would probably back off from such show-downs.

There are other complex issues. Whether the new institution is called the Supreme Court or the Constitutional Court, it will not fulfil its purpose if its judges replicate the House of Lords, staffed as it is by judges, many of them admirable, but also some of them seeking a respite from, or reward for, the rigours of the Court of Appeal. It is here that the British public would have their greatest qualms. A final court, presumably one that dealt with both public and private law, would need to be composed in a significantly different way from the current House of Lords. There would of course be places for former Lords Justice of Appeal from the Court of Appeal. To have it totally staffed in this way, however, would be a disaster. As a distinguished American professor of constitutional law said recently of the current Supreme Court of the United States: 'we have never had a court with more judicial experience [eight of the nine judges held prior judicial office] and we have never had a worse Supreme Court'. *Brown v*

---

[30] On the thorny issue of whether the Human Rights Act protects individuals retroactively, the House of Lords, by failing to sit *in banc*, has come close to making nonsense of consistency. A 3–2 decision in *R v DPP, ex p Kebiline* [2000] 2 AC 326 went one way; the 3–2 decision in June 2001, *R v Lambert* [2001] 3 All ER 577 another, while in November 2001, again 3–2, the House of Lords came close to overruling a decision given five months earlier: *R v Kawsal* (No 2) [2002] 1 All ER 257. The dilemma was best put by Lord Lloyd (at 263): 'In my opinion the only satisfactory way of resolving the present conflict of judicial opinion at the highest level would be to require the present appeal to be reargued before a panel of seven Law Lords. That is the traditional way in which problems of this kind are dealt with'. Lord Lloyd, a graduate of the Harvard Law School, invoked two US precedents. In *Planned Parenthood of Southeastern Pennsylvania v Casey*, 505 US 833, 854 (1992), O'Connor, Kennedy and Souter JJ said: '... no judicial system could do society's work if it eyed each issue afresh in every case that raised it ... Indeed, the very concept of the rule of law underlying our own Constitution requires such continuity over time that a respect for precedent is, by definition, indispensable'. In *Mitchell v WT Grant & Co*, 416 US 600, 610 (1974), Mr Justice Stewart had said: 'A basic change in the law upon a ground no firmer than a change in our membership invites the popular misconception that this institution is little different from the two political branches of government. No misconception could do more lasting injury to this court and to the system of law which it is our abiding mission to serve'.

Board of Education[31], in 1956, striking down segregation in the schools, was decided by nine Justices, none of whom had judicial experience before sitting on the Supreme Court. The unwise 2001 decision in *Bush v Gore*[32] was the product of nine Justices, eight of whom had prior judicial experience before being appointed to the Supreme Court. There will be a need for judges with a broader expertise, including that of politics[33] when the English (or British) supreme court is finally established.

As suggested, British commentators, even appreciating the important political work of such a court—human rights, administrative law, labour decisions, devolution, tax, international law—will feel nervous. They might admit that Dilhorne, Radcliffe, Reid, Scarman, and Somervell benefited from politics and public service, but could they be replicated? The answer is almost certainly 'Yes'.[34] In a generation now passing beyond the age limit, one can think of Lord Alexander of Weedon, Lord Lester and Lord Goodhart. Among the rising political figures one might name Lord Williams of Mostyn, Lord Kingsland, Lord Falconer, Lord Goldsmith, and Baroness Scotland.[35] This is merely a cull of those currently ennobled, but in the House of Commons there are others and outside Parliament still more. One could, for instance, think of leading public law silks like Michael Beloff and David Pannick who would obviously be strong candidates for a final appeal court. All would grace a Supreme Court. What is needed now is leadership in New Labour to produce the logical culmination to the remarkable constitutional changes over the last five years. A Supreme Court—and its related issues—ought to be the central plank in the constitutional settlement.

---

[31] 347 US 483 (1955).

[32] 531 US 98 (2001).

[33] In 1956 a quarter of all the senior judiciary had either been MPs or parliamentary candidates. Today, none of the English judges has. The Scottish judges normally include some who have had political experience and they normally make the better appeal judges.

[34] Lord Reid put it this way: 'If the law is to keep in step with movements of public opinion, then the judges must know how ordinary people of all grades of society think and live. You cannot get that from books or courses of study. You must have mixed with all kinds of people and get to know them. If you only listen to those who have hit the headlines you get quite the wrong impression. If we are to remain a democratic people those who try to be guided by public opinion must go to the grass roots. That is why it is so valuable for a judge to have given public service of some kind in his earlier days'. JSC Reid, 'The Judge as Law Maker' (1972) 12 *Journal of the Society of the Public Teachers of Law* 22, 27.

[35] On the significance of having women judges in the final court of appeal, see the arguments of AH Young, 'Feminism, Pluralism and Administrative Law' in M Taggart (ed), *The Province of Administrative Law* (Oxford, 1997) 331, especially at 349–56.

11

Post Script:
The Future is the Present

AS WE LEFT the story in the Spring of 2002, it looked as if the establishment of a Supreme Court was, in the long term, inevitable and the case for a Judicial Appointments Commission was becoming daily stronger. The Labour government had come to power in 1997 with a commitment to constitutional reform and joined-up government. New Labour has, as we saw, produced significant constitutional change: devolution to Scotland and Wales, the Human Rights Act, partial reform of the House of Lords, elected Mayors, a Freedom of Information Act, an Electoral Commission and more. Joined up it was not. Nothing better illustrated this than the botched Cabinet reshuffle on June 12, 2003. On that day, Downing Street announced the resignation (or sacking) of Lord Irvine, the Lord Chancellor since 1997[1], and the abolition—allegedly after 800 years—of his post, and, in its place, the establishment of a Department of Constitutional Affairs, the creation of a Supreme Court, and a Judicial Appointments Commission.[2]

---

[1] Baroness Kennedy, a Labour peer, explained it in these terms: 'It must have been a source of great distress to a Prime Minister who had known that Lord Chancellor (Irvine) so intimately and who had him as a mentor and pupil master. It must have felt like an act of patricide. It may be that, like many an employer, we would want to say that the person was now redundant because this post was abolished, rather than that one was sacking them.' Parl Deb , HL, Vol 657, col 1280 (12 Feb 2004). Baroness Kennedy is frequently off-message. She described David Blunkett's plans for terrorism trials 'an affront to the rule of law'. She compared the former Home Secretary to Robert Mugabe. 'He really is a shameless authoritarian'. *The Times*, Feb 3, 2004. The latter view was shared by David Pannick Q.C., 'Asylum: an abuse of power that would embarrass even Mugabe', *The Times: Law*, Feb 24, 2004. See also Helena Kennedy 'A good brand: is that all the Lord Chancellor is?' *Ibid*.

[2] As a former Editor of *The Times* put it: 'Nothing has been worse handled by the Prime Minister than his judicial reforms. He did not consult the law lords; he did not consult the Lord Chief Justice; he could not get the past Lord Chancellor's agreement; he did not perform his constitutional duty to tell the Queen. He mixed up the most important judicial reforms in a century with a panic reshuffle of his Cabinet. He thought he had abolished the Office of Lord Chancellor, which he did not have the power to do'. Lord Rees-Mogg, 'The supreme court: isn't there some law against it?', *The Times*, Aug 4, 2003.

A Tricky Plot

Piecing together that rather bizarre story is not easy.[3] The Prime Minister, although a barrister, had scant interest in constitutional reform. Despite the rhetoric, his historic sense of the constitution was limited. The bases of his actions were political, not comprehensive. As Robert Hazell has pointed out,[4] in most Cabinets there is potential for conflict between the civil libertarians and the forces of law and order. The decline in Cabinet Government and the move towards a presidential style probably highlighted the tensions[5], most obviously, between David Blunkett, the Home Secretary and Derry Irvine, the Lord Chancellor.

Derry Irvine was slowly becoming dispensable. In the first Labour government (1997–2001), Blair had deferred to him even as Irvine committed a series of political blunders over wallpaper, his claims of similarities to Cardinal Wolsey, and his solicitation of political contributions from members of the bar. By the time of the Second Labour Administration, Irvine was seen as less of a critical player. Alastair Campbell, the all-powerful press officer in No 10—some even saw him more as deputy Prime Minister—forbad Irvine to speak in the press. In the meantime, the Prime Minister increasingly relied on Charles Falconer—his old flatmate and colleague at the bar—for legal advice.[6] Falconer was not as powerful an intellect as Irvine, as is evident from the Consultation Papers on constitutional reform, but was a good advocate and showed he was far better adapted to politics than Irvine, after Falconer had been made a peer and Solicitor-General in 1997. Indeed, Falconer was rather like the traditional wooden doll; he might be pushed down, but immediately bounced back. That was no bad qualification for politics; his good nature and natural sense of advocacy stood him in even better stead.[7]

The friction between the law and order factions and the civil libertarian wing was primarily over immigration, crime and punishment. When Irvine supported the Lord Chief Justice over his view that first-time burglars should not be sent to prison, it not only infuriated Blunkett (he thought Irvine a 'buffoon'), it irritated Blair and his staff—especially Andrew Adonis and Jeremy Heywood. This time Blunkett was supported by the new junior minister in the Home Office, Charles Falconer. When Blunkett

---

[3] For the political background, I have relied on Anthony Seldon, *Blair* (London, 2004) 560–64 and Stephen Pollard, *David Blunkett* (2004) 284–89.
[4] e.g. The Select Committee on the Constitution Bill, House of Lords, *Evidence*, Q 182, 2004.
[5] Peter Oborne and Simon Walters, *Alastair Campbell* (2004) passim.
[6] Seldon, *Blair*, above n 3, chap 16.
[7] Lord Richard, Chair of the Select Committee, referred to 'his flexibility and natural charm'. Parl Deb, HL, Vol 663, col 1139 (Jul 13, 2004) See also Frances Gibb, 'The Cheerful chappie who rolls on undeflated', *The Times*, Jun 22, 2004.

demanded tougher sentencing, Falconer told his old profession 'it is right that Parliament should set the framework'. Over issues such as the introduction of previous convictions and altering the double jeopardy rule, the battles were between Lord Chancellor Irvine and the Attorney-General, Lord Goldsmith, on the one side, and Blunkett and Falconer on the other. Blair had several times to intervene in the battles between Blunkett and Irvine.

Blair was further alienated from Irvine when the Lord Chancellor—quite rightly in the view of most lawyers—whipped up the Senior Law Lord and the Lord Chief Justice to oppose the scheme—favoured by Blair—to put the administration of the courts under the Home Office. (Irvine's counter-proposal was to put criminal law under the Lord Chancellor's Department). Counselled by Adonis and Heywood, Blair had begun to think not only of replacing the progressively more difficult Irvine, who was also becoming vulnerable because of his increasingly iconoclastic judicial appointments, but to use the opportunity to make significant constitutional changes. A series of meetings between Blair and Irvine, early in June 2003, made it clear that Irvine was not interested in significant reform of his office or department and favoured, if anything, a 'rights' department. Blair favoured a more simplistic division between the judges and politics. It was a B-grade student's interpretation of the separation of powers. It was a simplistic notion that was to permeate the Consultation Papers; it was, however, scarcely a notion which caught the nuances and historical influences on the British constitution.

In the old days, such complex and sensitive ideas would have been honed and developed by a Cabinet Committee. Under the more presidential system that characterized the Blair years, and were later questioned by Lord Butler, the ideas were developed by the staff at No 10. Perhaps the staff feared that wider consultation would ensure that the proposed changes would not be radical. (In this sense the June announcement may have been more calculated than some commentators assumed.) All of these developments, however, were going on while the primary energy of the Prime Minister was absorbed by Iraq, and was further muddied by Blair's attempt to create a Minister for Europe—opposed by the Foreign Office—and hiving off criminal law from the Home Office to a new Ministry of Justice—opposed by Blunkett. At the same time, devolution, which had also been introduced without sufficient appreciation of its political and legal implications, was causing problems. The idea was floated that it would also be a good moment to abolish the posts of Secretary of State for Scotland and the Secretary of State for Wales. The idea of getting rid of these two posts and the Lord Chancellorship was agreed in No 10, but to say the implications of what was to happen to the functions of all three was not thought through would be an understatement. Few outside the Prime Minister's Office had been consulted. The episode gave the impression of being a most amateur affair.

Blair prevaricated, as he frequently did, with his strategy further confused by the decision of his Blairite Health Minister, Alan Milburn, to resign for personal reasons. It was a miserable week for Blair. He flew back from seeing President Chirac for the Cabinet Meeting of June 12, 2003, still without having had an opportunity of consulting widely, or even discussing the constitutional changes or their implications extensively. The Lord Chief Justice and Senior Law Lord were not consulted; nobody mentioned to the Queen that 'the keeper of her conscience' was about to be abolished. Even Lord Falconer was not consulted until the very morning of the Cabinet meeting and Lord Irvine got the news that afternoon when he was asked to stay behind after the Cabinet Meeting. The firing was believed to have come as a great shock to him.

Announcement and Implementation

The announcement of the changes was a shambles. Since nobody seemed to have realised that abolishing the Lord Chancellor would require legislation—his role was embodied in hundreds of statutes—or worked out how the loss of the Scottish and Welsh Secretaries would function, the Government appeared in embarrassing disarray. At first Falconer was announced as Secretary of State for Constitutional Affairs, as well as having the Scottish and Welsh portfolios. Within twenty-four hours, he accepted that he had to be Lord Chancellor as well, and the two other Secretariships were assigned to other Cabinet members. There was outrage after the announcement—especially in the House of Lords. The allegations were that the Government's real goal was to politicise the judiciary and destroy its independence.

It was a tribute to Charlie Falconer's charm and common sense that he managed to get the ship of state even marginally stabilised. Within a month a series of Consultation Papers[8] were published, outlining not only the end of the Lord Chancellorship, but a new Supreme Court with the law lords

---

[8]   The two most relevant for this analysis being *Constitutional Reform: a Supreme Court for the United Kingdom* CP 11/03 Jul 2003 and *Constitutional Reform: A New Way of Appointing Judges* CP 10/03 Jul 2003. A third paper was *Constitutional Reform: the future of Queen's Counsel*; a fourth, on the Lord Chancellorship, appeared in October: CP 13/03: *Constitutional Reform: reforming the office of the Lord Chancellor.* The document is not significant for this chapter. It is, however, a reminder that the Lord Chancellor's Office is, like the Smithsonian in the United States, 'the attic of the nation'. So much of the debris is the strange result of an established church and academic institutions seeking to be embraced by monarchy.

ceasing to sit in the legislature, together with a powerful Judicial Appointments Commission to choose the judiciary through a panel presented to the
Lord Chancellor. A later paper dealt with the rank of QC. The quality of
the consultation papers was not profound. Many of the constitutional
arguments were assumed; the jurisprudence was unsophisticated.

In the last months of 2003, the responses of the interested parties to the
Consultation Papers came thick and fast. For the profession—both barristers and solicitors—it seemed as if abolishing the rank of QC was foremost
in their minds.[9] The judges and the law lords delivered their responses. The
judges in the current Supreme Court—the High Court and the Court of
Appeal—were relatively calm. In their response they assumed the changes
would go through and wanted to make certain that things would be handled in a seemly way. They pushed for a statutory enactment of judicial
independence and a clear mandate for the Lord Chief Justice as head of the
Judiciary. They were conscious that the Heads of Division had played a significant role in the judicial appointments process and some judges looked
to a system in which neither Prime Minister nor Secretary of State was
involved; the Lord Chief Justice would nominate the new judge to the
Queen. Failing that, the judiciary would be heavily involved in the appointments process and the Secretary of State only nominally so. On the other
hand the majority of the judges apparently saw no problem with a Supreme
Court—indeed, reading between the lines there was an assumption that
this was something whose time had come.[10] On the other hand, the current
members of the House of Lords, the law lords, gave their own responses
and at least a majority were vigorously opposed to the changes, particularly
their ejection from the House of Lords.[11]

The Lord Chief Justice, too, was outspoken. The debate raged in the
press and in professional journals. The first serious breakthrough was the
Concordat between the Chief Justice and the Secretary of State. That was
agreed on January 26, 2004 and emphasised the boundaries between the
Secretary and Chief Justice. In particular, the Secretary/Lord Chancellor
would no longer be a judge and the leadership and discipline of the
Judiciary would pass to the Chief Justice who would become Head of the
Judiciary, with responsibility for administration and discipline. There was
also to be a statutory duty on the government to protect judicial independ-

---

[9] The rank now seems to have survived. 'Lawyers win fight to save QC rank', *The Times*, Feb
17, 2004.
[10] DCA, *Judges' Council Response to the Consultation Papers on Constitutional Reform*
(2003).
[11] House of Lords, *The Law Lords' response to the Government's consultation paper on Constitutional reform: a Supreme Court for the United Kingdom*, October 27, 2003. For a more
Conservative response, see Lord Hobhouse, *ibid*, November 7, 2003.

ence. There was even talk of a 'partnership' between government and judiciary[12]. Meanwhile the House of Commons Constitutional Affairs Committee had been taking evidence and producing a Report. It reported early in February 2004 urging caution and further consultation.[13] By this time, battle lines were being drawn in the Lords. Lord Kingsland, the shadow Conservative Lord Chancellor, suggested 'the real motive behind the Government's proposed Bill . . . is to weaken the judicial arm of the constitution.'[14]

The post of Lord Chancellor, which for decades had seemed to some a source of ridicule, suddenly began to take on mystical qualities, especially for the law lords and conservative politicians.[15] At this stage David Blunkett, frequently willing to irritate the judges as if they were aliens in the democratic process,[16] introduced his Immigration Bill, taking away the right of appeal to the judges in certain situations. Meanwhile the government announced plans to eject the last 92 hereditary peers, although its attempts to reform the House of Lords underlined New Labour's ability to bring confusion and lack of coherence to constitutional reform. Overall these developments, especially the Immigration Bill, appeared to encourage the Lord Chief Justice to doubt the whole proposed constitutional experiment in a Delphic public lecture in Cambridge on March 2nd.[17] The events

---

[12] See Parl Deb, HL, Vol 657, col 12 (26 Jan 2004). The Concordat is reproduced in the House of Lords, Select Committee on the Constitution Bill, Report, Appendix 6.

[13] House of Commons, Constitutional Affairs Committee, *Judicial Appointments and a Supreme Court* (court of final appeal), HC 48–1, 10 Feb, 2004. It took evidence from November 2003 to January 2004. It reported on February 10, 2004. Among other things, it concluded 'The Constitutional Reform Bill is a clear candidate for examination in draft . . . The consultation process has been too short and the legislative timetable is too restrictive to deal with changes which are so far reaching in their effect. The reason for haste seems to be primarily political.' *Ibid*, paras 188, 193.

[14] HL, Deb, Vol 657 col 929 (Feb 9, 2004).

[15] See the view of one law lord, Lord Millett: 'The Secretary of State in future, whatever he may be at the moment, is likely to be a middle-ranking, ambitious, career politician, with hopes of attaining yet higher office, dependent on the patronage of the Prime Minster and certainly subject to his discretion. Moreover, he can be removed easily and at a moment's notice, without causing the kind of outrage which greeted the announcement last June.' HL Deb Vol 657, col 1295 (Feb 12, 2004).

[16] Blunkett was reported as saying, 'what I don't understand is the assertion . . . that somehow there is the right of judges to be engaged in perpetual checking and overturning processes which a democratically elected parliament lays down. The judges are saying that they want to remain in the political debate. They are opposed to us removing them from the House of Lords. They want a supreme court which has the right to overturn the will of parliament.' Roy Hattersley, 'Home Truths', *The Observer*, Mar 7, 2004. For the reaction to Blunkett's demands for getting the judges out of asylum cases, see Jean Eaglesham, 'Blunkett's brinksmanship wins the day', *Financial Times*, Mar 5, 2004; Bob Shearwood, 'uneasy truce shattered as fears grow on asylum bill', *ibid*; Leader, 'Crying Woolf', *id*; Ministers are breaking the law', *The Times*, Mar 4, 2004; Joshua Rosenberg, 'The 'unthinkable' is coming true, *The Times*, Mar 4, 2004; 'Woolf fury at asylum curb on the courts', *ibid*.

[17] Dept of Constitutional Affairs, Lord Woolf, 'The Rule of Law and a Change in the Constitution', Cambridge University, Mar 2, 2004. He feared the Department of Constitutional

certainly left vague the question of who was the guardian of legal values in the legislative process.[18]

Meanwhile the Constitutional Reform Bill had been finally introduced into the Lords.[19] The debates were the traditional ones about the mysterious powers of the Lord Chancellor and the independence of the judiciary. While the Chief Justice—and the Liberal Democrats—were by then supporting the government's reforms, Lord Lloyd of Berwick, a law lord who was about to retire, called for the Bill to be referred to a Select Committee, arguing, among other things, that the House of Commons Constitutional Affairs Committee had called for further consultation. The debate on his motion came before a packed House of Lords on Monday, March 8. By the margin of 33 votes, the Bill was sent to a Select Committee, a rare parliamentary move.[20]

During the long evening of March 8th, political fortunes fluctuated. After the Lord Chief Justice spoke in favour of the Bill the government thought it would win. It was not to be. There were by then too many forces ranged against change. Lord McCluskey railed against Montesquieu and the separation of powers and gloried in the fact that law lords sometimes voted against the government.[21] On the role of the law lords there was concern that 'the judges themselves will lose a forum in which to defend the independence of the judiciary and fight measures which might damage the

---

Affairs would become a subsidiary of the Home Office. He opined that the Supreme Court would not be a 'real' Supreme Court apparently because it did not have the right to strike down statutes. 'Among the Supreme Courts of the world, our Supreme Court will, because of its more limited role, be a poor relation. We are exchanging a first class Final Court of Appeal for a Second Class Supreme Court.' He also patronised the Lord Chancellor by referring to Falconer as a 'cheerful chappie'. The Times commented that Lord Woolf 'cannot quite make up his mind whether he is a liberal reformer or the shop steward for the only trade union in the country whose members wear wigs and not hard hats or cloth caps'. 'Stage Two or Square One', *The Times*, Mar 10, 2004.

Woolf's talk of a second class Supreme Court obviously irritated Lord Bingham. The latter said in a public lecture: 'to describe a supreme court as 'second class' because it lacks the power to annul primary legislation is to disparage the principle of parliamentary sovereignty, which (subject to appropriate checks and balances) I would not wish to do.' 'At last judges find agreement.' *Daily Telegraph*, Mar 25, 2004. And see Roy Hattersley, 'Justice and the Enemies', *The Observer*, Mar 14, 2004. See too 'Scales of Justice', *The Times*, Mar 5, 2004.

[18] Robert Hazell, 'Who is the guardian of legal values in the legislative process: Parliament or the Executive?' (2004) *Public Law*, 495.

[19] Constitutional Reform Bill, HL Bill 30, 2004.

[20] 'Labour's Constitutional Mess', *The Economist*, Mar 13, 2004. Lord Hoffman, a Lord of Appeal, voted for the Lloyd motion. Hoffman had already said, in an earlier debate: 'It is sad that a great constitutional change should be adopted as a quick fix for personal squabbles in the Cabinet'. Parl Deb, HL, Vol 657, col 1259 (Feb 12, 2004). 'Labour vows to defeat Lords in power struggle', *The Times*, Mar 8, 2004; Leader, 'Day of Judgment', *The Guardian*, Mar 8, 2004; 'Lords Vote: 'a clash of wills'', *ibid*; 'Minister vows to force through law for supreme court', *The Times*, Feb 26, 2004.

[21] HL Deb, Vol 658, cols 1029–31 (Mar 8, 2004).

administration of justice. . .'[22]. Rather surprisingly the new system of appointing judges caused surprising little conflict, probably because the Concordat had ensured there would not be a majority of laymen on the Commission. There was surprisingly little disagreement over the Concordat and the issue of the independence of the judiciary. The debates and tension centred on the abolition of the Lord Chancellor, the establishment of a Supreme Court and the removal of the law lords from the legislature.

The hope of at least some of the opponents was that the vote to refer the Bill to a Select Committee would kill it. The Government talked of pushing the Bill through the Commons and then invoking the Parliament Act. That Act, resulting from the constitutional crisis of 1911, makes it possible for a Bill to become law without being passed by the Lords.[23] The truth was that that procedure was not available since this Bill had been introduced in the Lords. Passions were, however, running high. Baroness Amos, Labour leader in the Lords, said after the vote: 'We have witnessed an act of political opportunism by Conservative peers. Make no mistake, tonight's events have nothing to do with constitutional principle—and everything to do with political opportunism'. The Conservative leader, Lord Strathclyde, responded: 'Parliament has spoken. The government must now listen'. The proverbial gage had been thrown down.[24] The Lords, relying on the sense of increased legitimacy, with most of the hereditaries gone, as well as the political discontent flowing from the Iraq War, were in the mood for a fight. In so many ways, it was all ironic. By the beginning of the twenty-first century parliamentary sovereignty effectively lay in the House of Commons. The House of Lords, like the judges, were derogations from real parliamentary sovereignty. Such inconsistency did not deter the Lords' opposition.

In fact the Bill's defeat led to further concessions by the government—both in the Bill and in the political scene generally. In the Bill, for instance, the government gradually backed away from allowing the Secretary of State for Constitutional Affairs serious discretion in the appointment of judges—even for the Supreme Court. The worst he could do would be to ask for a new name. The Judicial Appointments Commission moved towards being an appointing body rather than a recommending one. Meanwhile, for the remainder of the then current Session, Prime Minister Tony Blair agreed to give up plans to axe the last 92 hereditaries, while David Blunkett agreed to restore to the courts the right to review

---

[22] Per Lord Waddington, *ibid*, cols 1034–35.
[23] E.g. Peter Hain, 'Stage two or Square One', *The Times*, Mar 10, 2004.
[24] 'Angry lords derail legal reform bill', *The Guardian*, Mar 9, 2004.

proceedings under his new Immigration Act.[25] In return, the Conservatives agreed to see that the work of the Select Committee was completed by June 2004—and each of the parties nominated some of their heavyweights to that Committee.[26] The pledge was honoured, the Committee was well chaired by Labour's Lord Richard,[27] and the Report of the Select Committee appeared on July 3, 2004. It was a Report which clarified rather than solved disagreements; but it was a useful legislative road map. New debates began that very month—with the assumption that they would restart in September 2004[28] and the government still hoped to have an Act by March 2005.

It is impossible to write about the Constitutional Reform Bill and its stormy passage in the Lords, without writing about the background political atmosphere. No doubt part of the opposition to the Bill was based on genuine concerns about the changes. Yet a wider political concern pervaded so much of the debate. Seen from the outside, Tony Blair seemed all powerful. Yet he was more admired outside the party than inside. He was dis-

---

[25] After a threat by Lord Irvine to oppose the Bill in the Lords. 'Irvine will attack new asylum bill', *Sunday Telegraph*, Mar 14, 2004. Lord Woolf claimed the proposal violated the Rule of Law. 'Profile: Lord Woolf', *Daily Telegraph*, Mar 7, 2004.

[26] The Conservatives were led by Lord Howe of Aberavon, a major and much respected player. He had served as Solicitor-General, Chancellor of the Exchequer, Foreign Secretary and Deputy Prime Minister. He had been seriously considered as Lord Chancellor in 1987. He was sceptical of change but not adverse to it. With Lord Howe were the Conservative shadow Lord Chancellor, Lord Kingsland, a liberal on reforming the Constitution; and Lord Windelsham, *inter alia*, an academic lawyer.

The more conservative group of Cross-Benchers was led by Lord Lloyd of Berwick. He had an impeccable establishment background: Eton, Coldstream Guards, Double First at Cambridge; Graduate Fellow at Harvard; Fellow of Peterhouse; Fellow of Eton; Attorney-General to the Prince of Wales; and Chairman of Glyndebourne. From earliest days he was regarded as both eloquent and elegant. Cynthia Gladwyn describes having tea at Eton while Lloyd was President of Pop: 'exquisite in his purple velvet waistcoat with three shields dangling from his watch-chain'. M Jebb (ed) *The Diaries of Cynthia Gladwyn* (1985) 77–78. He joined commercial chambers, survived the efforts of his clerk, Albert Smith, to persuade him to give up the Bar (the same advice that Smith had given to the young Lord Hobhouse), became a Commercial Judge and then a member of the Court of Appeal. When junior Lord Justices were promoted to the Lords ahead of him, many assumed his distinguished career was at an end, but Lord Mackay relented and he went to the Lords where he achieved distinction not only in commercial cases but in the legislative arena in security matters. For Lloyd's view on the Bill, see Lord Lloyd, 'Constitutional Reform or Vandalism?' *The Times: Law*, Sept14, 2004.

The Liberal Democrats were led by their spokesman, Lord Goodhart, a keen supporter of a Supreme Court and Judicial Appointments Commission: intelligent; urbane, low key and liberal.

Labour was led by the Lord Chancellor himself.

[27] Lord Kingsland suggested Lord Richard added 'a good helping of Welsh guile'. Parl Deb, HL, Vol 663, col 1142. Ironically, Lord Richard had been eased out of his role as Labour Leader of the House of Lords by the efforts of Lord Irvine. See p 101 above.

[28] Actually in October. The debate on October 11 confirmed the restoration of the title Lord Chancellor, but not as yet his powers, nor the requirement that he be in the Lords and be a lawyer. Later amendments in the Lords achieved the latter two requirements.

trusted by the left for what were seen as his right wing views. While the relationship varied, supporters of the Chancellor of the Exchequer, Gordon Brown, who saw himself as the next Prime Minister, resented Blair's clinging to office. Across the political spectrum there was anger about the war in Iraq and a feeling that the Prime Minister had not been entirely truthful, as well as being simple minded in following George W. Bush's messianic lead. These concerns, coupled with what many saw as Blair's somewhat unctuousness and presidential style, pervaded all parties. The problem was that the alternatives were not obvious. Until 2003 the Conservatives were led by Iain Duncan Smith, perhaps the least distinguished leader in that party's history. When, during the year, Smith was replaced by Michael Howard who, as Home Secretary, had clashed with the judges, the credibility of the party improved somewhat, but the party was so wounded by memories of the Major years and two weak leaders that serious opposition was difficult. Nor was the nation yet ready to trust Charles Kennedy and the Liberal Democrats.

The House of Lords too was in a state of flux. If the Constitutional Reform Bill had been introduced in the Commons it would have sailed through. Ironically Bagehot had predicted in the 1860's that if life peers were created, a reform he favoured, they would be more intellectual than the 'businessmen' in the Commons and would clash with them. In the Lords, moreover, Labour was in a minority and too many of those who had been created as Labour peers were either poor attendees or as likely to attack the government as support it. At the same time, the increasing number of Cross-bench peers were independent—the attacks on the Constitution Bill were more vicious from them than from the Conservatives. Overall, however, the House gave the sense of feeling that its privileges were under attack. Reform was in the air. Much of the Labour Party was demanding at least a partially elected House. The Conservative Party, under Iain Duncan Smith, had demanded that 80% of the House of Lords be elected. The current members of the House of Lords could smell the stench of the guillotine.

An Historical Excursus

The atmosphere was wonderfully reminiscent of the 1860s and 1870s. At the end of the great period of liberal reform, when substantive law and procedure had been radically reformed, it ultimately seemed as if it were time to reform the court system even at its apex. The Lord Chancellor, while an important officer of state, was not clearly thought of as head of the judiciary. The judges were seen as government appointees; there was not even a

Lord Chancellor's Office until 1880. The two Chief Justices (King's Bench and Common Pleas) and the Chief Baron of the Exchequer ran the judiciary. The intermediate court of appeal, known as the Court of Exchequer Chamber, was composed of the puisne judges of the three common law courts. Final appeals were the province of House of Lords and Privy Council. Writing in 1867, Walter Bagehot, basically a defender of the English Constitution, wrote:

> I do not reckon the judicial function of the House of Lords as one of its true subsidiary functions, first because it does not in fact exercise it, next because I wish to see it in appearance deprived of it. The supreme court of the English people ought to be a great conspicuous tribunal, ought to rule all other courts, ought to have no competitor, ought to bring our law into unity, ought not to be hidden beneath the robes of a legislative assembly.[29]

In that same year, Hatherley's Commission on the Judicature began its work and it was assumed that Bagehot's goal might be reached. In its first report in 1869, a Supreme Court composed of the High Court and Court of Appeal was recommended. Where the final appeal lay was still unclear; but to many in England that seemed irrelevant since the Lords was still predominantly a Scottish court. (In 1870, there were 19 English Appeals, one from Ireland and 31 from Scotland.) By 1871, however, the consensus seemed to be moving towards a supreme court for final appeals outside the Lords. Chief Justice Cockburn opined: 'Surely the time has come when the House of Lords may be asked to give up a jurisdiction which it has only in name.' Lord Westbury meanwhile called for an Imperial Court of Appeal as the apex of the system. In 1872, when Selborne finally became Lord Chancellor, he was determined to abolish the Lords' judicial functions. The Judicature Act, eventually passed in 1873, provided for a much stronger Court of Appeal. Cases of importance would be re-heard by all nine Lord Justices who would constitute the final court of appeal for England. For England, the House of Lords as an appeal court was gone. The issue of Scottish, Irish and overseas appeals was left until later.

There was some opposition in the Lords from such eccentric peers as Redesdale and Denman[30], but Lord Selborne noted the Lords parted with

---

[29] Walter Bagehot, *The English Constitution* (Oxford, 1963) 112.

[30] Behind the scenes, Lord Salisbury announced he could live with the Court of Appeal as the final appeal court, but he wanted its judges to remain members of the House of Lords. He felt that 'legal strength' was essential for the House to perform properly and he thought it was important for the judges also to sit as legislators: 'they are thereby saved from too technical and professional a spirit; and their decisions gain in breadth. Practically they often have to make law as judges, and they will do it all the better from also having to make it as legislators'. He also thought that having appeal judges as peers a 'fair reparation for stripping it (the House of Lords) of its ancient jurisdiction.' R Stevens, *Law and Politics: The House of Lords as a Judicial Body* (1978) 55.

the jurisdiction 'with less difficulty than might have been expected'. Politicians of all parties agreed that the time had come to separate the legislative and the judicial. In the Commons, a small group of Conservative MP's, led by William Charley, sought to retain the appeal, fearing for the Lords' 'loss of dignity'. With various vicissitudes the Bill passed and was set to come into force in 1874. By that time, however, the Gladstone administration had collapsed and Disraeli was Prime Minister. Disraeli at first appeared to support the changes, but he postponed the effective date of the Bill for one year. Meanwhile, Charley, together with Sir George Bowyer and Spenser Walpole, set up the Committee for Preserving the House of Lords. The emotional argument slowly converted Disraeli; he was a romantic. Moreover, when the Bill came back in 1875 a group of Conservative peers, this time under the leadership of the Dukes of Richmond and Buccleuch, led the assault to retain the privileges of the Lords and re-establish the final appeal. The dignity of the Lords was to take precedence over judicial reform. The way was open for the Appellate Jurisdiction Act, 1876 and the establishment of the 'modern' system. It was to survive largely untouched until 2005.[31]

A Disappearing Lord Chancellor?

In retrospect, it all seemed so simple. The office of Lord Chancellor had been something of a joke among intellectuals for over a hundred years.[32] The ironic thing was that the reforms of the 1870's had made the Lord Chancellor more important and more central to the system than before. Commentators across the spectrum saw some aspects of the Lord Chancellorship as particularly bizarre—especially the right to sit as a judge in the House of Lords. Had Derry Irvine been willing to forgo this right—it was last used in 2001—the office might well have survived intact. The Lord Chancellor's pride seemingly prevented it. A willingness not to act as Speaker in the Lords would also have helped. It was not to be. In June 2003 the whole edifice was destroyed. The Consultation Paper about the Lord Chancellor was solely about how to divide up the remains. Thus far the Select Committee agreed. No one wanted the Lord Chancellor to be a judge and it was assumed the House would determine for itself who would be Speaker.

---

[31] For a detailed description of the political battle see *ibid*, 44–67.
[32] The most thoughtful and perceptive analysis of the office of Lord Chancellor, is now Diana Woodhouse, *The Office of Lord Chancellor* (Oxford, 2001). See especially the critique in Chapter 8.

While critics over the previous decades had talked of a Minister of Justice to replace the Lord Chancellor, little thought had actually been given to the nuances and influences associated with the office. Increasingly intellectuals sought 'clear public principles'[33], while some in the legal establishment wanted to protect 'the important constitutional values which the office of Lord Chancellor protected'.[34] The government's position was that, with the judicial function and the Speakership stripped away, 'in performing his ministerial role, the qualities which will make him or her a success are the same as his other ministerial colleagues. Yet the current system involves the office holder being drawn from a restricted pool—those with senior legal and political standing.'[35] Such a glib view was not acceptable to a wide range of interested parties. It raised a number of fundamental problems.

The first was who would now be head of the judiciary. That had been answered by anointing the Lord Chief Justice. That, in its own way, was ironic, since it was partially restoring the political powers of the Chief Justice of Queen's Bench which, with respect to judicial administration and policy making, had withered between 1873 and 1880.[36] That still left a range of outstanding issues. One was the perennial issue of how those ethereal, but to many highly meaningful, issues of the Rule of Law and Independence of the Judiciary would be handled. The Lord Chancellor had been credited with protecting both. Both responsibilities received a partial solution in the Concordat between Chief Justice and Lord Chancellor early in 2004.

Assuming the Constitution Bill is ultimately passed, the changes agreed in the Concordat would be buttressed by a clause in the Act which would be a 'Guarantee of continued judicial independence', which would mandate that 'those with responsibility for the administration of justice must uphold the continued independence of the judiciary'.[37] Without unpacking the concept of independence of the judiciary, the statute would be largely meaningless, unless it were clear who had the duty to enforce the responsibility. Inevitably, independence of the judiciary remains a highly flexible concept eluding definition. More embarrassingly, the demand is all faintly reminiscent of another outburst of judicial chagrin about independence,

---

[33] E.g. Vernon Bogdanor, House of Lords Select Committee, *Evidence*, 336.

[34] Stevens, above n 30, 116.

[35] House of Lords, Select Committee on the Constitutional Reform Bill [HL] *Constitutional Reform Bill [HL]* Vol 2: Evidence, HL Paper 125–32.

[36] See p 92 above.

[37] 'Judicial independence "guaranteed"', *New Law Journal*, December 12, 2003, 1855. For support from the bar for this, see remarks of the chair of Bar Council, Stephen Irwin QC, 'Cabinet must back judges' authority', *The Times*, December 15, 2003. Apparently his view was that all members of the Cabinet must sign the pledge.

when the government sought to reduce judicial salaries during the financial crisis in the 1930s. In response to understandable judicial paranoia, the government introduced the Judiciary (Safeguarding) Bill, 1934. The Permanent Secretary to the Lord Chancellor, Sir Claud Schuster, urged the Statutory Draftsman: 'Begin with a recital, which should be as long and pompous as possible. . .the independence and all the rest of it. . .then declare that notwithstanding all this they are affected by the cut'. Schuster thought the whole thing 'extremely silly' and the Bill died[38]—possibly a useful precedent for the current crisis. The temper of the political age is the true protector of judicial independence.

The attitudes of leading members of bench and bar are, however, worth unpacking. As already suggested, just as the judges over the last forty years have been busy moving towards the centre of the political stage, the composition of the elected House of Commons has been changing. The intellectual quality of MPs and hence ministers, has not been maintained.[39] The arrival of a more presidential system of government, most obvious under Thatcher and Blair, is likely to produce even weaker MPs and ministers—including of course potential Secretaries of State for Constitutional Affairs. Critics suggest compliance has become more important than integrity in aspiring politicians. It is in this context that the legal establishment is worried about the absence of a legal heavyweight to protect the somewhat arcane concept of judicial independence. The Secretary of Defence is not expected to be a military person; the Secretary of Health is not expected to be a medical person; judges think that the Secretary of Constitutional Affairs must be a heavyweight lawyer. It may be an arrogant position[40]; it is also an understandable one.

It was this debate on the survival of the Lord Chancellor that absorbed so much of the time of the Select Committee. The Committee was split over whether the Minister for Constitutional Affairs should be a lawyer and needed to be in the Lords. The Government and the Liberal Democrats saw

---

[38] R Stevens, *Independence of the Judiciary*, 61–63.

[39] E.g. Lord Kingsland, 'in the 21st century, I am afraid, there will be almost no Lord Howes coming off the production line in another place. Sadly, very few lawyers of that quality are able to enter politics in another place'. Parl Deb, HL, vol 663, col 1145 (Jul 13, 2004).

[40] These concerns presumably explain the outburst by the Deputy Lord Chief Justice, Lord Justice Judge, at a press conference, seeing the possibility that in the future, dreadful things would happen in the democratic process from which the judges must be protected: 'I am not making a party political point against anybody, but we do have to remember the popularity of the second person in the recent presidential election in France. We do have to remember that Hitler came to power in a democratic country by getting a significant popular vote and then subverting the constitution. There are nasty people out there and there is no guarantee that because we are Great Britain none of them will ever, ever come to power'. Press Conference, Lord Chief Justice and Deputy Lord Chief Justice, November 6, 2003. And see 'Top judge fears legal reform will raise ghosts of Nazis', *Daily Telegraph*, November 7, 2003.

the need for neither. The Conservatives and the Cross-Benchers clearly did. Perhaps the greatest surprise was the fact that not only the 'usual suspects' were in favour of retaining the office of Lord Chancellor, but a wide range of independents including Lord Alexander of Weedon and his working party as well as Lord Bingham, the senior law lord.[41]

Despite the excitement, the opposition was on relatively limited grounds. No one seriously suggested that the Lord Chancellor should sit as a judge[42] and no one was particularly interested in his presiding in the Lords. There was general agreement, as we shall see, that judicial appointments should be primarily the responsibility of a Judicial Appointments Commission. The cynic might argue that the real issue was whether the Minister of Justice should be called Secretary of State for Constitutional Affairs or Lord Chancellor. Linked to the latter title was whether he had to be a lawyer and had to be in the Lords. Nevertheless, seen in that light it seemed a more manageable issue.[43] The rethinking of judicial appointments became all important.

---

[41] And the last Conservative Lord Chancellor, Lord Mackay. See Lord Mackay, 'Is there to be a Lord Chancellor no more?' *The Times*, Jul 13, 2004.

[42] Lord Lloyd was, however, a reluctant convert: 'I accept that there are problems with a judge sitting as a member of the Cabinet, particularly it seems, among the newly joined members of the European Union'. Parl Deb, HL, Vol 663, col 1146 (Jul 13, 2004). At the Committee stage he did, however, put down an amendment to return the Lord Chancellor to judicial duties.

[43] Some of the emotional attachment to the Office of Lord Chancellor can be seen in the debates in October 2004. The survival of the name rather than Secretary of State had effectively been conceded by July. In the October debates the Liberal Democrats announced they would allow a free vote on whether the Lord Chancellor would have to be a lawyer: col 31 (October 11, 2004). The strength of the mystical belief in the role of the Lord Chancellor was remarkable. It even infected colonial peers: e.g. Lord Cooke of Thorndon: 'What was the greatest legal office in the world? . . . his . . . high status has been an enduring symbol of the commitment of the United Kingdom to the rule of law and the independence of the judiciary' (*ibid*, col 38); and even the Episcopal bench. The Lord Bishop of Salisbury, distorting history, explained the arrival of the law lords: 'Due to the complexities of legislation in the 19th century, the institution of the law lords developed so that appeals could be heard by those who had judicial competence to hear them. However, never for one moment did we think that that was somehow a different function of our responsibilities; it was merely a devolved and in-gathering one. I believe it is very important we stick with that. It is the jury system of this House for hearing these appeals. It is through the Members of the House hearing appeals and being able to help in the process of the reform of the legal basis of our common life that I believe we stand the best chance of holding such matters together. We could go by way of dispersion into many dismembered fragments, but I believe that would undermine much of what our fragile and still largely unwritten constitution tries to do in holding our common life together' (*ibid* col 62).

A New Way of Appointing Judges

As we have seen, while Lord Irvine had been reluctant to encourage change, his years as Lord Chancellor had been marked by increasing encroachment on his unfettered right to appoint judges. The process had become increasingly transparent. The Peach Report, followed by the work of Sir Colin Campbell as Judicial Appointments Commissioner, had brought noticeable changes. The need for diversity had been accepted. In this sense Lord Falconer's consultative document on judicial appointments was both logical and disappointing. It was logical because it reflected the culmination of the reports over recent years seeking to make the process of appointment more transparent. The need for further powers had been powerfully underwritten while the debates were going on, by Sir Colin Campbell's analysis of the 2003 High Court Competition.[44] It was disappointing because the Consultation Paper neither thought in a sophisticated way about the judicial function, nor about the separation—or balance—of powers and what drove the increasing argument for further separation or balance.

With the Lords' defeat of that part of the Bill, the Lord Chancellor was forced to go with a Commission which is *de facto* an appointing one, sending only one name forward. If the limited precedent of Scotland is followed, this will mean that the final decision would really be that of the Commission. Power will have passed from the Lord Chancellor/Secretary of State to a quango. The change makes the composition of that body all important. Unlike Scotland and Northern Ireland, Judges and lawyers (including the JP) will be in the majority. Moreover, in addition to the Commission, there are to be two related bodies. First of all there will be a Committee to choose the members of the current Commission and an Ombudsman, to monitor that the appointments system is working fairly.

---

[44] See for example:

> Our observation was that those involved in the sifting process put a great deal of time and effort into attempting to assess the suitability of nominated candidates fairly, often on the basis of very limited information related to the appointment criteria. Perhaps inevitably this involved a high degree of inference, often based on broadly expressed comments . . . with little or no evidence relating specifically to some of the individual criteria. In these circumstances heavy reliance was placed on the seniority of those commenting on the nominated candidates.

H.M. Commissioners for Judicial Appointments, *Report of the Commissioners' Review of the High Court 2003 Competition* (2004) para 2.2. The Commissioners recommended: 'Appointments to the High Court bench, on the basis of the process used in the 2003 competition, which fall short of the requirements of an open, transparent and accountable process, in a number of regards, should cease to be made as soon as practicable'. *Ibid* para 8.3.11. Lord Lloyd of Berwick saw nothing wrong with the current system. Letter, *The Times*, Jul 6 2004.

It is arguable that the Consultation Paper on which the Bill was based represented the culmination of the utilitarian reforms of the nineteenth century. After all, the cult of competition for public appointments was parodied by Gilbert and Sullivan, suggesting that the peerage should be open to competitive examination; the new independent selection body for cross-bench peers goes some way to achieving that. Salisbury's sneering observation that one day the Master of the Rolls would be chosen by an examination in the Law Reports may, in one sense, not be unthinkable. Even Selborne and Cairns, however, would be surprised by the seemingly mechanical (or transparent) basis for judicial appointments, especially the disappearance of the right of the Secretary to choose from a panel.

Most of the criticism has gone to the mechanics of the proposed Commission. The current Commission for Judicial Appointments, through its Chairman, Sir Colin Campbell, called for the new Commission to be dominated by lay persons rather than judges and lawyers. Campbell saw this as vital in implementing one of Lord Falconer's main goals—a more diverse bench.[45] The Consultative Paper emphasises diversity, and some diversity could undoubtedly be produced by building on a wider recruitment base—including not only solicitors, but employed lawyers. The cult of 'independence', however, which has judicial independence lapping over to the Bar, will discourage such developments. Overall while all sections of the legal and lay community claim an interest in a more diverse bench, as criticism has mounted, Falconer has insisted that 'merit' must take precedence over diversity.

There are, of course, other criticisms of the vision of judicial appointments in the Consultation document. Can any Commission, no matter how wisely staffed, ever have the Solomonesque judgment of a good Lord Chancellor—or some appropriate single person? Lord Bingham, the senior law lord, has doubted it.[46] Lord Woolf has also pointed out the difficulties of having promotion to higher courts done by Committee; although the Bill provides that for the Court of Appeal, Chief Justice and heads of divisions there would be separate sub-committees of the Judicial Appointments

---

[45] 'People power to pick judges', *The Observer*, Aug 31, 2003. See Commission for Judicial Appointments, *Why should the Judicial Appointments Commission have a Lay Chair and Majority* (2004). See also *Reform of the Judicial Appointment System* (2004).

[46] This was put most elegantly and eloquently by Lord Bingham: 'I proceed to lay down as a rule that one man of discernment is better fitted to analyse and estimate the peculiar qualities adapted to a particular office than a body of men of equal or perhaps even superior discernment. The role and undivided responsibility of one man will naturally beget a livelier sense of duty and a more exact regard to reputation. He will, on this account, find himself under stronger obligations, and more interested to investigate with care the qualities requisite to the station to be filled, and to prefer with impartiality the persons who may have the fairest pretensions to them.' Justice, *Bulletin*, Autumn 2001, p 9.

Commission. Woolf argued that Committee promotions tend to lead to 'Buggins turn next'. He used the example of India and the selection of the Chief Justice[47]; he could just as easily used promotion to final court of appeal in Connecticut (the quaintly named Supreme Court of Errors and Appeals). It may well be more difficult for a Commission, no matter how distinguished its membership, to pass over less distinguished judges to make a promotion to the Court of Appeal than it was for a wise and unfettered Lord Chancellor.

In short, there are major objections to the long term solution that, as the Bill went through the Lords, was in the ascendant. First, the opportunity to make the imaginative appointment may well be disappearing. Will the complex web of Commission and panels be able to make innovative appointments? It will of course avoid a totally undistinguished nepotistic one. Will the new bureaucracy be able to replicate Lord Hailsham's decision to go against the advice of the judges and appoint Lord Donaldson as Master of the Rolls or Lord Mackay's decision to appoint Lord Bingham as Chief Justice? Will it be possible to reach outside the usual *cursus honorum* and appoint, as Lord Mackay did, a radical figure like Stephen Sedley to the High Court, or as Lord Falconer himself has recently done, to appoint Lady Hale as a law lord?[48]

Second, as the government has been forced to allow the Commission itself to define merit[49], is there any hope of greater diversity, for as Sir Thomas Legg has pointed out, depending how one defines the concept of merit, greater diversity may well call for *minimal* merit rather than *maximal* merit. In short the concepts may conflict.[50] During the Select Committee Hearings, Sir Colin Campbell argued that merit is but a threshold and a number of candidates may be meritorious.[51] There is little evidence that he convinced the House of Lords. This worry is compounded by the fear that the judges will be extremely powerful in the new Commission. The danger of a cloned judiciary is real. As Sir Colin Campbell noted, after Lord Falconer backed down on diversity and panels, 'after the Falconer capitulations, the new appointments system could end up looking a lot like

[47] Department of Constitutional Affairs, Lord Woolf, 'Speech at the Annual Dinner for HM Judges', Jul 9, 2003

[48] And for the view that Morris Finer and Peter Pain would not have been judges without Elwyn-Jones as Lord Chancellor, see Sir Michael Kerr, *As far as I Remember* (Oxford, 2002) 307.

[49] In their memorandum, the judges also warned of the dangers 'of becoming so anxious to achieve diversity that sight is lost of the primacy of merit. The justice system will be debased if the very best candidates are not appointed'. Para 80.

[50] Sir Thomas Legg, 'Brave New World: the new Supreme Court and judicial appointments' (2004) 24 *Legal Studies*, 45.

[51] Such a concept disturbed Lord Lloyd. See Letter to *The Times*, Jul 6, 2004.

the existing system, only without oversight'.[52] That may explain why from having been tense about the new system in the Autumn of 2003, the judiciary exuded the impression of feeling, by the Autumn of 2004, that it had triumphed.

The accepted wisdom among leading judges and lawyers is that the Secretary of State for Constitutional Affairs could not appoint the judges because he might not be a lawyer, therefore he would not know the legal profession and that he might pack the courts with government supporters.[53] This is not a totally convincing argument. A wise layman might well prove a more effective protector of judicial independence and a wiser selector (or final arbiter) of judicial appointments than have many Lord Chancellors. No Secretary—legal or lay—could know all 10,000 barristers and 90,000 solicitors. Lord Mackay had been at the Scottish bar, but he was remarkable as a selector of judges. Within the last one hundred years, Lord Halsbury packed the High Court bench with Tory supporters, although he was Lord Chancellor and sat regularly.[54] Chamberlain's Lord Chancellor in 1939–40, Caldecote, typified the mediocrity of some of the 'political hack' Lord Chancellors—he was an enthusiastic supporter of Munich. Churchill suggested that, in appointing Caldecote, Chamberlain had sought to choose as Lord Chancellor someone of inferior abilities to himself, while the young Michael Foot observed of his appointment that no more surprising announcement had been made since Caligula appointed his horse as consul. That of course did not prevent Caldecote being 'promoted' to Lord Chief Justice, when a place on the Woolsack was needed for Lord Simon.[55] As Lord Falconer has argued, would a layman like Roy Jenkins be less trustworthy than this?

---

[52] Bob Sherwood, 'Warning over move to reform selection of judges', *Financial Times*, October 7, 2004. The Third Annual Report of the Commission on Judicial Appointments also warned the new body 'perhaps not immediately but nevertheless pretty quickly (could) settle back into the traditional and familiar way of doing things.' For 2003, the Commission upheld half the complaints about the 'secret soundings' system.

[53] *Ibid.* And see Frances Gibb, 'Top Judge stays to fight politicians', *The Times*, Aug 1, 2003.

[54] In terms of lack of government pressure, it is worth remembering that Lord Haldane, Lord Chancellor in 1924, reprimanded Mr. Justice McCardie for criticising the government for its handling of the Amritsar Massacre. Henry Archer, *Mr Hardee* (London, 2003) 164–65. Lord Simon (Chancellor 1940–45) tried to persuade Lord Atkin to change his judgment in the famous civil liberties case of *Liversidge v Anderson*, although Simon had not been sitting in the House of Lords. RFV Heuston, *Lives of the Lord Chancellors*, 1940, 1970 (Oxford, 1987) 58–60. It is incidents such as these that throw doubt on the claims that Lord Chancellors, in their judicial work, are 'above politics'.

[55] R Stevens, *Law and Politics*, above n 30, 245.

Parliamentary Democracy and an Unelected Judiciary

In the broader political framework, the discussion of judicial appointments by the profession enables one to understand the frustration of the Howards and the Blunketts. The former Home Secretary David Blunkett went so far as to announce that he was 'fed up with having to deal with a situation where parliament debates issues and judges then overturn them'. He also took the view that 'if public policy can always be overridden by individual challenge through the courts, then democracy itself is under threat'.[56] David Blunkett demanded in the *Evening Standard*[57] that judges live in the 'real world'[58], apparently having in mind Mr Justice Popplewell[59] who had opined that Blunkett was 'whining about judges overturning what Parliament had enacted.' Popplewell was an admirable judge, but the world of Charterhouse and Cambridge University, cricket and the Oxford Circuit, was very different from Mr Blunkett's tough inner city politics in Sheffield: 'There are no newspaper editors, columnists or opinion formers living in my inner-city Sheffield constituency. If I don't speak about the experiences of my constituents and millions like them, they have no voice at all in the public arena.' The Home Secretary also took on the Lord Chief Justice—allegedly calling Lord Woolf 'a muddled and confused old codger'.[60]

When the Chief Justice warned that the judges are underpaid at £150,000 pa—with, in addition, a generous indexed non-contributory pension worth in excess of £1 million[61]—because the leaders of the profession are earning ten times that[62], it seemed to many that the judges and the leaders of the

---

[56] Speech of Lord Lester, Parl Deb, HL, Vol 648, col 894 (May 21, 2003).

[57] The article proclaimed: 'I won't give in to the judges . . . judges now routinely rewrite the effects of a law Parliament has passed'. They use 'ever more ingenious ways of getting what they want . . . we need a long hard look at the constitutional relationship between Parliament and the judges and be clear how it has changed.' See speech of Lord Rodgers, Parl Deb, HL, Vol 648, col 875, May 21, 2003. While the constitutional flap was going on, David Blunkett referred to Mr Justice Collins, chair of the Special Immigration Appeals Commission as 'bonkers'. 'Think, then talk', *Observer*, Apr 25, 2004. 'Judges accuse Blunkett over Terror Suspect', *Guardian*, Mar 9, 2004. See now Stephen Pollard *David Blunkett* (2004) 287–90.

[58] David Blunkett 'I won't give in', *Evening Standard*, May 12, 2003. At least he spared the judges Signor Berlusconi's view of the Italian judges: 'anthropologically divorced from the rest of humanity'. 'Forza Berlusconi!' *The Spectator*, Sept 6, 2003.

[59] See Sir Oliver Popplewell, *Benchmark: Life, Laughter and the Law* (London, 2003).

[60] Said Lord Ackner, a former law lord, 'Blunkett, with his megaphone politics, has gone out of his way to misconstrue, mischief-make and bully him as well', David Leppard, 'Chief Justice to quit in Blunkett row', *Sunday Times*, Oct 31, 2004.

[61] Increasingly difficult to justify in the light of the collapse of many final pension schemes in the private sector. 'The elephant in the room: the growing burden of generous public-sector pensions', *The Economist*, Sept 18, 2004.

[62] 'Woolf guards judges' pensions', *New Law Journal*, Aug 8, 2003, 1222. Indeed, in the Queen's speech in November 2004, there was a proposal that the judges should be exempted from the accumulations cap for pensions (£1.5m) imposed by the Chancellor of the

legal profession live in a cocooned corporatist other world. The average income in England is some £25,170 and MP's earn little more than twice as much; Justices of the Supreme Court of the United States earn appreciably less than UK law lords, who earn £180,000 per annum. Perhaps, in this climate, it is not surprising that too often MP's are sceptical of the judicial claims such as their allegation that precedent forced them to develop judicial review. The Conservatives opposed the Human Rights Act because it would pass too much power, and inevitably political decisions, to the judges. Labour backbenchers unwisely took the assurances from Blair and Irvine that all was well with parliamentary sovereignty when they passed the Human Rights Act. It is little wonder the mystique of judicial independence is under stress.

As always in the English scene, so much has depended on the strange interpretation of the words 'judicial independence'. The English have been late comers to the separation of powers, but they have all the zeal of converts. In the United States, where, since 1789, there have been clear divisions between the judicial, the executive and the legislative, there has also been a realisation that to make the system work there must be a system of 'checks and balances'. The English (or British), having merged the legislative and the executive in the 1720s, were happy to treat the judiciary as a poor cousin, subject to various public and private controls. Over the last thirty year period the obsession with the independence of the judiciary has been based on the assumption that it should be subject to no checks and balances at all. The traditional idea that independence of the judiciary meant that High Court judges had tenure under the Act of Settlement, were entitled to a decent salary, should be impartial with respect to decision-making, and free of political premises in their judicial work, has given way to a far more expansive doctrine.

This change is reflected in Lord Falconer's introduction to the Consultation Paper. He extols independence. 'The appointments system must be, and must be seen to be, independent of Government'; although at the same time 'those responsible for judicial appointments must be accountable to Parliament without it becoming part of the political process'.[63] The idea that this tenuous link with the democratic process will be enough to pro-

---

Exchequer. The proposal had been opposed by John Prescott in Cabinet: 'Prescott leads revolt over judges pensions' *Daily Telegraph*, Nov 5, 2004; while the judges threatened mass resignations unless they were exempted from the cap: 'Mass resignations threat by judges' *The Guardian*, Nov 27, 2004. Meanwhile senior civil servants were threatened with having their pensions cut: 'Civil Servants set to strike over loss of pension rights' *The Times* Dec 6, 2004; 'Top Civil Servants to lose thousands of pounds in retirement benefits', *ibid*, 9 Dec, 2004.

[63] One of the mysteries of all this is that government departments still consult the judges as they draft legislation. For instance, Lord Woolf's Cambridge speech reveals that the judges were consulted by the Home Office as they drafted the Immigration Act. The problem for the

tect the judges from the claim of being a 'unelected' is dubious. The judges thought having an ombudsman would be enough to protect their political flank. Since Michael Howard and David Blunkett started attacking the judges for being 'unelected', 'undemocratic' and 'elitist', the response of the legal profession has been to suggest that 'our' judges are independent of politics. If what is meant is that judicial decisions are significantly determined by legal rules, that is true. If, however, those making the claim are taking the Italian concept of corporatism as their model, they are likely to be doomed to failure.

As Americans readily accept but the British do not, judges do have their own personal and political views which·they take on to the bench with them and help shape their decisions; the law is not a value-free process. In a democratic society, the elected legislature, and those legislators who serve in the executive under the system of responsible government, need to be involved in the selection of the judiciary in more than a tangential way, if only to protect the judiciary from political attack. This will be all the more important now the office of Lord Chancellor has taken on an attenuated form. The theory behind this was put most persuasively by Richard Posner of the Federal Court of Appeals in the U.S.. He argued that it is the political involvement in the appointments process that protects the tenure of judges during their judicial life.[64] The refusal to address this issue in the UK may well be storing up long-term trouble for the judiciary. It will only add to the Lord Chief Justice's concern 'about the relationship between the different branches of government'.[65]

The mere mention of matters such as the 'democratic deficit'[66] is enough to make the English profession and bench nervous. One of the obvious parallels is the United States Federal bench. The debates at Philadelphia had centred on the legislature making the appointments to the Supreme Court. The ultimate compromise was appointment by the President, with

judges was that the Home Office then ignored their advice. Woolf, 'The Rule of Law and a Change in the Constitution', *op cit.*

[64] And see generally William M Landes and Richard A Posner, 'The Independent Judiciary in an Interest-Group Perspective', (1975) 18 *Journal of Law and Economics*, 875.

[65] Lord Woolf, Parl Deb, HL, Vol 648, col 879 (May 21, 2003). In Israel, which boasts of its non-political system of appointment, the 9 person Commission is composed of 3 Supreme Court judges (with the President of the Court as Chair), 2 lawyers, the Minister of Justice and one other Cabinet minister, and 2 members of the Knesset.

[66] One of the lamest parts of the Judges' submission is the brief paragraph on 'Democratic Accountability': ' . . . we recognise the need for democratic accountability. This will be provided by the continuing role of the Ombudsman, who will scrutinise the appointments process and publish an annual report. In addition, the Chairperson of the Judicial Appointments Commission should be required to report annually to Parliament. We would also expect the Constitutional Affairs Select Committee regularly to scrutinise the appointments process.' Para 113.

confirmation by the Senate. The appointment process is a political tussle; but it has ensured over the last decades representation in the judiciary for women, African-Americans, Hispanics, Jews and Westerners. Superficially this would seem to support Lord Falconer's demand for 'more women, more minority members, and lawyers from a wider range of practice'. The idea of a potential judge being subjected by politicians to the kind of grilling leading members of the bar inflict on members of the public daily is, however, anathema to bench and bar alike.[67]

Moves in that direction run into the distaste created by the televised hearings on Robert Bork and Clarence Thomas before the US Senate. Indeed, Lord Falconer has moved to cut off any suggestion that Parliament itself might be involved. In the Consultation Paper, the simplistic assumption is made that any political considerations (as opposed to gender, race and social considerations) are out of the question. Any legislative involvement is, rather naively, thought to be inconsistent with judicial independence. The American Federal System is raised briefly only to be dismissed: 'Due to the pivotal role played by the legislature, appointment arrangements at federal level are not relevant to the issues raised in this consultation and are not discussed further here'.[68] There is greater discussion of the selection of U.S. State judges, with emphasis on how the States now seek to avoid the election of judges. There is no mention of the fact that the system of election was developed in the nineteenth century, during the period of Jacksonian Democracy, because the judges were thought to have taken over too many political tasks and were not sufficiently representative of society at large. That parallel would be too uncomfortable.

The die is now cast. Despite the scepticism of the Senior Law Lord it is difficult to see how, at the very least, effectively an executive Appointments Commission, can be avoided. Indeed during the House of Lords debates the government accepted that the Secretary would be presented with only one name. Instead of the government monitoring diversity and quality, the responsibility will have been handed to a legally dominated quango. This may well ensure quality but will it ensure diversity?[69] The current

---

[67] Although Lady Hale, the first woman Lord of Appeal, implies that such a procedure would help avoid cloning on the bench. Brenda Hale, 'A Supreme Court for the United Kingdom?' (2004) 24 *Legal Studies*, 36, 42. For a contrast with accountability of the Monetary Policy Committee, see now Charles Goodhart and Ellen Meade, 'Central Banks and Supreme Courts' (2004) *Moneda y Crédito*, No. 218, p. 11.

[68] *A New Way of Appointing Judges*, 75.

[69] See, for instance, Professor Robert Hazell, 'to present ministers with a single name in my view assumes too simplistic a notion of merit'. Select Committee, *Evidence*, § 152. See also Professor Diana Woodhouse, 'I am concerned that if only one name is given the Commission might always produce, or is in danger of producing, the 'no risks' candidate at all times because they would be so scared of getting it wrong. If this is a degree of choice then in the

Commissioner fur Judicial Appointments, Sir Colin Campbell, thinks the new system may be worse than the old in terms of diversity. Presenting a panel to the Secretary would have been far preferable.[70] In common with other European countries, England is increasingly judicialising political issues[71]; the tectonic shift of power reflected by the Human Rights Act is slowing being recognised.[72]

The 'democratic deficit' is now more associated with the judiciary than with Parliament. There is a danger that judges, with their influence on what is effectively an appointing committee, will be seen by their critics as representing a self perpetuating oligarchy. Nowhere in these procedures is there any room for injecting democratic legitimacy, unless one counts the right of the Secretary to demand another name. For those who fear, as judges become more obviously powerful, that there is a democratic deficit in a judiciary, appointment without any effective political input is hazardous. We have seen the attacks by Michael Howard and David Blunkett; ten years down the road, unless there is real input by a politician to provide political cover, these attacks could seem mild. The judges claim that the Ombudsman will provide the democratic input will seem naïve. Having discretion in the hands of the Secretary, as proposed in the Consultation Paper, not only ensured the monitoring of quality and diversity, it gave the judges

---

end it is still going to be the minister who gets the blame, as it were, if he chooses the wrong one. After all, he is the one who is accountable ultimately to Parliament, so I think that putting the onus on the minister is not a bad thing': *ibid* § 382. That had originally been the view of the Lord Chancellor: 'appointing judges is a central function of the State. Parliamentary accountability for the appointments system must therefore be retained, through the Secretary of State. It follows that a Secretary of State who is accountable for the appointments system should have a real, albeit carefully tempered, discretion in those appointments'. Select Committee, *Written Evidence of the Lord Chancellor*, 18. He later capitulated.

[70] In a recent debate in the Lords, Lord Lester suggested that the Attorney-General might act as a substitute Lord Chancellor, while Lord Alexander made a plea for the retention of a scaled-down Lord Chancellor. See Parl Deb, HL, Sept 8, 2003 at cols 112 and 117 respectively. Lord Mackay is also now on record suggesting the Attorney-General as a substitute Lord Chancellor. 'Law Diary', *The Times*, Sept 23, 2003. See also Bob Alexander, 'A brazen challenge to the separation of powers', *Financial Times*, Jan 8, 2004.

[71] E.g., A Stone Sweet, *Governing with Judges* (Oxford, 2000); C Guarnierni and P. Pederzoli *The Power of Judges* (Oxford, 2002); M Shapiro and A Stone Sweet (eds) *On Law Politics and Judicialisation* (Oxford, 2002).

[72] For a sample of recent writing, see Aileen Kavanaugh, 'Statutory Interpretation and human rights after *Anderson* : A more contextual approach', (2004) *Public Law*, 537; Maurice Sunkin, 'Pushing Forward the Frontiers of Human Rights Protection: The Meaning of Public Authority under the Human Rights Act, *ibid*, 643; Ian Loveland 'The impact of the Human Rights Act on Security of Tenant in Public Housing, *ibid*, 594. See now also, Danny Nicol, 'The Human Rights Act and the Politicians', (2004) 24 *Legal Studies*, 451. For a useful survey of declarations of incompatibility see per Lord Steyn in *Ghaidan v Godin-Mendoza* [2004] 2 AC, 557, 578–82.

political legitimacy. The judicial pressure to have the Commission offer only one name to the Secretary may well be a judicial own goal.[73]

The elected representatives may also need a role in the selection of judges. Perhaps the political parties could have nominated three members for the Committee choosing the Commission. Failing that, assuming there is to be a Commission, then if not immediately, at least shortly, the House of Commons, as the representatives of the people, will, like the Cabinet and Knesset in Israel, demand representation on the Commission. After all, in France, both the Senate and the National Assembly nominate members of the Conseil Superieur de la Magistrature and in Portugal the seven non-judges on the Conselho Superior da Magistradura are nominated by the legislature. In this country, if the judiciary continues to expand judicial review and if the Human Rights Act becomes ever more popular, the demands for a more politicised Commission will grow. The irony is that judicial appointments may become more political than they have been under the last forty years of the Lord Chancellor system.

A Supreme Court for the United Kingdom

If the consultation paper on the appointment of judges was both radical and naïve, the consultation paper on the Supreme Court was both conservative and cautious. In so many ways, what it was recommending was what the Judicature Commission recommended in the 1860's and the Judicature Act of 1873 provided through an Imperial Court of Appeal. Of course things are now different, but the unsatisfactory solution in the Appellate Jurisdiction Act, 1876, of having the House of Lords continue as the final court of appeal will be ended. Some critics have seen a separate final court of appeal as inevitable as a result of pressure coming from Article 6 of the European Convention on Human Rights. Sceptics—and they have included both Lords Irvine and Woolf—see the changes as architectural, of less importance than new court buildings in Manchester.[74] The majority of law

[73] Sir Thomas Legg, QC, former Permanent Secretary of the Lord Chancellor, expressed it in these terms: 'because I for my part believe the appointment of judges is a political and governmental act in which the Executive should play a real, important and accountable part. If it is going to do that I think Ministers should have a choice.' Select Committee, *Evidence*, question 679.

[74] Lords Nicholls, Hoffman, Hope, Hutton, Millett, Rodger. On the other side were Lords Bingham, Steyn, Saville and Walker. The latter regarded 'the functional separation of the judiciary at all levels from the legislature and the executive as a cardinal feature of a modern, liberal, democratic state governed by the rule of law.' See House of Lords, *The Law Lords' response to the Government's consultation paper on Constitutional Reform: A Supreme Court for the United Kingdom*, p.1 Some law lords were becoming increasingly outspoken in their opposition to the proposed constitutional changes. Lord Lloyd referred to the changes as

lords believe the changes are both 'unnecessary' and 'harmful'[75] and with a commendable concern for the public fisc, something not always shown where legal aid or judicial salaries are involved, 'they consider that the cost of the change would be wholly out of proportion to any benefit.' The absence of an obvious building to house the new Supreme Court did not make things easier. That does not appear to be the view of Lord Falconer. With the exception of the severing of the link with the House of Lords as a legislative body, there are precious few other changes proposed in the Consultation Paper—which is a disappointment to critics, although it may well be politically wise for the Lord Chancellor. At least it made it possible to defeat the combined forces of the Conservative peers and many cross benchers (including various law lords) in December 2004. Support from the Chief Justice (who was worried about losing the other part of the Bill) and, oddly enough, the bishops, eventually saw a majority for a Supreme Court.

The Consultation Paper rightly announced that the severing of the link with the legislature 'will reflect and enhance the independence of the Judiciary from both the legislature and the executive'.[76] It was after all following the suggestions of the senior law lord and the Chairman of the Bar, and reflects the rational side of independence of the judiciary. It was seen as a logical tidying up of the Constitution by Bagehot a hundred and fifty years ago. As the Consultation Paper continued, however, it became caught up in the mythological side of judicial independence. After discussing the expansion of judicial responsibilities through devolution (to be transferred from the Judicial Committee of the Privy Council to the new Supreme Court), 'the considerable growth of judicial review' and the Human Rights Act, the paper argues that 'It is essential that our systems do all they can to minimise the danger that judges' decisions could be perceived to be politically motivated'. The logical way to do that would be to follow the advice of Michael Howard, now leader of the Conservative Party, and repeal the Human Rights Act[77]; and there are no doubt members of his party who would like to repeal the devolution legislation.

'constitutional vandalism'. Lord Nicholls noted, of the efforts to evaluate other democracies: 'Legal uniformity adds nothing. It is not a virtue.' 'Senior Law Lord attacks Supreme Court move', *Daily Telegraph*, December 2, 2003.

[75] The dispute is now focussing more on whether the Supreme Court should have a new building along the lines of the U.S. Supreme Court or a renovated existing building. There was also talk of the new Supreme Court sitting in both Belfast and Edinburgh. 'Trial of wills as judges battle over site of supreme court', *The Times*, Jan 2, 2004. Finding a suitable home for the new Supreme Court now seems fairly advanced. Eg Frances Gibb, 'No rough justice at the Supreme Court', *The Times*, Apr 14, 2004; 'Law Lords reject chosen site for supreme court', *ibid*, May 7, 2004.

[76] For criticism of the logic of this by a political scientist peer, see Lord Norton, Parl Deb, HL, Vol 652, col 122 (Sept8, 2003)

[77] 'Tories push to scrap Human Rights Act', *The Independent*, Aug 24, 2004.

The judges have been handed political issues. The English judges are adept at providing the fig leaf of judicial objectivity, but how long will the public be hoodwinked? Lord Falconer's view of all this was relatively simplistic. 'The Law Lords are judges and not legislators: the separation between the two roles should be made explicit'[78]. The most recent of the law lords, Lady Hale, gave a more sophisticated explanation: 'this (the House of Lords) is an intensely political place. This may have become more apparent since the party political balance become closer and the House of Lords has felt much freer to engage in serious challenges to the House of Commons. This is none of our business as judges: yet if we take an interest we risk compromising our neutrality and if we do not we are seen as humble and stand-offish.'[79] Lords Bingham, Steyn, Saville and Walker saw 'the separation of the judiciary at all levels from the legislature and the executive as a cardinal feature of a modern, liberal democratic state governed by the rule of law'. Sir Thomas Legg, former Permanent Secretary to the Lord Chancellor added that the establishment of a Supreme Court 'is an item of long unfinished business from 1875 and I am sure it is a good move'[80].

Lord Falconer's approach, effectively developing the separation of powers, is no bad abstract goal, but it is to be achieved by pretending nothing has changed. The reasoning is that if we say often enough that our judges are apolitical, they will be. The UK will be different, unlike the United States and Germany which have Supreme Courts, as the Consultation Paper, puts it:

> to protect the written constitution. In our democracy, Parliament is supreme. There is no separate body of constitutional law which takes precedence over other law. The constitution is made up of the whole body of the laws and settled practice and convention, all of which can be amended or repealed by Parliament. Neither membership of the European Union nor devolution nor the Human Rights Act has changed the fundamental position. Such amendment or repeal would certainly be very difficult in practice and Parliament and the executive regard themselves as bound by the obligations they have taken through that legislation, but the principle remains intact.

The principle may remain intact to formalists, but the reality is that the European Community Act, 1972, the Scotland Act 1998 and the Human Rights Act 1998 have imposed a form of fundamental law, well known to American and German lawyers. The European Court and the Court of

---

[78] Lord Chancellor, HL Select Committee, *Evidence*, written evidence, 9.
[79] *Ibid, Evidence*, 364
[80] *Ibid* Q 679. And see H.L., Select Committee on the Constitutional Reform Bill, *Report*, p.33.

Human Rights has led to the judicialisation of political issues throughout Europe. Intelligent commentators are not deceived. As *The Economist* said of the appeal by nine foreign detainees in Belmarsh Prison, without trial, under the Terrorism Act, the case 'provided the best illustration yet of how European human-rights legislation is turning Britain's House of Lords into an American-style Supreme Court.'[81]

The Consultation Paper continues the concern about how to appoint the judges of Supreme Court. It continues, however, to work on the premise that these are legal appointments of persons who have no political role. At least it manages to overcome one prejudice; this time the recommendation will be to the Prime Minister, who will consult the First Ministers in Scotland and Northern Ireland, who will make the decisions. The concern shown in the *Appointing Judges* paper over the fear that a non-lawyer might be involved (i.e. a layman being Secretary of State for Constitutional Affairs) appears to be overcome, noting that the First Minister in Scotland is involved in the appointment of the Lord President of the Court of Session.[82]

What the Paper is clear about is that it is opposed to any suggestion that Parliament might have more confidence in the judiciary if there were confirmation hearings:

> The Government sees difficulty in such a procedure. MPs and lay peers would not necessarily be competent to assess the appointees' legal or judicial skills. If the intention was to assess the more general approach to issues of public importance, this would be inconsistent with the move to take the Supreme Court out of the potential political arena. One of the main intentions of the reform is to emphasise and enhance the independence of the Judiciary from both the executive and Parliament. Giving Parliament the right to decide or have a direct influence in who should be the members of the Court would cut right across that objective.

Superficially, this sounds impressive. It, however, confuses the legitimate aspect of judicial independence—having the judges independent of executive and legislature—and accepts the more naïve side of the alleged value-free aspect of judicial independence. If the judging process is value free, apolitical and isolated, why the obsession with changing the composition of the judiciary? *Appointing Judges* complains that 'the current judiciary is overwhelmingly white, male from a narrow social and educational background' so that 'the Government is committed to setting up a system of appointments, to attract suitably qualified candidates both from a wider

[81] 'Supremely Important', *The Economist*, October 9, 2004.
[82] The demands of the *Judges' Council Response to the Papers on Constitutional Reform* are somewhat extravagant. Para 164 seems to suggest that the Supreme Court Appointments Commission should consist only of Supreme Court judges, chaired by the President.

range of social backgrounds . . .'.[83] (Quite how one reconciles this with Falconer's recent incantation that merit will be the only criterion is unclear.)[84] South Africa has similarly been broadening the composition of the bench, yet it is a little more realistic about the justification for such diverse appointments. As Mr Justice Cameron of the South African Supreme Court put it: 'Judges do not enter public office as ideological virgins. They ascend the Bench with built-in and often strongly held sets of values, preconceptions, opinions and prejudices. They are invariably expressed in the decisions they give, constituting inarticulate premises in the process of judicial reasoning'.[85]

The 'inarticulate premise' argument comes from Mr Justice Holmes of the US Supreme Court more than a hundred years ago. It is a concept, however, that English lawyers have traditionally claimed does not apply in England. Little has changed since Harold Laski wrote to Justice Holmes in 1932, explaining why he dissented in the Scott-Donaghmore Committee, established in the wake of Hewart's *New Despotism*: 'my fight was the old one against regarding a judge as an automatic slot-machine into whom you put the statute and from whom you get a construction in which there is no articulate major premise'. The reason England needs a more diverse bench is partly the issue of political acceptability, but more importantly because there needs to be greater diversity in the 'inarticulate premises'[86], especially in the final court of appeal[87].

While every effort is made to hide the real nature of the judicial process in the discussion papers, the truth occasionally breaks through. The Supreme Court paper does admit that 'the selection of the judge to hear the case may at least in theory affect the outcome', naively adding that, 'It is impossible to tell after the event whether it has done so or not'. (What of *Pinochet?*[88]) The paper concludes that it is more important to have the

---

[83]   At 4

[84]   Parl Deb, HL, Jan 26 2004.

[85]   Clare Hogan, 'In search of justice fit for a Rainbow Nation', *The Times: Law*, Sept 9, 2003. And see Edwin Cameron, 'Judicial Accountability in South Africa', (1988) *South African Journal of Human Rights*, 251 (1988), and Michael Kirby, '*Judicial Activism*'; *Authority, Principle and Policy in the Judicial Method*, (London, 2004) passim.

[86]   M de W. Howe (ed) *Holmes-Laski Letters*, 1368.

[87]   See, for example, Lady Hale arguing that the Supreme Court will continue to have 'a role in shaping the law which is quite different from that of the first tier appeal courts in any of the three jurisdictions. It is often involved in questions of legal policy. It needs a variety of legal and life experiences to feed into that discussion'. *Select Committee on the Constitutional Reform Bill* [HL], 2004. *Evidence* §175.

[88]   For a discussion of how the various panels affected the outcome in Pinochet see pp 107–12 of this volume. Lord Hoffman himself reflected elsewhere on cases in which one feels that a slight change in the composition of the Appellate Committee would have set the law on a different course'. David Pannick, 'Why Naomi Campbell's privacy case is not a model judgment', *The Times*, May 18, 2004

Court sit in panels, so the Court can get through more work, than it is worrying about the remote possibility that the composition of the panel might affect the outcome. There is the traditional British casualness about allowing retired judges to sit if needed. It is a system which encourages the potential for specific outcomes in decisions to be based on the vagaries of judicial composition. Then, sounding rather like the Pharisee, the discussion concludes: 'In the United States, appointments to the Supreme Court are more political, and therefore there is a stronger possibility that the composition of the court might affect the outcome. This is not the case in the United Kingdom.'[89] In England the stiff upper lip of objectivity will prevail[90].

In short, on most issues, the Paper—and now the Bill—is conservative. Obviously the new Supreme Court could not sit *in banc* as the United States Supreme Court does: 'The reason for this (in the US) is to prevent the possibility that the composition of the panel will affect the outcome of the case'—something that could not be relevant for apolitical English judges. Panels are needed to get through the work. Another important unarticulated reason is that to sit *in banc*, the orality of English proceedings would have to be curbed. That would deeply offend the Bar and cause irritation among the retired law lords who would attack the government for undermining the independence of the bar. The mythology goes deep![91]

The same conservatism permeates the search for judges. The agenda appears to encourage appointing Supreme Court judges from the lower courts. 'The criteria for selection for members of the Court must be consistent with those for selection to the lower courts. The principles will be that selection must be made from a pool of properly qualified candidates on merit alone. The impartiality of the Judiciary must be maintained, and appointment must be free from improper influence.'[92] Memory is short. Many of the more successful appeal judges have been promoted directly from the bar—Radcliffe, Reid, Mackay (during his period as a Lord of Appeal), all with experience of politics in the broad or narrow sense. It also

---

In September 2004 government lawyers requested that Lord Steyn recuse himself from hearing the appeal of foreigners detained at Belmarsh Prison without trial under the Terrorism Act. Steyn had publicly criticised the detentions in Guantanamo. Clare Dyer, 'Lords to rule on terror suspects held in jail', *The Guardian*, October 4, 2004; Marcel Berlins, 'I was wrong about Steyn', *ibid*, Sept 29, 2004.

[89] *Supreme Court*, Para 51.

[90] Even apparently when the Privy Council reverses itself on the death penalty in appeals from Trinidad. Sir Louis Blom-Cooper QC 'One death penalty after another, and, still it isn't right'. *The Times*, Jul 20, 2004.

[91] Lord Bingham was more realistic. He noted that the Lord Chancellor 'used to set the panels, the constitution which sat, and in amazingly recent memory was willing to manipulate the panels to achieve a certain result'. *HL Constitutional Reform Bill, 2004, Evidence*, §402.

[92] *Appointing Judges*, para 47.

ignores the American experience. Currently eight of the nine justices of the US Supreme Court were judges before they were appointed, but as a distinguished academic, and former Solicitor-General put it, 'we have never had so many Justices with previous judicial experience, or such an undistinguished Supreme Court.'[93] In fairness, however, when Lord Cullen, before the Select Committee, demanded that for appointment to the final court the candidate must already be a member of an intermediate court of appeal, a shameless restrictive practice proposed by the Scottish judiciary, that suggestion was rejected.[94]

The unspoken assertion in the Consultation Papers and in all Lord Falconer's statements, was that the new Supreme Court would operate in much the same way as the old House of Lords—the same law lords doing the same old thing. Lord Rees-Mogg's evidence to the Select Committee that Britain might be faced with *Dred Scott* or a Warren Court were treated with disbelief. No doubt the former Editor of *The Times* was exaggerating, but a truly independent Supreme Court may well feel a psychological freedom not at work on the current final Court of Appeal[95]. One day the UK, assuming that the court will be a UK court, will have to face the issue of the role of a Supreme Court in a democracy. There is unlikely to be the kind of searching analysis provided by Aharon Barak, President of the Supreme Court of Israel[96], but, *pace* Lord Falconer, an intellectual *status quo* is highly likely to be challenged. As Lady Hale put it, any final appeal court is likely to have 'a role in shaping the law which is quite different from that

[93] See, for instance, Lord Lester in a recent debate on the new Supreme Court: 'The quality of independence is well provided by judges drawn from the independent Bar, for the Bar is a profession of self-governing and inner-directed individuals, trained to be robustly independent. But the Bar still lacks diversity and it has no monopoly for providing judges with such qualities. Judges and barristers need to recognise that experience of advocacy is not a necessary condition for a good judge. The qualities needed can be well provided on the basis of wider professional experience beyond the Bar, including solicitors, those who have chaired tribunals or who have been distinguished academics and civil servants.' Parl Deb, Vol 652, col 113 (Sept8, 2003).

[94] Cullen agreed that 'In other words, somebody should demonstrate a proven track record bringing up qualities that show he or she is suitable for promotion to an appellate job. In other words, I see this as a promoting post'. House of Lords, Select Committee on the Constitutional Reform Bill [HL], *Evidence*, §884.

[95] A view accepted by Lord Mackay. Lord Rees-Mogg said in the Lords: 'We have at present 'joined up' constitution in which there is no complete separation of powers: not from the legislature to the executive; not from the legislature to the judiciary. In those instances in which the Supreme Court of the United States has been in repeated conflict with the legislature, and has sometimes been disastrously mistaken, our judges and Parliament have been able to work together in harmony. We would do better to stay with a system that has preserved the ultimate supremacy of Parliament and of democracy.' Parl Deb, HL, Vol 657, col 1271 (Feb 12, 2004).

[96] Aharon Barak, 'Forward: A Judge on Judging: The Role of a Supreme Court in a Democracy', (2002) 116 Harvard Law Review, 19. In rejecting the Dworkin thesis—once popular with English judges—that, even in 'hard cases', judges have only one 'right choice', based on fundamental principles, Barak argues 'whatever the philosophical answer may be, the reality is

of the first tier appeal courts in any of the three jurisdictions. It is often involved in questions of legal policy. It needs a variety of legal and life experiences to feed into that discussion'[97]. That made the government nervous. Best not to frighten the horses.

Final thoughts on the Judges

That the English are a long way from re-thinking the role of the judges is exemplified by the Consultation Papers' views on the use of judges for public inquiries. The issue does raise challenging problems. In a society which increasingly treasures openness, something akin to an inquiry mentality has emerged. Whether it is Gulf War Syndrome, deaths at Deepcut Barracks, the MMR jab or an increasing multitude of matters, the demand for an independent inquiry is becoming the norm. The idea that parliamentary questions provided this independent watchdog has faded. For more serious general matters even the Ombudsman system is regarded as too specific.

that the large majority of judges in supreme courts think, as I do, that in some cases they do have a choice. In such cases, it is not that their decisions legitimate the rulings. Their judicial discretion is an expression of their legitimacy' (at 22).

'One element of the judicial role is bridging the gap between law and society. I regard the judge as a partner in creating law. . . . The extent of this partnership varies with the type of law being created. In creating common law, the judge is the senior partner. In creating enacted law, the judge is the junior partner. Nevertheless, he is a partner and not merely an agent who carries out the orders of his principal. The second major task of the judge is to protect the constitution and democracy' (at 25–26).

'The role of the judge is to understand the purpose of law in society and to help the law achieve its purpose' (at 27).

He was sceptical of the UK solution in the Human Rights Act of allowing judges to hold legislation incompatible, but not strike it down (at 40).

'My position is that every norm—whether expressed in a statute or in case law—lives. . .replete with values and principles. These values create a 'normative umbrella' for the operation of the common law and a framework for interpreting all legal texts' (at 41–42).

'The judge is a product of his times – living in, and shaped by a given society in a given era. The purpose of objectivity is not to sever the judge from his environment. Rather, its purpose is to allow him to ascertain properly the fundamental principles of his time. The purpose of objectivity is not to rid the judge of his past, his education, his experiences, his belief, or his values. Its purpose is to encourage the judge to make use of all these personal characteristics to reflect the fundamental values of the society as faithfully as possible' (at 38).

Fundamental principles 'include the principles of equality, justice and morality. It may expand to the social goals of the separation of powers, rule of law, freedom of speech, freedom of movement, worship, occupation, and human dignity, the integrity of judging, public safety and security, the democratic values of the State and its very existence' (at 85).

'Substantive democracy is based on the separation of powers. It is in the backbone of [the] constitutional system. . . . It is not designed to ensure efficiency. The purpose of the separation of powers is to strengthen freedom and prevent the concentration of power in the hands of one government actor in a manner likely to harm the freedom of the individual' (at 120).

[97] House of Lords, Constitutional Reform Bill, *Evidence*, 364.

In a system of responsible government with executive and legislature merged, the spotlight often falls on the judges. After all they, in their judicial work, have successfully established the constitutional myth—in the anthropological sense of that term—that they can decide policy issues without being political. The Supreme Court Consultation Paper and the Appointments Paper play into this. One of the reasons for having as many as twelve judges in the final court of appeal is 'to allow for the continued release of members of the Court to undertake other functions such as the chairing of public enquiries'. Lord Falconer in his introduction to *Appointing Judges*, explained that judges 'are very often entrusted to chair major inquiries whenever an impartial, independent investigation is required'.[98] In one sense this assumption is odd. The Consultation Papers are full of homilies about the importance of separating the judges from politics. Except in the most factual inquiry, however, such inquiries almost inevitably lap over into policy areas, which inevitably shade into political issues. The nature of such inquiries varies, with excursions beyond the finding of facts varied. In policy-oriented inquiries, the hope is always that judges will be able to draw lines under crises, something politicians can rarely do. When Britain was a more deferential society, that may have been possible. It is less possible today.

As we saw, the regular use of judges as chairs of 'independent' inquiries is relatively recent, with the 1921 Act encouraging them and the period of judicial quiescence in terms of law making after 1945 giving legitimacy to the process. In those days, judges were active in pay awards, industrial disputes, colonial misadventures and the like.[99] With a far more activist judiciary over the last thirty-five years, the system may well be ripe for re-examination, as Lord Bingham has noted.[100] Other countries which take the separation of powers seriously have traditions of not allowing judges to take on political roles like this. US Supreme Court judges have been used twice in the last century to chair Commissions—Mr Justice Roberts on Pearl Harbour and Chief Justice Warren on the Kennedy Assassination. Both lived to regret their decisions as their Reports were increasingly seen

---

[98] *Appointing Judges*, 3.

[99] For a journalistic survey of these roles, see David Aaronovitch, 'The end of the poisoned embrace', in D Aaronovitch et al (eds) *The Hutton Enquiry and its Impact* (London, 2004) 336. For an admission that judges were not appropriate for determining pay claims, see R Wilberforce, *Reflections on My Life* (2003) 77–80. Wilberforce had recommended an inflationary pay award in the coal industry in 1972.

[100] See also Lord Morris of Aberavon, discussing the Scarman and MacPherson inquiries: 'When a judge enters the marketplace of public affairs outside his court and throws coconuts, he is likely to have the coconuts thrown back at him. If one values the standing of the judiciary . . . the less they are used the better it will be.' Parl Deb, HL, Vol 648, col 883 (May 21, 2003).

as political.[101] In Canada, Chief Justice Duff regretted chairing the enquiry into Canadian activities in Hong Kong during World War II. The Constitutional Court in South Africa recently refused permission to Mr Justice Heath to chair a commission on corruption and in Australia such activities are allowed only if 'compatible' with the judicial role. (In Victoria judges do not take on such roles.) In comparison, the English approach has been, at the very least, casual.

It is not merely the changing function of the English judiciary that justifies a serious rethink of the role, but the changes within and around Parliament. While Parliamentary Sovereignty is trotted out as an excuse for many things, in fact there are various brakes on 'elected dictatorship'—the independent Civil Service and the House of Lords itself are non-democratic brakes on the democratic House of Commons. As Parliament agonises over judges becoming more activist, since they are unelected, members of the House of Lords are remarkably complacent about their own greater political activism although it is arguable that they have even less 'democratic legitimacy' than the judges.

The continued use of the judges for Commissions and Committees also overlooks the changes within the House of Commons. This is particularly true as the departmental parliamentary committee system has developed since 1979. The recent Report on Higher Education by the Select Committee on Education of the House of Commons fulfils what would have been a Royal Commission in former days. The House of Commons Foreign Affairs Committee would in theory be the right place to discuss whether the UK should have gone to war in Iraq.[102] How far the system has to go can be seen by comparing Congressional committees. In the United States, Congress has been looking not only into intelligence but how it was used to justify the War. In both House and Senate Republicans as well as Democrats have been rigorous in their questioning of the Military, the Secretary of Defence and his underlings as well as the Intelligence establishment. The effect of their inquiries was, for instance, to end the career of George Tenet, Director of the CIA.[103] There are of course limits on how far there can be parallel developments in the UK. Parliamentary Committees are poorly resourced, find it difficult to get government co-operation and are largely ignored by the media. Most important of all in the UK, the party whips have, as part of the system of responsible government, extraordinary power in keeping Committees in line; something rarely relevant to the United

---

[101] Roberts exonerated President Roosevelt; Warren found only one assassin was involved.

[102] Simon Jenkins, 'No more inquiries, now Parliament must do its job', *The Times*, Feb 4, 2004. And see now, Jack Beatson, 'Should Judges conduct public inquiries?', Lionel Cohen Lecture, Hebrew University of Jerusalem, June 1, 2004.

[103] 'Intelligence tested', *Financial Times*, Jun 5/6, 2004.

States. The House of Commons Foreign Affairs Committee may have mauled Dr Kelly; it did not dare to maul the government.

Nevertheless, the pressure for an independent inquiry into the circumstances surrounding Dr Kelly's death was so obviously strong, a judge had to be appointed—but only to inquire into the circumstances surrounding the death of Dr Kelly. The Hutton Report showed the strengths and weaknesses of the use of the judges. Factually it was impeccable. Indeed its published evidence illuminated the process of decision-making in government. The judgments it gave—effectively exonerating the Prime Minster and his spin doctor, Alastair Campbell, as well as the Ministry of Defence, while laying heavy blame on the BBC and to some extent on Dr. Kelly himself, caused surprise.[104] The media were clearly irritated and there was much talk of a whitewash.[105] Suddenly some saw the prejudices—or more politely the basic assumptions—of a member of the Ulster Protestant Ascendancy coming to the fore. Readers were reminded that Hutton had been counsel to the Widgery Committee on Bloody Sunday.[106] Some suggested he had thought as a criminal judge and applied the inappropriate criminal burden of proof.[107]

Greg Dyke, the Director-General of the BBC, who was pushed into resignation by the Report was unforgiving:

> Hutton clearly knew little about journalism, had spent many years living closely with the security services, and was naïve about the way Blair's Downing Street operated—all of which would explain why he made the mistakes he did. He certainly had no experience of running a major public enquiry. The nearest he had come to it before was an inquiry in Northern Ireland in relation to drainage works in a river. But does this explain why he did what he did? What I do know is that Philip Gould, one of the architects of New Labour and very much part of Blair's inner circle, was asked by one Labour peer before the Hutton Report was

---

[104] *The Times*, Feb 2, 2004. Editorially, however, *The Times* was supportive of the Report. 'The Hutton Verdict', *ibid*, Jan 29, 2004. See also Leader, 'In defence of Hutton', *Sunday Telegraph*, Feb 1, 2004.

[105] Matthew Parris, 'Shade of grey would have been better than whitewash for Blair', *The Times*, Jan 31, 2004.

[106] For Hutton's defence of his work, see House of Commons, Public Administration Committee, *Effective Inquiries, Evidence*, May 13, 2004.

[107] 'It was not suited to an investigation of the kind which cried out for examination of the broader context of the decisions made, and the interesting constitutional principles governing matters such as the role of government advisors in relation to the intelligent services, or whether the secretary for defence could validly hide behind his officials or should take full ministerial responsibility for his actions. Hutton scarcely asks how independent MI6, or indeed the joint intelligence committee, should be.' Jeffrey Jowell QC, 'The wrong man for the job', *The Guardian* Feb 3, 2004. Conor Gearty, 'Hutton missed the mark', *The Times: Law*, Feb 24, 2004. D Aaronovitch et al (eds), *The Hutton Inquiry and its Impact* (London, 2004) *passim*. Peter Oborne, 'A disaster for British Public Life', *The Spectator*, Jan 31, 2004; Rod Liddle, 'The great whitewash', *ibid*.

published if he thought the Government faced a problem over the Kelly affair. Gould replied: Don't worry we appointed the right judge.[108]

At a more general level, beyond the analysis of facts, however, judicial inquiries cannot determine legal liability, much as the public and media demand it. Judges do, however, inevitably allocate blame. So it was with Hutton. Even the Conservative Lord Rees-Mogg declared that the Hutton Report was 'one of the most one-sided public documents of my lifetime . . . (it) exonerated the Prime Minister in the teeth of the evidence, and put the blame squarely on the BBC.'[109] Polls reported that the Hutton Report was second only to the war in Iraq as a reason for the loss of trust in government.[110]

Certainly the Report led to a rapid retreat by both Conservative and Liberal Democrat parties, who had been demanding a judicial inquiry into why the country had gone to war. By this time, however, even President Bush had been pushed on to the defensive and forced to concede an independent commission to investigate these matters, but following U.S. practice without any judges. When Blair felt he had no alternative but to follow suit, he reluctantly chose a Committee chaired by Lord Butler of Brockwell, a former Head of the Civil Service, by then head of an Oxford college, with

---

[108] Greg Dyke, 'How Blair betrayed me—and the BBC', *Observer*, Aug 29, 2004. Excerpted from Greg Dyke, *Inside Story* (2004). Hutton was reported to have been recommended by Peter Mandelson, disgraced former Secretary of State for Northern Ireland. For a portrayal of No 10's Press Secretary—Alistair Campbell's—distasteful reaction to the Hutton Report, see Peter Oborne and Simon Walters, *Alastair Campbell* (2004). Eg at 4 and 5: '. . . better than my best case scenario . . . what the report shows very clearly is this . . . the prime Minister told the truth, this government told the truth, and I told the truth. The BBC from the chairman and the director-general on down did not.' Dyke called Campbell 'a deranged vindictive bastard'. *Financial Times*, Aug 30, 2004. Lord Rees-Mogg, former editor of *The Times* and Governor of the BBC claimed that Dyke had 'a social chip the size of the Tay Bridge'. William Rees-Mogg,, 'Despite all their bonding ceremonies, Tony's cronies are coming unstuck', *The Times*, Aug 30, 2004. Later Dyke claimed he was the victim of an establishment conspiracy rather than a New Labour one.

[109] For a more balanced approach see William Twining, 'The Hutton Inquiry: Some Wider Legal Aspects', in WG Runciman (ed) *Hutton and Butler: Lifting the Lid on the Workings of Power* (Oxford and London, British Academy/OUP, 2004) 29; and Louis Blom-Cooper QC and Colin Munro, 'The Hutton Inquiry' (2004) *Public Law*, 472. Note also Lord Howe's view: 'Surely his (Hutton's) wisdom would have been the greater if he had been flanked on one side by someone with media experience and on the other by someone with experience of government'. Quoted by Tony Wright, Chair of the House of Commons Public Administration Committee, during the evidence of Lord Hutton to the Committee's investigation of Inquiries, May 13, 2004. Hutton felt his findings were misinterpreted by the media. He was astonished about allegation of a whitewash. 'Top BBC resignations astonished Hutton', *The Guardian*, Mar 4, 2004.

[110] 'Watchdog reveals our distrust of MPs' *Evening Standard*, Sept 7, 2003. Published by the Committee on Standards in Public Life.

a Committee in theory to be appointed by political parties.[111] The Butler Report was described by the press as largely exonerating 10 Downing Street on misleading the nation about Iraq's WMD. In fact the Report, on closer reading, was excoriating about the casual, Presidential-like, decision-making in 10 Downing Street. Some would even have read the Report to suggest that the Prime Minister might consider resigning. As with so many such reports, however, it was rapidly swept under the carpet, and, where it was not, glosses substituted for the Report itself.

If one were to contrast the relative skills of Butler—who had political members of his Committee—and Hutton who sat alone—it was clear that Butler's Committee understood the nuances of politics and administration, while Hutton approached his task as a journeyman criminal lawyer, seeking proof beyond all reasonable doubt. It is true the Butler mandate was broader than Hutton's, but the contrast in style was clear. Hutton also reflected the more sophisticated style developed by Scott, moving away from the Salmon principles which had previously assumed a similarity between an inquiry and a trial. It is scarcely surprising that Geoffrey Howe, understandably nursing grievances about his perceived shabby treatment by the Scott Committee, recommended that judges should never be allowed to chair committees involving policy issues without at least two other members of the Commission.[112]

Certainly this is a period when much thought is going into the use of judges. While the Public Administration Committee of the House of Commons has been asking, among a variety of important questions, whether judges should be chairing inquiries, and if so, alone[113], there is, little evidence that the Department of Constitutional Affairs is carrying through the logic of its claims about the separation of judges and politics. In the Department's Consultation Paper and response to the House of Commons Public Administration Committee, *Effective Inquiries*, no serious—or any—thought is given to the constitutional implications of using judges to

[111] The Liberal Democrats refused to join; the Conservatives agreed and then changed their minds, although their nominee refused to resign. Charles Kennedy, 'There is only one question the public want an answer to. And Lord Butler won't provide it.' *Independent on Sunday*, Feb 8, 2004.
[112] For the argument that even in a factual enquiry judges need expert colleagues or assessors, see Lord Howe, 'Remember three wise men will always be better than one', *The Times*, Feb 5, 2004. Harold Wilson, in opposition, said after the Denning Inquiry into the Profumo Affair, using judges for such inquiries blurred 'the edge which marks the sharp definition of the function of the judiciary, on the one hand, and the executive and legislative on the other'. David Pannick, 'Prime Minster, I'm a member of the judiciary, get me out of here', *The Times: Law*, Feb 10, 2004.
[113] House of Commons, Public Administration Committee, *Government by Inquiry*, Issue and Questions Paper, Feb 24, 2004.

chair inquiries, although there was concern about their length and cost. The rather simplistic constitutional arguments were put thus:

> the Government believes that it can be appropriate for judges to chair inquiries, because their experience and position make them particularly well suited to the role. The Judiciary has great experience in analysing evidence, determining facts and reaching conclusions, albeit in an adversarial rather than an inquisitorial context. The judiciary also has a long tradition of independence from politics, and judges are widely accepted to be free from any party political bias.[114]

Lord Falconer's justification for appointing Lord Hutton was similar:

> The reason why . . . judges of this eminence and calibre of the noble and learned lord, Lord Hutton, are appointed to look into such issues is because dispassionately—away from politics, from trying to establish the point of view of a particular political persuasion, from trying to change the political party in power or score political points—it is possible to come to a firm and final conclusion about what happened.[115]

It is a little surprising, however, that leaders of the profession, from the Senior Law Lord down—although not including the Lord Chancellor—have voiced increasing scepticism about the use of the judges for enquiries. Jeffrey Jowell QC would, apparently, exclude the judges from all such enquiries. Michael Beloff QC has taken the view that 'judges ought not to be asked to undertake tasks that are properly those of our elected representatives', citing in support the US Canons of Judicial Conduct: 'A judge should not accept appointment to a government committee or other position that is concerned with issues of fact or policy or matters other than the improvement of the law, the legal system or the administration of justice'.[116] Finally, Lord Woolf, appearing before the Public Administration Select Committee in December 2004, announced that the Judges' Council had agreed that he would decide when a judge might be allowed to chair an inquiry:

> In these days of the separation of powers, the executive should not be able to say what a judge is going to do. . .The Lord Chief Justice should be entitled to say not only who but whether a judge should conduct the inquiry at all. The subject matter of the inquiry may be so political that it would damaging to the judiciary for a judge to be involved. In addition, the question of whether there should be

---

[114] DCA, Consultation Paper, *Effective Inquiries*, CP 12/04 (2004). The Paper was produced in response to the Public Administration Select Committee of the House of Commons, *Government by Inquiry*. That Select Committee has produced other thoughtful and relevant papers, for example *Taming the Prerogative: Strengthening Ministerial Accountability to Parliament*, HC 422 (2004).

[115] Parl Deb, HC, Vol 657, col 786 (Feb 4, 2004).

[116] Michael Beloff QC, 'Discussion' in Runciman (ed) above n 109, 51.

an inquiry at all may be highly controversial, and if a judge is appointed, the judiciary, as a result of the appointment, may be seen as siding inappropriately with the government.

It was clear that the aftermath of Hutton was having its effect. When an inquiry was needed that same month to investigate whether David Blunkett had fast-tracked the visa of his mistress's nanny, it was Sir Alan Budd, a former Permanent Secretary, who was chosen. The world was indeed changing.[117]

Conclusion

It is ironic that a series of documents—the Consultation Papers—that insist that the judiciary and politics live in totally different systems and never the twain should meet, should offer the judges on the sacrificial altar of public inquiries, which inevitably have a greater or lesser political content. Yet there is a theme. To Conservatives, these Consultation Papers seem dangerously radical; hence the heated debates in the Lords over the Constitutional Reform Bill. Yet, in so many ways they are immensely conservative and unimaginative, too often reflecting the completion of Victorian reforms coupled with 1950s views of the judicial process, rather than fulfilling the claims of modernisation, so beloved of New Labour.

By December 2004, however, the Concordat between Lord Chief Justice was set and apparently the method of appointing the judges, now to be heavily influenced by the existing judges. The Supreme Court, which had threatened so many peers, was through. The title 'Lord Chancellor' was secure. Whether he must remain a lawyer and peer, even if shorn of many of his responsibilities, remained very much alive.[118] While the Lords had demanded these qualifications, they did not appeal to the Commons, where the Bill was introduced in January 2005. For a somewhat renewed Conservative Party there was hope that the changes would provide political fodder. At the Party Conference in October 2004, the Conservative Leader in the Lords, Lord Strathclyde, announced: 'On our first day, Michael Howard

---

[117] 'Woolf wants final say over inquiries', *The Times*, Dec 15, 2004. See also the Inquiries Bill, introduced into the House of Lords in November 2004; and Iain Steele, 'Judging Judicial Inquiries' (2004) *Public Law*, 738.

[118] Lord Howe said of Lord Falconer: 'I have to say that I do not find it easy to respect someone, however personally agreeable, who has the privilege of being appointed to such an historic and constitutionally vital office and is then disposed, at little more than a month's notice, to set about its demolition. In order to prevent such constitutional vandalism – I make no apology for repeating the phrase – the office now has to be recreated, preserved and strengthened'. Parl Deb, HL, Vol 663, col 1156 (Jul 13, 2004).

(the putative Prime Minister) will name a Lord Chancellor. He will be a lawyer and he will sit in the House of Lords'. With more enthusiasm than accuracy he announced 'the office of Lord Chancellor protected judicial independence for centuries. There has never been a whiff of political bias or corruption. So why are Labour meddling with the appointment of judges? I think we all know the answer.'[119] There were battles ahead for Lord Falconer when the Bill returned to the Lords. The government still hoped to have the Bill through before the Spring election. If not, the changes would be included in the Manifesto and the Bill reintroduced in the Commons, assuming a Labour victory. This time the Parliament Act would be available.

---

[119] 'Lord Chancellor is safe in our hands, promises Strathclyde', *Daily Telegraph*, October 8, 2004.

Bibliography

Abel-Smith, B, and Stevens, R *Lawyers and the Courts: A Sociological Study of the English Legal System* (London, 1967)

——, and —— *In Search of Justice: Society and the Legal System* (London, 1968)

Ackerman, B 'Revolution on a Human Scale' (1999) *Yale Law Journal* 2279

—— 'The New Separation of Powers' (2000) 113 *Harvard Law Review* 633

Anderson, B, 'Being Derry Irvine Means Never Having to Say You're Sorry', *Spectator* 24 February 2001

Barber, NW 'Prelude to the Separation of Powers' (2001) 60 *Cambridge Law Journal* 59

Barendt, E 'Constitutional Law and the Criminal Injuries Compensation Scheme' [1995] *Public Law* 357

—— 'Separation of Powers and Constitutional Government' [1995] *Public Law* 599

Bennion, F 'A Naked Usurpation?' [1999] *New Law Journal* 421

Bergen, F *The History of New York Court of Appeals, 1847–1942* (Columbia NY, 1985)

Bingham, T 'Anglo-American Reflections', First Pilgrim Fathers' Lecture, Plymouth Law Society, 29 October 1994, reprinted in *The Business of Judging: Selected Essays and Speeches* (Oxford, 2000)

—— *The Business of Judging: Selected Essays and Speeches* (Oxford, 2000)

—— 'Dicey Revisited' [2002] *Public Law* 39

Blom-Cooper, L 'Tribunals under Inquiry' [2002] *Public Law* 1

—— and Drewry, G *Final Appeal: A Study of the House of Lords in its Judicial Capacity* (Oxford, 1972)

Blunkett, D 'At Times Like These the Majority Must be Protected from the Minority', *The Times*, 4 October 2001

Bowman, J 'Dead End?', *Legal Week*, 24 May 2001

Boyle, K, Hadden, T, and Hilliard, P *Law and the State: The Case of Northern Ireland* (London, 1975)

Bresler, F *Lord Goddard: A Biography* (London, 1977)

Browne-Wilkinson, N 'The Independence of the Judiciary in the 1980s' [1988] *Public Law* 44

—— 'The Infiltration of a Bill of Rights' [1992] *Public Law* 405

—— 'The Impact of Judicial Reasoning' in B Markesinis (ed), *The Impact of the Human Rights Bill on English Law* (Oxford, 1998)

Butler, D, and Kavanagh, D *The British General Election, 2001* (London, 2002)

Campbell, J *Lives of the Lord Chancellors* (London, 1869)

Ching, F *The Li Dynasty: Hong Kong Aristocrats* (Hong Kong, 1999)

Clark, G *The Later Stuarts 1660–1714* (Oxford, 1955)

Clark, JCD *English Society 1660–1832* (Cambridge, 2000)

Coleridge, EH *Life and Correspondence of John Duke, Lord Coleridge, Lord Chief Justice of England* (London, 1904)

Cornes, R 'McGonnell v UK, the Lord Chancellor and the Law Lords' [2000] *Public Law* 166

—— 'Time for a Home of their Own?' [2002] *New Law Journal* 63

Cosgrove, R *The Rule of Law: Albert Venn Dicey, Victorian Jurist* (N Carolina, 1980)

Cottrell, J, and Ghai, Y 'Between Two Systems of Law: The Judiciary in Hong Kong' in D O'Brian and P Russell (eds), *Judicial Independence in the Age of Democracy* (Virginia, 2001)

Craig, P 'Sovereignty of the United Kingdom Parliament after *Factortame*' (1991) 11 *Yearbook of European Law* 221.

Curtis, S (ed) *The Journals of Woodrow Wyatt* (London, 1998) vol 1

Davies, PW 'Howard Punished in each Sentence', *The Independent*, 24 May 1996

Davis, G *The Early Stuarts 1603–1660* (Oxford, 1937)

Denning, A *The Closing Chapter* (London, 1983)

Dicey, AV *Introduction to the Study of Law of the Constitution* (London, 1885)

—— *Lectures on the Relation between Law and Public Opinion in England during the Nineteenth Century* (London, 1905)

Drewry, G 'Judicial Appointments' [1998] *Public Law* 1

Duman, D *The Judicial Bench in England 1727–1875* (London, 1982)

Eaglesham, J 'Lord Chancellor Shows He is Not Afraid to Fight Fire with Ire', *Financial Times*, 15 April 2002

Egan, D *Irvine: Politically Correct?* (London, 1999)

English, R 'Acorns of Wisdom from Oakington' [2001] *New Law Journal* 1629

Epstein, R 'The Human Rights Act—Will the Law Ever be the Same Again?' [2001] *New Law Journal* 1558

Gearty, C 'Unravelling Osman' (2001) 64 *Modern Law Review* 159

Gibb, F 'The Supreme Sacrifice', *The Times*, 17 July 2001

—— 'Strong Seas but a Sure Touch at the Helm', *The Times*, 16 April 2002

Gilbert, WE *Iolanthe or the Peer and the Peri* (London, 1982)

Gill, F 'Judge Dismayed Tory Ministers', *The Times*, 8 September 2001

Goldsworthy, J *The Sovereignty of Parliament: History and Philosophy* (Oxford, 1999)

Grant, H 'Commissions of Inquiry—Is There a Right to be Legally Represented?' [2000] *Public Law* 377

Greene, W 'Law and Progress' (1994) 94 *Law Journal* 349

Griffith, JAG 'Who Will Referee the Refs?', *Times Literary Supplement*, 25 September 1998

—— 'The Open Conspiracy', *Times Literary Supplement*, 20 April 2001

—— *The Politics of the Judiciary*, 4th edn (London, 1991) and 5th edn (London, 1997)

—— *Judicial Politics since 1920: A Chronicle* (Oxford, 1993)

—— 'Judges and the Constitution' in R Rawlings (ed), *Law, Society and Economy: Centenary Essays for the London School of Economics* (Oxford, 1997)

—— 'The Brave New World of Sir John Laws' (2000) 63 *Modern Law Review* 159

—— 'The Common Law and the Political Constitution' (2001) 117 *Law Quarterly Review* 42

Guarnieri, C, and Pederzoli, P *The Power of Judges: A Comparative Study of Court and Democracy* (Oxford, 2002)

Gubbay, AR 'Judicial Independence in Zimbabwe' [2001] *New Law Journal* 357

Gwyn, W *The Meaning of the Separation of Powers* (Tulane, 1967)

Hale, B 'Equality and the Judiciary: Why Should We Want More Woman Judges?' [2001] *Public Law* 484

Hare, I 'Prerogative and Precedent: The Privy Council on Death Row' (2000) 60 *Cambridge Law Journal* 1

Hargreaves, I 'Kingmaker: The Truth about Derry Irvine', *Observer Sunday Review*, 11 October 1998

Hartley, TC, and Griffith, JAG *Government and the Law*, 2nd edn (London, 1991)

Harvey, J 'HRA "Flood" is More of a Trickle', *Legal Week*, 11 October 2001

Havinghurst, A 'The Judiciary and Politics in the Reign of Charles II' (1950) 66 *Law Quarterly Review* 62, 229

—— 'James II and the Twelve Men in Scarlet' (1957) 69 *Law Quarterly Review* 522

Heuston, RFV *Lives of the Lord Chancellors 1885–1940* (Oxford, 1964)

Hill, C *The Century of Revolution* (London, 1981)

Hirschon, RE 'Defence: Judges Deserve Our Respect—And Salaries That Support Their Independence' (May 2002) *ABA Journal* 10

Hoffmann, L 'Human Rights and the House of Lords' (1999) 62 *Modern Law Review* 159

Hoppit, J *A Land of Liberty? England 1689–1727* (Oxford, 2000)

Horne, A *Harold Macmillan 1957–1986* (London, 1989) vol 2

Horwitz, H *Public Policy and Politics in the Reign of William III* (Manchester, 1977)

Howe, G 'A Judge's Long Contest with Reality', *The Spectator*, 27 January 1996

—— 'Procedure at the Scott Inquiry' [1996] *Public Law* 445

Hughes, A and Pilling, B 'The Arbitration Act Five Years On', *New Law Journal*, 5 October 2001

Hunt, M 'Constitutionalism and the Contractualisation of Government in the United Kingdom' in M Taggart (ed), *The Province of Administrative Law* (Oxford, 1997)

Hurd, D 'A Vessel Destined to Founder', *Financial Times*, 8 January 2002

Institute of Public Policy Research *The Constitution of the United Kingdom* (London, 1991)

Irvine, A 'Judges and Decision Makers: The Theory and Practice of Wednesbury Review' [1996] *Public Law* 59

Jenkins, P *Mrs Thatcher's Revolution: The Ending of the Socialist Era* (Cambridge Mass, 1987)

Jenkins, S *Accountable to None: The Tory Nationalization of Britain* (London, 1995)

Johnson, B 'The Long Arm of the Law', *Spectator*, 17 June 1995

Johnson, F 'Blair's First Crony Emerges Unscathed', *Daily Telegraph*, 25 January 2002

Jones, J *Labour of Love: The Partly-Political Diary of a Cabinet Minister's Wife* (London, 1999)

Kahn-Freund, O 'Labour Law' in M Ginsberg (ed), *Law and Opinion in England in the 20th Century* (London, 1959)

Kentridge, S 'The Highest Court: Selecting the Judges', *Cambridge Law Journal* (forthcoming)

Klug, F, and Starmer, K 'Incorporation Through the "Front Door": The First Year of the Human Rights Act' [2001] *Public Law* 654

Labour Party *A New Agenda for Democracy: Labour's Proposals for Constitutional Reform* (London, 1997)

Langford, P *A Polite and Commercial People: England 1727–1783* (Oxford, 1989)

Laws, J 'Is the High Court the Guardian of Fundamental Rights?' [1993] *Public Law* 59

—— 'Judicial Remedies and the Constitution' (1994) 57 *Modern Law Review* 213

—— 'Law and Democracy' (1995) *Public Law* 80

—— 'The Constitution: Morals and Rights' [1996] *Public Law* 622

—— 'The Limitation of Human Rights' [1998] *Public Law* 254

Legg, T 'Judges for the New Century' [2001] *Public Law* 62

Lemmings, D *Gentlemen and Barristers: The Inns of Court and the English Bar 1680–1730* (Oxford, 1990)

—— 'The Independence of the Judiciary in Eighteenth Century England' in P Birks (ed), *The Life of the English Law* (London, 1993)

Lester, A 'Fundamental Rights: The United Kingdom Isolated?' [1986] *Public Law* 46

—— ' The Mouse that Roared: The Human Rights Bill 1995' [1995] *Public Law* 198

—— 'Acceptance of the Strasbourg Jurisdiction: What Really Went on in Whitehall in 1965' [1998] *Public Law* 237

Le Sueur, A 'The Judicial Review Debate: From Partnership to Friction' (1996) 31 *Government and Opposition* 8

Lewis, G *Lord Hailsham: A Life* (London, 1997)

Lightfoot, E, and Prescott, M 'Too Big for their Wigs?', *Sunday Times*, 5 November 1995

Lobban, M *The Common Law and English Jurisprudence* (Oxford, 1991)

Loveland, I 'Alconbury in the House of Lords' [2001] *New Law Journal* 713

Macaulay, TB *History of England (London, 1688–1832)* (London, 1997)

Major, J *The Autobiography* (London, 1999)

Malleson, K *The New Judiciary: The Effects of the Expansion and Activism* (Aldershot, 1999)

—— 'Assessing the Performance of the South African Judicial Service Commission' (1999) 116 *South African Law Journal* 36

—— 'Safeguarding Judicial Impartiality' (2002) 22 *Legal Studies* 53

Mandelson, P 'The Future of Ireland', *GQ*, January 2002

Marr, A *Ruling Britannia* (London, 1995)

Maxwell, P 'The House of Lords as a Constitutional Court—The Implications of *ex parte EOC*' in B Dickson and P Carmichael (eds), *The House of Lords: Its Parliamentary and Judicial Roles* (Oxford, 1999)

Mears, M 'Lawspeak' [1999] *New Law Journal* 34

Miles, A 'Is the Home Secretary Really Above the Law?', *The Times*, 14 November 2001

Money-Kyrle, R 'Forum', *Legal Week*, 20 September 2001

Moore, C 'Everyone Deserved Better', *Daily Telegraph*, 2 March 1999

Mount, F 'From Major to Maurras' *Prospect*, March 1996

Mullan, K 'The Impact of *Pepper v Hart*' in B Dickson and P Carmichael (eds), *The House of Lords: Its Parliamentary and Judicial Roles* (Oxford, 1999)

Mustill, MJ 'What Do Judges Do? (1996) 3 *Sartryck ur Juridisk Tidskrift* 622

—— 'Margins: A Right to be Wrong?' *Law Quarterly Review* (forthcoming)

Naughtie, J *The Rivals: The Intimate Story of a Political Marriage* (London, 2001)

Newman, WJ *The Quebec Secession Reference* (Ontario, 1999)

Nicol *EC Membership and the Judicialization of British Politics* (Oxford, 2001)

O'Brien, D, and Carter, V 'Constitutional Rights, Legitimate Expectations and the Death Penalty' [2000] *Public Law* 573

O'Neill, A 'Judicial Politics and the Judicial Committee: The Devolution Jurisprudence of the Privy Council' (2001) 63 *Modern Law Review* 603

Oliver, D 'The Lord Chancellor, the Judicial Committee of the Privy Council and Devolution' [1999] *Public Law* 5

Pannick, D *Judges* (Oxford, 1988)

—— 'Why Judges Cannot Avoid Politics', *The Times*, 7 November 1995

—— 'Lord Chancellor Should Leave the Judging to the Pros', *The Times*, 12 March 2002

Patten, J 'Let's Reform the Lord Chancellor', *Daily Telegraph*, 10 July 1996

Peach, L *An Independent Scrutiny of the Appointment Process of Judges and Queen's Counsel in England and Wales* (London, 1999))

Pierson, CG *Canada and the Privy Council* (London, 1960)

Pimlott, B *Harold Wilson* (London, 1992)

Plowden, P, and Kerrigan, K 'Judicial Review—A New Test?' [2001] *New Law Journal* 1291

Pook, S 'The Woman Who Hit Boycott for Six', *The Daily Telegraph*, 13 November 1998

Radcliffe, Lord *Not in Feather Beds* (London, 1968)

Rawlings, R 'Courts and Interests' in I Loveland (ed), *A Special Relationship* (Oxford, 1995)

Reid, JSC 'The Law and the Reasonable Man' (1968) *Proceedings of the British Academy* 193

—— 'The Judge as Law Maker' (1972) 12 *Journal of the Society of Public Teachers of Law* 22

Resnik, J 'Judicial Independence and Article III' (1999) 72 *Southern California Law Review* 353

Rice, R 'Former Star of the Bar Papers Over the Last Cracks in his Image', *Financial Times*, 7 December 1998

Riddell, P 'Lord Chancellor's Deviousness Could Haunt New Labour', *The Times*, 14 November 2001

Roberts, A *Salisbury: Victorian Titan* (London, 1999)

Robertson, D *Judicial Discretion in the House of Lords* (Oxford, 1998)
—— 'The House of Lords as a Political and Constitutional Court: Lessons from the Pinochet Case' in D Woodhouse (ed), *The Pinochet Case: A Legal and Constitutional Analysis* (Oxford, 2000)
Rozen J 'Recipient's Choice', *New Yorker*, 11 January 1999
Rozenberg, J *Trial of Strength: The Battle between Ministers and Judges over Who Makes the Law* (London, 1997)
—— 'Lords Need Common Touch', *The Daily Telegraph*, 17 April, 2001
—— 'When Does a Hotel Become a House?', *Daily Telegraph*, 3 July 2001
—— 'I Saved Judges From Blunkett Says Lord Irvine', *Daily Telegraph*, 15 April 2002
Schrag, P *Paradise Lost* (University of California Press, 1998)
Schwoerer, LG *The Declaration of Rights* (Baltimore, 1981)
Scrutton, TE 'The Work of the Commercial Courts' (1923) 1 *Cambridge Law Journal* 8
Sedley, S 'Charter 88: Wrongs and Rights' [1991] *Citizenship*
—— 'Air Transport 2: Noisy Flights', *Economist*, 17 June 1995
—— 'Human Rights: A Twenty-First Century Agenda' [1995] *Public Law* 386
—— 'The Common Law and the Political Constitution: A Reply' [2001] 117 *Law Quarterly Review* 68
Seldon, A *Major: A Political Life* (London, 1997)
Sergienko, G ' "A Body of Sound Practical Common Sense": Law Reform Through Lay Judges, Public Choice Theory, and the Transformation of American Law' (1997) 41 *American Journal of Legal History* 175
Shetreet, S *Judges on Trial* (Amsterdam, 1976)
—— *Between Three Branches of Government: The Balance of Rights in the Matter of Religion* (Jerusalem, 2000)
—— 'The Critical Challenge of Judicial Independence in Israel' PH Russell and DM O'Brien (eds), *Judicial Independence in the Age of Democracy* (Virginia, 2001)
Simon, J *Rufus Isaacs, DNB 1931–1940* (Oxford, 1949)
Simpson, AWB *In the Highest Degree Odious: Detention Without Trial in Wartime Britain* (Oxford, 1992)
—— *Human Rights and the End of Empire: Britain and the Genesis of the European Convention* (Oxford, 2001)
—— 'The Devlin Commission (1959): Colonialism, Emergencies and the Rule of Law' (2002) 17 *Oxford Journal of Legal Studies* 22.
Smith, JH *Appeals to the Privy Council from the American Colonies* (Columbia NY, 1950)
Stevens, R '*Hedley Byrne v Heller*: Judicial Creativity and Doctrinal Possibility' (1964) 14 *Modern Law Review* 27
—— 'The Final Appeal: Reform of the House of Lords and Privy Council, 1867–1876' (1964) 80 *Law Quarterly Review* 343
—— *Law and Politics: The House of Lords as a Judicial Body 1800–1976* (N Carolina, 1978)
—— *The Independence of the Judiciary: The View from the Lord Chancellor's Office* (Oxford, 1993)

—— 'Judges, Politics, Politicians and the Confusing Role of the Judiciary' in K Hawkins (ed), *The Human Face of Law: Essays in Honour of Donald Harris* (Oxford, 1997)

—— 'The Case for Banishing M'Lud from the Lords', *The Times*, 22 December 1998

—— 'Judicial Independence: The Case of England' (1999) 72 *University of Southern California Law Review* 101

—— 'Loss of Innocence: The Separation of Powers and Judicial Independence' (1999) 19 *Oxford Journal of Legal Studies* 365

—— 'Judicial Independence in England: A Loss of Innocence' in P Russell and D O'Brien (eds), *Judicial Independence in the Age of Democracy: Critical Perspectives from around the World* (Virginia, 2001)

Stevens, R, and Yamey, BS *The Restrictive Practices' Court: A Study of the Judicial Process and Economic Policy* (London, 1965)

Steyn, J 'Does Legal Formalism Hold Sway in England?' (1996) *Current Legal Problems* 43

—— '*Pepper v Hart*: A Re-examination' (2001) 21 *Oxford Journal of Legal Studies* 59

—— 'The Case for a Supreme Court' (2002) 118 *Law Quarterly Review*

Sugarman, D 'The Pinochet Case: International Criminal Justice in the Gothic Style?' (2001) 64 *Modern Law Review* 933

Taylor, P 'Howard's Production Line Justice', *The Times*, 23 May 1996

Tompkins, A *The Constitution After Scott: Government Unwrapped* (Oxford, 1998)

Utley, T 'Bring Back Stop and Search, For the Sake of All of Us', *Daily Telegraph*, 4 January 2002

Van Gerren, W 'Bridging the Gap Between Community and National Laws: Towards a Principle of Homogeneity in the Field of Legal Remedies' (1995) 32 *Common Market Law Review* 579

Vile, MJC *Constitution and the Separation of Powers* (Oxford, 1967)

Wadham, J 'The Human Rights Act: Sufficient Protection?' [2001] *New Law Journal* 1411

Wadham, J, and Chakrabarti, S 'Infinite Detention without Trial' [2001] *New Law Journal* 1564

Wadham, J, and Mountfield, H *Blackstone's Guide to the Human Rights Act 1998* (London, 2000)

Ward, S 'Judges vs. the Government', *The Independent*, 3 November 1993

Wicks, E ' The United Kingdom Government's Perception of the European Convention on Human Rights at the Time of Entry' [2000] *Public Law* 438

Williams, B *The Whig Supremacy, 1714–1760*, 2nd edn (Oxford, 1962)

Woodhouse, D (ed) *The Pinochet Case: A Legal and Constitutional Analysis* (Oxford, 2000)

—— *The Office of Lord Chancellor* (Oxford, 2001)

—— 'The Office of Lord Chancellor: Time to Abandon the Judicial Role—The Rest Will Follow' (2002) 22 *Legal Studies* 128

Woolf, H 'Droit Public—English Style' [1995] *Public Law* 57

—— 'Judicial Review—The Tensions Between the Executive and the Judiciary', (1998) 114 *Law Quarterly Review* 579

Woolf, H, and Jowell, J (eds) *De Smith's Judicial Review of Administrative Action* (London, 1995)

Wyn Ellis, N *John Major* (London, 1991)

Young, AH 'Feminism, Pluralism and Administrative Law' in M Taggart (ed), *The Province of Administrative Law* (Oxford, 1997)

Young, H *One of Us: A Biography of Margaret Thatcher* (London, 1989)

—— 'When Judges Put Ministers in the Dock', *The Guardian*, 17 October 1995

Zander, M 'More Louis XIV than Cardinal Wolsey' [1998] *New Law Journal* 1084

—— 'The Anti-Terrorism Bill—What Happened?' [2001] *New Law Journal* 1880

Index